# The College of Law
*of England and Wales*

### LIBRARY SERVICES

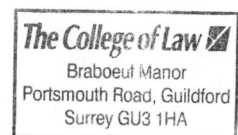

The College of Law
Braboeuf Manor
Portsmouth Road, Guildford
Surrey GU3 1HA

# PROPERTY AND THE LAW OF FINDERS

Are finders keepers? This most simple of questions has long evaded a satisfactory legal answer. Generally, it seems to have been accepted that a finder acquires a property right in the object of her find and can protect it from subsequent interference, but even this turns out to be the baldest statement of principle, resting on obscure and confused authority.

This first full-length treatment of finders sets them in their legal-historical context, and discovers a fascinating area of law lying at the crossroads of crime, obligations and property. That on the same facts a finder might be thief, bailee and/or property right holder has clouded our conceptual analysis, and prevented us from stating simply our rules about finding. Nonetheless, when the applicable doctrines and policies of our property law (particularly the central concept of possession) are explored and understood in the light of countervailing rules of crime and tort, we can argue confidently that, despite centuries of doubt and confusion, English law has succeeded in producing a body of law that is theoretically and practically coherent. *Property and the Law of Finders* makes this argument, and will appeal to anyone specifically interested in the law of personal property, and also to those with broader concerns about the evolution of common law concepts and their ability to yield workable, practical solutions.

# Property and the Law of Finders

Robin Hickey

·HART·
PUBLISHING
OXFORD AND PORTLAND, OREGON
2010

Published in North America (US and Canada) by
Hart Publishing
c/o International Specialized Book Services
920 NE 58th Avenue, Suite 300
Portland, OR 97213-3786
USA
Tel: +1 503 287 3093 or toll-free: (1) 800 944 6190
Fax: +1 503 280 8832
E-mail: orders@isbs.com
Website: http://www.isbs.com

Hart Publishing Ltd, 16C Worcester Place, Oxford, OX1 2JW
Telephone: +44 (0)1865 517530 Fax: +44 (0)1865 510710
E-mail: mail@hartpub.co.uk
Website: http://www.hartpub.co.uk


British Library Cataloguing in Publication Data
Data Available


ISBN: 978-1-84113-575-5


Typeset by Compuscript Ltd, Shannon
Printed and bound in Great Britain by
TJ International Ltd, Padstow, Cornwall

# ACKNOWLEDGEMENTS

This book is a revised version of my doctoral thesis, completed at Queen's University Belfast. I am deeply grateful to Norma Dawson and David Capper, who acted respectively as first and second supervisors. Each was unfailingly generous with time, enthusiasm and encouragement; each was a stern critic when necessary, saving me from many errors, and opening wide avenues of more fruitful thought. I doubt I shall ever repay their patience with me and with this project, but I hope we do some justice to their commitment.

Brice Dickson acted as first supervisor for one academic year while Professor Dawson was on research leave. He read and commented usefully on many parts of this work. Fiona Marshall kindly proofread the final draft. Bill Swadling, Sarah Worthington and Alan Dowling were thorough examiners. I have found their comments enormously helpful. The final sections of Chapter 5, and the Epilogue, have been prompted by our discussions.

Parts of Chapters 3, 6 and 7 were prepared during research visits to Harvard Law School in March 2005 and March 2007. I wish to express my thanks to James Cavallaro, Paul MacMahon and Deirdre Mask.

An earlier version of Chapter 4 appears as 'Curbing the Enthusiasm of Finders' in E Cooke (ed), *Modern Studies in Property Law—Volume 4* (Oxford, Hart Publishing, 2007). Some material in Chapters 2 and 6 was published in 'Stealing Abandoned Goods: Possessory Title in Proceedings for Theft' (2006) 26 *Legal Studies* 584.

It has been a great pleasure to work with Richard Hart, and everyone at Hart Publishing. They too have shown unfaltering patience with a first-time author, forgiving many delays and encouraging me at every step of the way.

Finally, I owe thanks to my parents for their unreserved support and interest over the many years of this project; and to Caroline, for whom there are no words to express the depth of my love and appreciation.

# CONTENTS

*Contents*

# ABBREVIATIONS

Certain standard or frequently cited texts are abbreviated as follows:

| | |
|---|---|
| Ames, HT | JB Ames, 'The History of Trover' (1897–98) 11 *Harv LR* 277; 374 |
| Am.Jur.2d | *American Jurisprudence* 2nd edn (Thomson West, 1962–2008) |
| B & M | JH Baker and SFC Milsom, *Sources of English Legal History: Private Law to 1750* (London, Butterworths, 1986) |
| Baker, *Introduction* | JH Baker, *An Introduction to English Legal History* 4th edn (London, Butterworths LexisNexis, 2002) |
| Baker, *OH* | JH Baker, *The Oxford History of the Laws of England*, vol VI, *1483–1558* (Oxford, OUP, 2003) |
| Bl Comm | E Christian (ed), *Commentaries on the Laws of England by Sir William Blackstone* 15th edn (London, Cadell & Davies, 1809) |
| Bracton | GE Woodbine (ed), *Henri De Bracton on the Laws and Customs of England* (SE Thorne (trans), Cambridge MA, Harvard University Press, 1968) |
| *Clerk and Lindsell on Torts* | AM Dugdale *et al* (eds), *Clerk and Lindsell on Torts* 19th edn (London, Sweet & Maxwell, 2006) |
| Co Inst | E Coke, *Institutes of the Laws of England* (London, Lee and Pakeman, 1660) |
| D | T Mommsen, P Krueger and A Watson (eds), *The Digest of Justinian* (University of Pennsylvania Press, 1985) |
| *EPL* | A Burrows (ed), *English Private Law* (2nd edn, Oxford, OUP, 2007) |
| East PC | EH East, *A Treatise on the Pleas of the Crown* (London, J Butterworth, 1803) |
| *Goff and Jones* | G Jones (ed), *Goff and Jones: The Law of Restitution* 7th edn (London, Sweet & Maxwell, 2007) |
| Hale PC | G Wilson (ed), *The History of the Pleas of the Crown by Sir Matthew Hale* (London, J Butterworth, 1800) |
| Hawk PC | J Curwood (ed), *A Treatise of the Pleas of the Crown by William Hawkins* (London, Sweet, 1824) |
| Holdsworth, *HEL* | WS Holdsworth, *A History of English Law* 3rd edn (London, Methuen & Co, 1923) |

| | |
|---|---|
| Holmes, *CL* | OW Holmes, Jnr, *The Common Law* (New York, Dover Publications, 1991, an unabridged reproduction of the original text: Boston, MA, Little Brown, 1881) |
| J Inst | JB Moyle (ed), *The Institutes of Justinian* (JB Moyle (trans), Oxford, Clarendon Press, 1945) |
| P & M | F Pollock and FW Maitland, *History of English Law* 2nd edn (Cambridge, Cambridge University Press, 1923) |
| P & W | F Pollock and RS Wright, *An Essay on Possession in the Common Law* (Oxford, Clarendon Press, 1888) |
| Palmer, *Bailment* | NE Palmer, *Bailment* 2nd edn (London, Sweet & Maxwell, 1991) |
| *Russell on Crime* | JWC Turner (ed), *Russell on Crime* 12th edn (London, Stevens & Sons, 1964). References to earlier editions appear with full citations. |
| SS | Selden Society (annual volumes, 1887–) |

# TABLE OF CASES

## English Cases Cited By Year

## Table of Cases

### Northern Ireland Cases

### Republic of Ireland Cases

### US Cases

### Australia Cases

# Table of Cases

## Canada Cases

## New Zealand Cases

# TABLE OF LEGISLATION

# Introduction

'The next matter of consideration was, whether, in buying the coat as it stood, the papers [found in the coat pocket] belonged to me, or the old flunkie waiting-servant with the peaked hat. James and me, after an hour and a half's argle-bargleing pro and con, in the way of Parliament-house lawyers, came at last to be unanimously of opinion, that according to the auld Scotch proverb of

'He that finds keeps,

And he that loses seeks',

whatever was part or pendicle of the coat at the time of purchase, when it hung exposed for sale over the white-headed Welshman's little finger, became according to the law of nature and nations, as James Batter wisely observed, part and pendicle of the property of me, Mansie Wauch, the legal purchaser'.[1]

I f the maxim 'finders keepers' has long been evident in popular consciousness, no less is it thought to have real significance at law. Modern cases on finding rather take it for granted that a finder has some property right in the object of her find, and consider the proposition to be of considerable legal heritage. In *Parker v British Airways Board*, Donaldson LJ spoke of an 'ancient common law rule' to this effect;[2] in *Waverly BC v Fletcher*, Auld LJ thought it was a 'firm principle established … long ago',[3] and described the maxim 'finders keepers' as a 'familiar notion of English law'.[4] In framing their propositions, both judges relied on the 1722 case of *Armory v Delamirie*.[5] There, allowing a young boy to recover damages for the value of a jewel from a goldsmith who refused to redeliver it to him, Pratt CJKB ruled that:

the finder of a jewel, though he does not by such finding acquire an absolute property or ownership, yet he has such a property as will enable him to keep it against all but the rightful owner.[6]

There is no question that *Armory* remains the 'jural icon' of our law of finders,[7] but the law is much more complicated and much more open to doubt than

---

[1] From *The Life of Mansie Wauch*, a novel by DM Moir first published in 1828, which the *Oxford English Dictionary* gives as an early written source of the 'finders keepers' maxim. The extract reproduced here is taken from a later edition: (London/Edinburgh, TN Foulis, 1911) 83–4.
[2] [1982] QB 1004, 1008.
[3] *Waverly Borough Council v Fletcher* [1996] QB 334, 339.
[4] *Ibid* 338.
[5] (1722) 1 Stra 505. A decision of the court of Pratt CJKB at *nisi prius* in Middlesex.
[6] *Ibid*.
[7] S Roberts, 'More Lost Than Found' (1982) 45 *MLR* 683.

this short and simple judgment suggests.[8] On the issue of rights acquisition, finding disputes continue to produce difficult litigation. Questions remain about the extent to which a finder's rights should prevail over those of certain other non-owning claimants (most obviously, over those of the possessor of the land where the find occurred), and there are real doubts about whether a finder's acquisition of right should be qualified or denied according to the presence of certain extraneous facts related to her behaviour or status.[9] There are also doubts about what the law requires finders to do. Must they report losses? May they make any use of the things that they find? Must they make an effort to redeliver lost items to their loser? And must they take care of them in the meantime? To these questions, and more, as yet, English law has provided no concise or indisputably authoritative answers.

A great part of the difficulty in understanding and articulating clearly the English law of finds is attributable to the range of its sources. There has been no general legislation regulating the legal position of finders, as has been the fashion in some jurisdictions, notably Scotland.[10] Instead, the law of finds depends on the common law, and on certain scattered legislative provisions. Teasing out its main propositions involves an appreciation of our legal history, and a willingness to transgress traditionally discrete categories of legal thought. Our laws of property, obligations, and crime all have something to say on the legal position of finders, and many of these propositions cannot be understood without some reference to the old common law procedure from which they have evolved. The first major aim of this work is to identify and explain the various propositions clearly and authoritatively. The second is to show that, when the full range of applicable laws is appreciated, and specifically when rules of property are understood in the light of rules of crime and tort, the English law of finds, as it stands, can be shown to be based on coherent legal doctrine and sound public policy.

This argument is developed as follows. In order to introduce the various categories of legal thought relevant to the modern law, Chapter 1 considers the legal history of finders until 1722 and the decision of *Armory v Delamirie*. We will see that historically the question of the rights acquired by a finder was not much at issue. Allegations of finding in litigation were generally relevant to the liability of a defendant, who was counted (or himself pleaded) to have found certain goods, but they were not commonly relevant to the ability of a plaintiff to maintain an action. Of course, *Armory* did allow the ability of the boy to maintain trover, but by then it was already well established that trover was available to a wide class of other non-owning possessors, and there is nothing in the judgment to suggest that

---

[8] 'The popular saying that "Finding is keeping" is a dangerous half-truth, which needs a good deal of expansion and qualification to make it square with the law': PH Winfield, *A Textbook on the Law of Tort* 1st edn (London, Sweet & Maxwell, 1937) 382.

[9] ie that she was (a) dishonest; (b) a trespasser to land; (c) an employee; or (d) in a private, as opposed to a public, location.

[10] Civic Government (Scotland) Act 1982, Pt VI.

any further finder-specific proposition was contemplated in granting recovery of the value of the jewel. On the contrary, the legal rhetoric of a finder's rights has most fully been developed in more recent disputes between a finder and the possessor of the land where the find occurred. Chapter 2 traces the development of these cases from *Bridges v Hawkesworth*,[11] arguing that their legal basis has changed over time. It demonstrates that the modern cases depend on a theory of common law possession which emerged late in the nineteenth century, well after *Bridges*, which accordingly is shown to have been decided on other grounds. These modern cases are often thought to contain discrete propositions which are exceptions to the general rule in *Armory*. Here it is argued that they establish only that the finder's right is necessarily subject to the claims of those who can assert a better right by virtue of a prior possession. According to the ordinarily accepted meaning of possession in the common law, this entails proof of an earlier factual control of the goods, and an earlier intention to possess them.

The commensurability of the finder's right with those of prior possessors suggests a correlative proposition which has never fully been explored: the finder's right is consequent only on her possession. This proposition is supported in Chapters 3 and 4, which together offer an argument for not treating finding as a *sui generis* event outside the normally applicable rules of possession. Chapter 3 establishes that the facts of finding have no bearing on the finder's acquisition of right. Referring to doctrine and commentary developed in US state jurisdictions, which appear to have exerted some influence in our leading modern case,[12] it distinguishes four separate kinds of losing event, ie (a) unintentional, accidental loss of custody ('loss'); (b) intentional temporary removal of goods from custody, followed by an omission to retake ('mislaying'); (c) intentional removal from custody with a concomitant intention to conceal ('hiding'); and (d) intentional removal from custody with a concomitant intention to divest ('abandonment'). In contrast to the US states, where often it has been determinative of the matter, it is argued that in English law the designation of goods as lost, mislaid, hidden or abandoned does not have any bearing on the kind of right acquired by the finder. It might have an impact on the exigibility of that right insofar as it is indicative of the presence or absence of a greater right in someone else. It might influence too the criminal liability of the finder. But there is nothing to suggest that it operates per se on the finder's acquisition of right; or to put the matter another way, the facts of loss have no proprietary significance in English law.

Chapter 4 considers the frequently made contention that finders owe obligations to losers of goods. If this is right, it might offer a reason to distinguish finders from possessors generally, but it will be argued that the proposition cannot be supported in English law. There is no authority to warrant the imposition of specific obligations on finders in virtue of their status; finders are not properly to be regarded

---

[11] (1851) 15 Jur 1079.
[12] *Parker v British Airways Board* [1982] QB 1004, 1017.

as bailees; and general duties of tort and unjust enrichment, without more (and, in the latter case, if they exist on the facts of finding), do not compel the kind of conduct desired of finders. It is suggested that, where it has occurred, the proposition of finder-obligations has been premised on an attempt to ensure that the law of finds aims at sound policy objectives, facilitating the discovery of the loser of goods, and creating the conditions for a reunion of loser and lost goods. The objection here is not to the policy conclusions drawn, but rather to the manner in which their realisation has been conceived. It is suggested that, when the full range of laws applicable to finders is properly understood, English law can indeed be shown to encourage a finder to act in favour of the loser, but it does not do so by the imposition of specific obligations. Accordingly the temptation to bend existing common law doctrines to impose those obligations must be resisted.

Having established that, in the modern law, a finder's claim to goods depends only on the facts of her possession, Chapter 5 considers the nature and quality of the right which arises in consequence of those facts. This issue has not received much express treatment in the finding literature. When Pollock considered the rights of possessors, he started with the general availability of legal protection to possessors (through trover in the case of goods, and ejectment in the case of land), and abstracted to offer a very substantive account of the rights involved. We will see that, on his view, the right resulting from possession was a property right in a very full sense, attracting the standard advantages of ownership, and vulnerable only to the extent that it might be defeated by one who could prove a better, because earlier, possession. Moreover, it will be argued further that, once acquired, this right has the potential to outlast the facts of its creation, and so the finder acquires a property right which will withstand the subsequent loss of her possession. Since the content of this right is equivalent to ownership, it seems reasonable to say that a finder acquires an ownership interest in the object of her find, or that (albeit relatively) she is *an* owner of the asset in question. The terminology of personal property law is far from satisfactory in this respect (an issue to which we return in the Epilogue), but the conceptual relation between possession and ownership is very clear. 'Possession' denotes a set of facts (the facts of physical control of some asset, with the intention to possess it). The significance of these facts is that, when demonstrably present, they result in the acquisition of a legal right. This legal right has the content of ownership. So possession generates an ownership interest in goods. Possession is a causative event.

Chapter 6 argues that there is no ground for suggesting that a finder's acquisition of right should be qualified on the basis of extraneous facts related to her behaviour or status. Specifically, the finder's acquisition of right is not altered where at the time of the find she is (a) dishonest; (b) committing a trespass to land; (c) an employee; or (d) in a private (as opposed to a public) location. Coupled with the conclusions in Chapter 5, this establishes a wide proposition in favour of the finder: in every case where a finder takes possession of goods, she acquires an ownership interest in respect of those goods. Chapter 7 considers this proposition in the light of countervailing rules of crime and tort, arguing that

4

taken together, and despite the width of the rule of property acquisition, English law provides incentives for a finder to take reasonable steps to identify the loser of goods. It compares the structure of English law to legislative provisions in force in Scotland and the United States, and demonstrates that, properly understood, English law reflects the same two-tiered policy, facilitating the restoration of lost goods to their loser in the first instance, but providing alternative arrangements in favour of the finder in the event that the loser cannot be found. Inasmuch as it accords with the legislation of these comparator jurisdictions, English law is shown to be coherent from the perspective of public policy, and does not present itself as a candidate for urgent (legislative) reform.

As a final note of introduction, we will see throughout this work that our modern understanding of possession and finders owes a heavy debt to the intellectual rationalisation of the old forms of action which occurred towards the end of the nineteenth century. For a long time we have been content to accept *Armory v Delamirie* as authority for the proposition that possession generates a property right, but there is some reason to believe that *Armory* was not about possession at all; or at least that, in 1722, the boy's right to proceed would not have been justified on the basis of his possession alone. Possibly the most interesting and significant feature of a general work on the law of finders is that it forces us to evaluate the dominant concept of possession in the common law. It seems that Holmes and Pollock were responsible for its first elucidation, but it is equally certain that the cases on finders provided the necessary conditions for its development. In the course of this book we begin to explore its emergence and evolution.

# 1

## The Legal Context of *Armory*

For the greater part of our legal history the question of a finder's rights was not an issue. The law did not delineate or protect the rights of finders as such. Neither at first did it delineate or protect ownership as such, nor possession as such,[1] but it would remedy an involuntary loss of possession. Thus, the earliest cases involving finders are concerned almost exclusively with a loser's recovery of lost goods from a subsequent possessor. More specifically, allegations of finding might have been relevant to legal proceedings in one of three respects. First, from the middle of the fifteenth century until its abolition in 1852, a fictitious allegation—that the plaintiff casually had lost and the defendant subsequently had found certain goods—dominated civil procedures for the recovery goods. Secondly, an allegation that the defendant had found certain goods might afford a substantive plea in defence to a charge of trespass. Thirdly, an allegation that the defendant had found certain goods might afford a defence to a criminal charge of larceny, insofar as it served to deny a constituent element of that liability. This chapter explores fully each of these three distinct kinds of finding allegation, and for context's sake begins with a general account of the early procedures for recovery of lost goods. Later we come to *Armory v Delamirie*,[2] which is conversely related to the first allegation. It confirms the ability of a finder to bring trover. That is, it allows a finder herself to count loss and finding against a defendant who converts the object of her find to his own use.

## Recovery of Lost Goods at Common Law

It is difficult to find any authority prior to *Armory v Delamirie* that expressly discusses the property rights of finders. Doubtless for many years the issue did not arise at all, at least not in our terms. It is well suspected that early lawyers did not trouble themselves with theories as to the meaning of ownership and possession.[3] From the outset, however, they were concerned to remedy involuntary losses of possession.

---

[1] Holdsworth, *HEL* 3, 89.

[2] (1722) Stra 505.

[3] Holdsworth, *HEL* 2, 78. Maitland notes the absence of information about ownership and possession in the early periods of the common law: P & M, II, 149.

The early actions of the common law developed in an age where cattle were the typical example of goods and cattle lifting the typical form of theft.[4] Indeed, it has been suggested that if only this kind of physical interference with goods could have been suppressed, 'the [early] legislators will have done all or almost all that they can hope to do for the protection of the owner of movables'.[5]

It seems that our law of lost goods began not with formal legal proceedings as such, but with lawful out of court procedures for the recovery of *res addiratae* ('lost things'). Ames identifies an early practice for the recovery of lost animals potentially estray.[6] The lord of a manor would proclaim a found animal to be his, but bind himself to restore it or its price if it was claimed by its loser within a year and a day.[7] The loser would have his recovery if he produced a sufficient body of witnesses (or *secta*) to swear to his ownership or loss of the animal, though he must pay the lord for keeping the animal. The same procedure seems to have been available to obtain recovery of stolen goods from a subsequent possessor.[8] It was common practice for the *secta* to be composed of bailiffs (unless the possessor was himself a bailiff or other official) and the claimant would rely on their executive powers to have his claim enforced.[9]

If the possessor refused to hand over lost goods claimed in this manner, the claimant's legal recourse would be to the law of theft, which from the earliest days lay against anyone who detained goods (whether or not the original taker).[10] Bracton's account of theft[11] seems to disclose two methods of proceeding, one criminal, the other civil, although the latter could be augmented to a criminal charge. Thus:

> he who sues may from the outset sue civilly or criminally, whichever he pleases. For he may claim his property as lost (*rem suam petere ut addiratum*), supporting his claim by the testimony of reasonable men, and thus sue to recover his property though it is stolen. If he who is seised will not comply with his demand he may augment his action and claim it as stolen.[12]

There is some debate about the precise meaning of these words. Holdsworth thought that the civil claim countenanced was a formal action ('the action for *res addiratae*') which existed in parallel to the criminal appeal, except that it omitted the words of felony.[13] Others have likewise considered it a formal claim, though

---

[4] Holdsworth, *HEL* 2, 79. Such proceedings are thought common: 'An action for the recovery of cattle seems as typical of the Anglo-Saxon age as an action for the recovery of land is of the thirteenth century, or an action on a contract is of our own day': P & M, II, 149.

[5] P & M, II, 157.

[6] Ames, HT, 379.

[7] (1281) 2 SS 31. If the waif was not claimed within a year and a day it became the property of the lord: Fleta, Ch 45, 72 SS 100.

[8] JM Kaye, '*Res Addiratae* and the Recovery of Stolen Goods' (1970) 86 *LQR* 379, 380–1.

[9] *Ibid* 380.

[10] Holdsworth, *HEL*, 3, 270.

[11] Bracton, f 150b *et seq*.

[12] *Ibid*. It was not possible conversely to charge the possessor as a thief, and later reduce the prosecution to a claim for lost goods.

[13] Holdsworth, *HEL*, 3, 269.

doubted its nature. Baker, for example, noting the existence of doubt, suggests that it might have been a petition in eyre, at gaol delivery, or alternatively that it was a complaint in trespass.[14] Ames certainly thought it was trespassory in nature.[15] He also construed literally the permissibility of augmenting the complaint to an appeal of larceny, and for that reason thought it a necessary preliminary to criminal proceedings, in the sense that the latter could only be commenced in the event that the possessor refused to redeliver the lost thing on proof and demand.[16] Maitland, by contrast, thought that Bracton was not giving two separate actions but only alternative methods of counting within the same action.[17] Latterly, caution has been urged in pursuing the differences between these several opinions, each of which is said to be 'based on rather slender evidence', and 'marred, to some extent, by misconceptions as to the scope of the appeal of larceny'.[18] Nonetheless, whichever view is taken, it seems certain that the claim was tortious in nature, at least in the general sense of existing to remedy a wrong done to the claimant.[19] This is clearly evident in an entry in the Year Book of 1294, which Ames takes to be the count for a lost thing:

> Note that where a thing belonging to a man is lost (*endiré*), he may count that he (the finder) tortiously detains it, etc, and tortiously for this that whereas he lost the said thing on such and such a day, etc, he (the loser) on such a day, etc, and found it in the house of such a one and told him, etc, and prayed him to restore the thing, but that he would not restore it, etc, to his damage, etc; and if he will, etc. In this case the demandant must prove by his law (his own hand the twelfth) that he lost the thing.[20]

There is also the following precedent in the *Novae Narrationes*.[21] Although in its terms it concerns the recovery of a lost horse, it is clear from the subsequent entry that it can apply equally to other tangible chattels:[22]

> W, who is here, lays before you this: that whereas he had his horse of such a colour, price so much etc, in such a vill, such a day, such a year, such a place, there was this horse lost

---

[14]  Baker, *Introduction*, 391. The view that the action is a complaint in trespass is here attributed to Britton's treatise on the laws of England, which was produced at the end of the 13th century: see FM Nichols (ed) *Britton* (Oxford, Clarendon Press, 1865), vol I, 57, 68.

[15]  Ames, HT, 380–1.

[16]  *Ibid* 380.

[17]  P & M, II, 161.

[18]  Kaye, above n 8 at 380.

[19]  Specifically wrongful detention of goods: FW Maitland, *Bracton's Note Book* (London, CJ Clay & Sons, 1887) case 824. Note, however, Baker's opinion, writing of trespass and case in the fifteenth century, that the idea of wrong 'was perhaps the broadest and least well-defined concept in the common law': *OH*, 753.

[20]  (1294) YB 20 Ed I 466, trans Ames, HT, 380. See also E Shanks and SFC Milsom (eds), *Novae Narrationes* (1963) 80 SS clxxix.

[21]  The *Novae Narrationes* was a mediaeval collection of counts and defences available in the King's courts. It is thought to have first been published towards the end of the fifteenth century. For an overview see 'General Introduction' in *Novae Narrationes*, above n 20 80 SS ix. On this kind of legal literature generally, see Baker, *Introduction*, 177.

[22]  The specific examples given of other things caught by the precedent are loads, cloths, and vessels: *Novae Narrationes*, above n 20 80 SS 120 at B 234.

to him; and he went seeking his horse from place to place and caused it to be asked for at church, at market, and at fair, from such a day etc, and he could hear nothing of his horse until (a certain) day when he came and found his horse in the keeping of one Robert de C, who is there, to wit in the house of this same Robert in the same vill, and he hold him how his horse was lost to him, and asked that he should deliver it up, (but) he would not do so and still will not, wrongfully and to his damages etc.[23]

If successful in such a claim, it seems that the plaintiff would have return of his goods, though possibly this depended on the acquiescence of the finder, and was not required of him as such.[24] If he wanted to be sure of recovering his goods *in specie*, he would need to elevate his action to an appeal of larceny. That was a private prosecution,[25] in which a victim alleged that his goods had been thievishly taken by the appellee, contrary to the King's peace.[26] The law required that immediately upon the discovery of his loss, the victim raised hue and cry, and, with his neighbours, made fresh pursuit of the thief. A thief caught red-handed was dealt with in the most summary means imaginable: he would be put to death without hearing immediately upon an oath from the victim that the goods had been stolen from him. A hearing was allowed where the thief was not caught in hot pursuit. Initially trial was by battle,[27] though eventually the appellee could elect to put himself upon a jury.[28] He might also claim to hold the goods as the bailee or vendee of someone else, and vouch this third person as a warrantor to defend the appeal in his place.[29] In the event of conviction, the appellee would be put to death, and his goods forfeited to the Crown, except those forming the subject of the appeal, which were returned to the victim.

The availability of specific restitution of the victim's chattels shows that the appeal of larceny was 'recuperatory' in nature. We might say that it served to achieve twin criminal and civil objectives of punishing thieves and allowing those wronged to have recovery of their goods.[30] The availability of a defence by voucher of warranty also fulfilled an important commercial policy objective,

---

[23] *Ibid* 80 SS 119 at B 233.

[24] Bracton, f 150b; Ames, *HT*, 380. Holdsworth says that the plaintiff must accept damages: *HEL* 3, 270.

[25] There was no public prosecution of crime until the Assize of Clarendon in 1166. Larceny was included in this list of felonies that could be tried by indictment: Holdsworth, *HEL*, 3, 286.

[26] Bracton says that the victim appealed that the appellee 'took the said property (*rem illam*) feloniously and stealthily and larcenously and against the King's peace and thievishly bore it away': Bracton, f 150b–151.

[27] Bracton, f 151.

[28] P & M, II, 165.

[29] A rule which benefited the honest possessor, and meant that the rules laying on him the burden of disproving his guilt 'did not press so hardly … as might first appear': *HEL*, 2, 81, 83.

[30] P & M, II, 157, 159–60. Of course, the labels 'criminal' and 'civil' are latter day rationalisations of the functions of this appeal, and are not readily applicable in the period in question. The appeals were private actions against wrongdoers (whether criminals or tortfeasors), and depended upon the initiative of the injured party: Ames, HT, 278.

insofar as it ensured publicity in dealings with goods. As Holdsworth says,[31] a prudent man, lest he be appealed of certain things, would know how his goods came to be in his possession, and would ensure that his neighbours knew the same. Maitland applied this logic directly to finders: a prudent finder would have taken the witness of his neighbours to the finding, so that he might escape any appeal by waging his law with their testimony.[32]

## Development of Forms of Action at Common Law

In the twelfth and thirteenth centuries, the appeals gradually fell into disuse owing to the availability of public prosecution and, no doubt, an increasing distaste for the onerous procedures of the appeal of larceny.[33] At the same time, a host of new actions were being developed to remedy losses of possession. All of these 'standard medieval remedies' were based on wrongful interferences with goods.[34] The first of them was the writ of trespass for goods taken and carried away (*de bonis asportatis*). The writ itself was simple, directing the sheriff to attach the defendant to answer the plaintiff for an act of force (*vi et armis*) contrary to the King's peace, the latter count explaining the jurisdiction of the royal courts in the matter.[35] The count in trespass was thus equivalent to the appeal of larceny, except that it omitted the words of felony, and likewise the offer of trial by battle. For this reason, many have thought the origin of trespass no more than the logical historical development of the appeal,[36] although this is by no means uncontroversial.[37]

In some respects it seems counter-intuitive that trespass should have lain for the recovery of lost goods. At the least, it is difficult to construe a non-felonious assumption of lost goods as an act of taking contrary to the King's peace.[38] Yet exactly this seems to have happened in a case of 1372, where the plaintiff brought trespass for a quantity of gold and silver taken and carried away.[39] The defendants

---

[31]  Holdsworth, *HEL*, 2, 81.

[32]  P & M, II, 175.

[33]  For a useful summary of the difficulties of prosecuting such an appeal, see Ames, HT, 280–2.

[34]  Baker, *OH*, 801.

[35]  Lest the royal courts be swamped with litigation, a statute of Edward I provided that no one should have a writ of trespass unless he swore by his faith that his goods were worth 40 shillings or more: (1278) 6 Ed I c8.

[36]  Holdsworth, *HEL*, 3, 271-273; P & M II, 165.

[37]  Questioning this theory, Fifoot contended that 'the evidence marshalled in its support is more slender than its frequent repetition would suggest': CHS Fifoot, *History and Sources of the Common Law* (London, Stevens & Sons Ltd, 1949) 44. See also TFT Plunkett, *A Concise History of the Common Law* 5th edn (London, Butterworths, 1956) 369–71.

[38]  See Ibbetson for the view that breach of the peace was a jurisdictional term, and did not necessarily depend on violence: DJ Ibbetson, *A Historical Introduction to the Law of Obligations* (Oxford, OUP, 1999) 39.

[39]  (1372) YB 46 Ed III, f 15, pl 1.

pleaded that they had found the goods at sea, and ultimately sought judgment against the writ because it counted a taking against the peace where there was none on the facts. Nonetheless, the court allowed the plaintiff to maintain the action, and so held, notwithstanding the lack of violence contemplated by the literal form of the writ, that taking lost goods was trespass.[40] The position seems to have been the same in the case of animals lost and potentially estray. Indeed, even when faced with a counter demand from his lord, the loser of an animal might have a writ of trespass, or with addition of words of felony, an appeal.[41] So we read:

> No person can detain from another birds or beasts *ferae naturae*, which have been domesticated, without being guilty of robbery or of open trespass against our peace, if due pursuit be made thereof within the year and day, to prevent their being claimed as estrays.[42]

Professor Tay rationalised the availability of trespass in such matters by holding that the early common law knew of no conceptual category of 'lost' goods.[43] Once in human possession goods might be abandoned, but otherwise they continued in that possession until they passed out of it by violence or consent. There was no intermediate category of goods not abandoned but out of the present physical control of anyone. Thus, constructively, the act of taking found goods carries the appearance of an immediate interference, because at the time of such assumption they were legally in the possession of the loser; or, to put the matter from the other end, as did Tay, 'since I did not consent to the finder's taking up of the object I dropped, he is a trespasser'.[44] Possibly there is a good deal of truth in this rationalisation, but it is by no means certain that the common lawyers of the day thought about or argued cases of loss in such conceptual terms. As likely an explanation for allowing losers of goods to maintain trespass is to be found in a general tendency towards expansion of the jurisdiction of the King's courts, or a desire to occasion liability in cases where defendants were perceived to have behaved improperly or dishonestly.[45]

---

[40] See also (1484) YB 2 Rich III, f 15, pl 39, where Donnington J would have allowed a loser to elect between trespass or detinue to recover from a finder. There might yet be an earlier case than that of 1372: see RC Palmer, *English Law in the Age of the Black Death* (Chapel Hill NC, University of North Carolina Press, 1993) 357, citing *Stok v Palfreyman* (1369) CP 40/433 m 68, where the count alleged that the defendant with force and arms 'took the plaintiff's certain horse found at Settrington and rode that horse with such hurry that the horse could not serve for further labour'.

[41] FM Nichols (ed), *Britton* (Oxford, Clarendon Press, 1865) 68.

[42] *Ibid* 215–16. Ames notes additionally that either an owner or his lord might bring trespass for an estray carried off by a third hand: Ames, HT, 288, citing (1504) YB 20 Hen VII, f 1, pl 1.

[43] AES Tay, '*Bridges v Hawkesworth* and the Early History of Finding' (1964) 8 *American Journal of Legal History* 223, 226.

[44] *Ibid* 226.

[45] For an example paralleling the availability of trespass against a finder, see the doctrine of breaking bulk developed to allow larceny against bailees, drawn from *The Carrier's Case*, discussed below.

## Detinue

Whilst it seems certain that a loser of goods could have a writ of trespass to recover their value, it is equally certain that soon there were other forms of legal recovery available to him. Detinue was an action born of debt,[46] sounding in damages, although the defendant could satisfy the judgment by delivering up the disputed goods.[47] In its original form it depended on the existence of a bailment,[48] and lay between a bailor and his bailee for the latter's refusal to return goods on a demand from the former.[49] However, by the middle of the fourteenth century, it was settled that demand and refusal was the essence of the action,[50] and it was good enough for the plaintiff to count that the goods in question came into the hands of the defendant (*devenerunt ad manus defendentis*) without alleging any bailment.[51]

To proceed in this manner, it seems that initially the plaintiff must have explained how in fact the goods came to be in the hands of the defendant, which explanation could be denied by the defendant.[52] But soon the allegation was considered non-traversable, and the plaintiff need only count his prior possession of the goods, and that these were in the hands of the defendant. This general form of detinue was well established by the end of the fourteenth century, and it lay against finders. Ames says that the first case between a loser and a finder was in 1370, where the plaintiff brought detinue for an ass which strayed to the seignory of the defendant, and which the defendant refused to return in spite of the plaintiff's offer of money for the animal's keep.[53] In a case of 1429 for detinue of a deed, Paston J thought the plaintiff need not show how the defendant had come to it because 'it may be the defendant found the deed'.[54] Of course, that the trespass case of 1372 existed concurrently with this new claim in detinue suggests that, at least for a time, multiple remedies were

---

[46] P & M, II, 173; Ames, HT, 375.

[47] Bracton, f 102b. In his count the plaintiff would be obliged to put a value on the thing, although the value would also be assessed by the jury: P & M, II, 174.

[48] The count in detinue alleged a bailment, and a traverse of that allegation was an answer to the action.

[49] The writ commanded the sheriff to order the defendant to deliver up certain goods of the plaintiff, which the defendant 'unjustly detained' (*quae injuste detinet*): Baker, *Introduction*, 391; P & M, II, 173–4.

[50] Baker, *Introduction*, 392. Baker there notes the presence of earlier examples of detinue against a third hand, the earliest defendants being the executors of bailees, or those who detained title deeds.

[51] It might be more accurate to say that the action of detinue bifurcated into two forms. Where the plaintiff could point to the existence of a bailment, he had his writ on that basis, but where there was no bailment he could count simply that the goods had come to the hands of the defendant. Thus, there might be respectively detinue sur bailment and detinue *ad manus devenerunt*. Milsom considers these to be two quite different liabilities: SFC Milsom, 'Not Doing is No Trespass' (1954) *Camb LJ* 105, 113.

[52] *Ibid.*

[53] Ames, HT, 381, citing (1370) YB 44 Ed III, f 14, pl 30.

[54] (1429) YB 9 Hen VI, f 58, pl 4.

available against a finder of lost goods. In the middle of the fifteenth century, however, the court considered whether it was more appropriate for a loser of goods to count a finder in trespass or detinue. In answering the question it gave birth to the fictitious form of finding that would influence the common law for the next 400 years.

# The Fiction of Finding

In a case of 1455, a bailiff alleged his possession of certain charters, and that these had come to the defendant by finding.[55] Prisot CJ thought that the proper action was in trespass, but Littleton (then of counsel) argued the contrary, without further dissent from the court. The argument is interesting, because the court seems to have assumed that taking by finding was lawful, and not trespassory.[56] Littleton pressed an analogy between a finder and a distrainor. In the event that a distrainor refused to return the distress on payment of the monies owed, the proper remedy for the distrainee was in detinue rather than trespass,[57] since the initial taking was lawful. Likewise, said Littleton, 'when [the defendant] found the charters it was lawful, and although he would not deliver them on the request I shall have no trespass but only detinue, for no trespass is yet done'.[58]

This case is something of a high water mark in the history of finding. From this time onwards, in a writ of detinue not alleging a bailment, the general *devenerunt ad manus* count was replaced by the allegation that the defendant found the goods (*devenerunt ad manus per inventionem*), and so the fictional count of detinue sur trover was born.[59]

There is no doubt that in some respects this trover count in detinue was advantageous to plaintiffs. The court would not allow a defendant to traverse the allegation unless he could show that he came by the goods by some lawful means,[60] and possibly the writ was allowed and intended to do the work of the old action *de re adirata*.[61] But detinue also had its disadvantages, two of which have generally been accepted. First, the defendant might evade liability completely by electing to wage

---

[55] (1455) YB 33 Hen VI, f 26, pl 12.

[56] 'per le invencio il ne filt ne tort' (Prisot CJ, *ibid*). This emergence of a view that honest finding was not trespassory is discussed further below.

[57] Originally the proper remedy for a distrainee was replevin: see generally Ames, HT, 374–5.

[58] (1455) YB 33 Hen VI, f 26, pl 12.

[59] *Trouver* being the verb 'to find' in French.

[60] Baker, *Introduction*, 393.

[61] Though Ames notes, by way of distinction, that in the count for *res addiratae* given in *Nova Narrationes*, the plaintiff alleged that he found the goods in the defendant's possession, but the trover allegation supposed that the defendant found the goods. In other words, the count for a *res addirata* did not allege that the defendant found the goods: Ames, HT, 382.

his law.[62] Secondly, it was not always possible for the plaintiff to receive the full measure of his loss. As we have seen, a judgment in detinue called for damages, but the defendant had always the option of returning the goods to the plaintiff in satisfaction of the claim. This caused a problem when the defendant had damaged the goods, or used them to such an extent that they became worthless. B might find A's horse and work it to exhaustion, but satisfy a judgment in detinue (or evade liability altogether) by returning it. A would recover an exhausted horse, but could have no damages in detinue for the depreciation in its value.[63] Moreover, in the event that B had completely destroyed the goods, it is arguable that detinue was frustrated altogether because it could not truthfully be asserted that B detained A's goods.[64] Probably for these reasons, detinue fell out of use in the fifteenth century,[65] though the fiction of finding would quickly reassert itself, albeit in a different action.

## Trover and Conversion

To remedy plaintiffs suffering from the disadvantages of detinue, counsel and courts experimented with new forms of liability, and particularly with actions of trespass on the case.[66] The essence of case was its flexibility. It was a special form of trespass, available at the King's Bench or the Common Pleas,[67] special in the sense that it omitted the allegation of forceful taking (*vi et armis*) that ordinarily was the backbone of the writ.[68] Instead, plaintiffs could use the introductory part to count various facts and various wrongs, and could rely on alleged rights and duties not otherwise established at common law.[69] Quickly, however, certain identifiable species of case began to emerge,[70] one of which was the action on the case for conversion, undoubted forerunner of our modern tort of the same name.

The origins of the action on the case for conversion are not exactly known and a matter of some dispute. Milsom thought that it emerged to deal with the situation where the plaintiff's goods were accidentally lost by a subsequent possessor who was not his bailee, including, relevantly for our present enquiry, accidental

---

[62] Though Simpson thinks that too much is made of the possibility of fraudulent waging of law: AWB Simpson, 'The Introduction of the Action on the Case for Conversion' (1959) 75 *LQR* 364, 365.

[63] He might have a second claim for damages for this loss, with a special action on the case.

[64] Baker, *OH*, 801.

[65] It was not formally abolished until 1977: Torts (Interference with Goods) Act 1977, s 2(1).

[66] In a case of 1479, Bryan CJ specifically objected to the use of case to supplant detinue because it denied the defendant an opportunity to wage his law: Baker, *OH*, 801.

[67] Baker, *OH*, 751.

[68] Baker, *Introduction*, 394.

[69] Milsom, above n 51 at 106.

[70] Examples include actions on the case for defamation, malicious prosecution, breach of contract, and conversion. It is probably inaccurate to think of these as different species of case, though Baker says it is 'almost irresistibly convenient, and not too misleading' to give names to the main variants: Baker, *OH*, 752.

loss by a finder.[71] Simpson has vigorously resisted this contention,[72] and pressed an alternative argument using the doctrine of *specificatio*.[73] Whichever of these is correct, it is certain that, though the development of the action was 'slow and interesting', it would eventually stand to remedy positive misconduct by the defendant, where the latter had misappropriated the goods of the plaintiff to his own use.[74]

Soon the action operated by repeating the fictions of detinue. In a case of 1519, a plaintiff brought conversion for goods alleging that they had come to the hands of the defendant.[75] Quickly the general count was replaced by an allegation of trover, again borrowed directly from detinue.[76] Baker suggests that the earliest actions for trover and conversion may well have originated from cases of genuine loss and finding.[77] He gives a case of 1531 in which the plaintiff lost a purse and obtained judgment, having 'framed his action in terms of an accidental loss, a coming to the hands of the defendant by finding, and a felonious sale and conversion'.[78] Nonetheless, as with detinue sur trover, it is certain that the allegation soon became non-traversable,[79] and a fiction so liberal in scope that it could lie against a bailee, a taker with force and arms,[80] and other subsequent possessors who could not in the term's ordinary usage have been said to have 'found' anything.[81] But the height of the fiction is most clearly illustrated in that for some time there was doubt about whether trover should be allowed against *actual* finders. We find disagreement about this across the various courts.[82] In 1595, the Exchequer Chamber allowed it. The short report of *Eason v Newman*[83] records a special verdict that one Pepper was possessed of goods, and that the

---

[71] Milsom, above n 51 at 114. The argument is said to follow from the impossibility of bringing detinue sur trover in these circumstances, where by reason of the defendant's loss the plaintiff could not show his lost thing in the former's hands.

[72] '[O]n the face of it seems unlikely that a finder of goods who was sued in detinue sur trover could defend himself by showing that he lost the goods *in any way whatsoever* before he was asked to return them': AWB Simpson, 'The Introduction of the Action on the Case for Conversion' (1959) 75 LQR 364, 371 (original emphasis).

[73] *Ibid* 372–4.

[74] *Ibid* 380; *Isaack v Clark* (1614) 2 Bulst 306. Like detinue, the standard remedy in conversion was damages, though the defendant could satisfy judgment by returning the thing.

[75] *Audelet v Latton (No. 1)* (1519) KB 27/1030, m 39; (1977) 94 SS 252.

[76] Baker, *Introduction*, 397.

[77] This is consistent with a question about lost money in the Inner Temple in the 1490s: 'Query, if someone finds money which I have lost out of a bag, what action lies? I may not have detinue or debt, as it seems to me': JH Baker (ed), *The Notebook of Sir John Port* (1986) 102 SS 80.

[78] *OH*, 806. Baker adds that, apart from the count of felony, which would be dropped in later proceedings, this was the form of the standard count in trover: *OH*, 806.

[79] JH Baker, 'Actions on the Case for Wrongs', ch VIII in *Introduction to the Reports of Sir John Spelman* (1977) 94 SS 23, 252.

[80] *Bysshoppe v Viscountess Mountague* (1604) Pas 1601: Cro Eliz 824, pl 1; Mich 1604: Cro Jac 50, pl 21; reported in B & M, 540.

[81] Baker gives examples of the action being used for recovery of a ship 'lost and found in London', and for long lists of the contents of houses: Baker, *Introduction*, 398.

[82] See generally Baker, *Introduction*, 388–99.

[83] (1595) Cro Eliz 495.

defendant found them. Pepper made the plaintiff his executor, and the defendant denied to deliver the goods to the plaintiff upon the latter's request. The justices (Popham CJ dissenting) thought that the finder's denial was a conversion. The King's Bench oscillated in its conclusions. In an anonymous case of 1579, after some disagreement, an action on the case was allowed for conversion of a horse, because detaining and using a horse was a conversion.[84] In the later case of *Isaack v Clark*, the court would refine this opinion and hold that conversion would not lie for a refusal to redeliver goods lawfully acquired,[85] because this action was a nonfeasance, and conversion required misfeasance.[86] For this reason Coke CJ expressed the opinion that there could be no action of conversion against a finder:

> [I]f a man finds goods, an action upon the case lieth, for his ill and negligent keeping of them, but no trover and conversion, because this is but a non feasans.[87]

Coke CJ rationalised this proposition by pressing a distinction between 'trover in law' and 'trover in fact'.[88] A person whose lost goods were actually found had his remedy in detinue, but not trespass or case, the latter being a fiction ('a trover in law') to be counted against misfeasors. If this opinion had prevailed, it would have entailed that losers of goods bring claims against finders in detinue, with all its procedural and substantive disadvantages. Fortunately this does not seem to have been the case.[89] We are not helped by a lack of recorded disputes between finders and losers in the civil law reports from the time of Coke onwards,[90] but generally it is accepted that by the end of the eighteenth century, trover had become 'theoretically concurrent with ... [the] appeal of larceny, trespass, detinue, and replevin', and in practice was the standard remedy used in all cases of interference with goods.[91] Thus the fiction of finding remained at the centre of cases on wrongful inferences with goods until its express abolition by the Common Law Procedure Act 1852.[92] That statute provided a new form of declaration by which a plaintiff alleged: 'That the defendant converted to his own use, or wrongfully deprived the plaintiff of the use and possession of the plaintiff's goods'.[93] We will return to consider this modern tort of conversion in Chapter 4, but for now it is enough to note that, inasmuch as it was fictional and concerned to facilitate the return of goods to those that had lost them, the allegation of

---

[84] (1579) LI MS Misc 488, pl 44, trans B & M, 533.

[85] Hence the development of the specific statutory wrong of conversion by a bailee.

[86] (1614) 2 Bulst 306.

[87] (1614) 2 Bulst 306, 312.

[88] *Ibid* 313.

[89] J Williams, *Principles of the Law of Personal Property* 11th edn (London, H Sweet, 1881) 30; Simpson, above n 72 at 378–9.

[90] Tay, above n 43 at 232.

[91] Ames, HT, 386. For a sketch of its assumption of the role of these other forms, see 383–6.

[92] Common Law Procedure Act 1852, s 49.

[93] *Ibid* sch A, No 28; Supreme Court of Judicature Act 1875, App A, pt 2, s 4; RSC 1883, App A, pt 3, s 4.

finding that featured in the old common law forms of action has got little, if anything, to say about the acquisition of rights by a finder.

# Finding as a Justificatory Excuse: 'The Law of Charity'

Whilst allegations of finding were a prevalent fiction in the old forms of action at common law, they also had a non-fictitious, substantive role to play. It seems that a plea of finding could work to the advantage of a defendant charged with trespass or detinue sur bailment. In *Isaack v Clark*, Coke CJ declared that a finder who kept goods in safe custody for their owner committed no wrong:

> it is the law of charity, to lay up the goods which do thus come to his hands by trover, and no trespass shall lie for this.[94]

We do not know much about the origins of this proposition. Certainly it was contemplated *arguendo* by Littleton in the case of 1455 discussed above,[95] and implicitly accepted by the court in allowing the plaintiff his writ of detinue. In the years that follow, we find many opinions in the same terms, and it may be that initially the expression of charity was a fiction designed to move proceedings out of trespass and into detinue.[96] In a case of 1467, the plaintiff brought trespass for certain goods carried away.[97] The defendant pleaded to the action that he was executor for a testator who was co-owner with the plaintiff; that he had found the goods complained of amongst those of the testator; that he had taken them to keep them safely for the plaintiff; and that for this reason the plaintiff should have brought his claim in detinue rather than trespass. Nedham J allowed the plea:

> This is a plea to the action, for it is a good justification, for it was lawful for him to take them when he found them among his testator's goods, for if a man lose a thing in the road and I come and find the thing in the road and take it to guard it for the use of him that lost it, if he bring trespass against me of this thing I shall plead this to the action and not to the writ, for it was allowable for me to take it for the use of him that lost it.[98]

Soon this idea of lawfulness was developed to give the plea a more substantive flavour. In 1485, Donnington J characterised the finder's justification as an invocation of jeopardy: a finder might justify himself, and so escape a writ of trespass,

---

[94] (1614) 2 Bulst 306. In the clause preceding this quotation, the learned Chief Justice had expressed the concomitant view that such conduct did not amount to a conversion.

[95] Although it was a view held 'in the face of all authority': Tay, above n 43 at 230.

[96] As we have said, in the years before Littleton's innovation the courts seemed to allow a plaintiff an election between trespass and detinue: (1429) YB 7 Hen VI, f 22, pl 3.

[97] (1467) YB 7 Ed IV, f 3, pl 9.

[98] (1467) YB 7 Ed IV, f 3, pl 9 (Littleton J concurring); P & W, 175.

by taking goods 'for the sake of saving them'.[99] This was followed in 1505, where Kingsmill J refused to allow a defendant to justify for trespass of a quantity of corn carried away because the corn was not 'in peril of perishing'.[100] By the time of *Isaack v Clark* we have the beginnings of a doctrine of rightful and wrongful finding, such that one who takes goods for the sake of their owner cannot be charged in trespass, but 'where one takes goods, where there is no such danger of being lost, or findes them before they are lost, otherwise it shall be'.[101] In substantive law, this amounted to holding that a finder of goods could not excuse himself in trespass merely by claiming that he found the goods. Something must be 'lost' before it could be found. This proposition was not much developed in the civil courts of the seventeenth century, but the same question would arise again in the criminal context of larceny, to which now we turn.[102]

# Larceny by Finding

To complete our contextual picture of finding allegations, we must note that they have always been significant to criminal liability for theft offences. Bracton defined theft as 'the fraudulent mishandling (*contrectatio*) of another's property without the owner's consent, with the intention of stealing'.[103] In Roman law *contrectatio* was a term with many meanings.[104] In England, its import was restricted to the situation where the actions of a thief effected a physical change in the possession of the goods stolen,[105] and for that reason there came quickly to be an association between larceny and trespass, such that the former would not lie without the latter.[106] Once it was established through the 'law of charity' that it was not trespass

---

[99]  (1484) YB 2 Rich III, p 15, pl 39; P & W, 176.

[100]  (1505) YB 21 Hen VII, f 27, pl 9.

[101]  (1614) 2 Bulst 306, 312. An argument of the Inner Temple in 1494 says that a finder is not liable in trespass 'as long as he behaves as a finder', though the focus here is on subsequent wrongdoing after finding: (1989) 105 SS 293.

[102]  It is worth noting that in Pollock and Wright, the principal treatment of 'the law of charity' occurs in the context of a discussion on the requirement of trespass in theft: P & W, 172–80.

[103]  Bracton, f 150b.

[104]  Literally it seems to translate as 'handling', and Buckland describes the central case as an 'actual meddling' with possession of goods, but it is equally clear that the term covered a much wider variety of interferences, including apparently consensual transfers of possession. See generally J Inst 4.1, and WW Buckland, *A Textbook of Roman Law* 2nd edn (Cambridge, Cambridge University Press, 1932) 577–8.

[105]  3 Co Inst 107; Holdsworth, *HEL*, 3, 287. It seems probable that this was due to the fact that in its earliest form, as we have seen, the central case of theft contemplated removal of goods by force and a hot pursuit after the thief.

[106]  *R v Ashwell* (1885) 16 QBD 190; *Russell on Crime*, vol II, 907; JP McCutcheon, *The Larceny Act 1916* (Dublin, Round Hall Press, 1989) 25; J Edwards, 'Possession and Larceny' (1950) 3 *Current Legal Problems* 127. Of course, if it is right, as has been contended, that actions in trespass were born of the appeal of larceny, then the connection is even more readily apparent: JH Beale, Jnr, 'The Borderland of Larceny' (1892–93) 6 *Harv LR* 244, 245.

to take up lost goods, it was neither larceny. So, in the seventeenth century, Coke declared confidently that there could be no larceny where goods were acquired by trover or finding, even when they were acquired dishonestly:

> If one lose his goods, and another finde them, though he convert them, *animo furandi*, to his own use, yet it is no larceny, for the first taking is lawfull.[107]

Yet the ultimate root of this proposition, ie that larceny involved a trespassory violation of possession, as opposed to a more abstract interference with property, was far from uncontroversial. Consistently it was regarded as the principal difficulty of the law of theft,[108] and the history of larceny might well be understood as a series of attempts by the courts to circumvent the requirement in cases where it was felt that the dishonest conduct of the defendant demanded punishment. One notorious example is *The Carrier's Case* of 1473,[109] where the Star Chamber convicted a carrier of larceny of the contents of certain bales of dyer's weed. The objection that there was no taking on the facts[110] was overcome by holding that the bales entire had been bailed to the defendant, and not their contents, so that when he broke open the bales and removed the contents he committed a trespass.[111] In the fifteenth and sixteenth centuries, the concept of taking was extended to allow larceny in cases where servants took away goods entrusted to them by their masters,[112] and there was a similar extension in later cases where goods were obtained under false pretences. In *R v Pear*,[113] the defendant hired a horse from the prosecutor saying that he intended to go from London to Surrey, but later sold the horse at Smithfield market. The jury found that the defendant's intentions were fraudulent from the start. With this, the judges thought him guilty of felony because 'the parting of the property had not changed the nature of the possession … [which] remained unaltered in the prosecutor at the time of the conversion'.[114]

---

[107] 3 Co Inst 108, citing (1348) 22 Edw 3 cor 265. Hale and Hawkins are in the same terms. Thus: 'If A finds the purse of B on the highway, and takes it and carries it away, and hath all the circumstances that may prove it to be done *animo furandi*, as denying it or secreting it, yet it is not felony' (1 Hale PC 506); and: 'One who finds such goods as I have lost, and converts them to his own use, *animo furandi*, is no felon' (1 Hawk PC 142).

[108] Baker, *OH*, 566–7; Plunkett called it 'the great defect in the common law of larceny': *A Concise History of the Common Law* 5th edn 9 London, Butterworths, 1956) 449. Compare modern difficulties with the meaning of appropriation.

[109] (1473) YB 13 Ed IV, f 9, pl 5.

[110] Bryan CJ took this objection to be decisive.

[111] In truth, the several justices of the court offered varying formulations of this rationale, but generally the rule was accepted until the nineteenth century, though it was far from immune from criticism: see generally GP Fletcher, 'The Metamorphosis of Larceny' (1976) 89 *Harv LR* 469, 483–5.

[112] '[I]f any such servaunt or vauntes withdrawe hym or them from their said Masters and Maystresses and g awaye with the said caskettes jewels money goodes or other catelles … and defraude his or their said Maysters or Maystresses therof … or otherwise convert the same to his owne use with lyke purpose to stele yt … frome hensforth [this] shalbe demed and adjudged felony': (1529) Statute 21 Hen VIII, c 7.

[113] (1779) 1 Leach 212.

[114] *Ibid* 213–14.

Similar circumvention of the requirement of trespassory taking can be seen from the late seventeenth century onwards in cases involving finders. The earliest known case is *R v Lamb*,[115] in which the driver of a hackney coach was convicted of stealing a trunk left behind by a passenger. Eventually the criminal law would come to recognise a specific offence of larceny by finding,[116] but its development was extremely incremental, and the rationale for counting a trespass on the facts of finding was never entirely clear. One solution was to extend the doctrine of breaking bulk to finding cases. There are traces of this from the late eighteenth century. *R v Wynne*[117] was another hackney coach case, where the driver made off with a box left under a seat, despite the shouts of the passenger who ran into the street after the coach on realising his loss. Eyre B directed the jury that it should only return a guilty verdict if it was satisfied that the driver had opened the box with an intention to embezzle its contents.[118] If he had simply detained the box in the hope of a reward, however much a breach of his moral duty to the passenger, yet it would be no larceny, since it was no taking to keep that which had been 'thrown upon him by the negligence of the prosecutor'.[119] In *Cartwright v Green*,[120] where the defendant found 900 guineas hidden in the secret drawer of a bureau sent to him for repair, Lord Eldon confirmed the requirement of felonious taking,[121] but thought it would certainly exist if the defendant had broken open any part of the bureau which it was not necessary to touch for the purpose of repair.[122] This application of breaking bulk to the facts of finding was criticised in *R v Thurborn*,[123] in a passage which is relevant to our present study because it makes reference to the existence of a property right in a finder. Parke B considered it 'difficult to apply a doctrine which belongs to bailment, where a special property is acquired by contract, to any case of goods merely lost and found, where a special property is acquired by finding'.[124] Probably this view depends too much on a contractual theory of bailment, which was then, and is now, much disputed, but in any event, despite Parke B's view, *The Carrier's Case* doctrine certainly played a part in the development of larceny by finding.

An alternative analysis followed *R v Pear* and used the increasingly fluid concept of legal possession to hold that, although goods were in fact out of the immediate custody of their owner, in law they continued in his possession, such that any assumption of them was a trespassory interference. This rationale is evident in a series of US cases that would later become significant in the determination

---

[115] (1694) 2 East PC 664.
[116] Larceny Act 1916, s 2(1)(d).
[117] (1786) 1 Leach 413.
[118] *Ibid* 415.
[119] *Ibid* 414.
[120] (1803) 8 Ves Jun 406.
[121] *Ibid* 409.
[122] *Ibid.*
[123] (1849) 2 Car & K 831.
[124] *Ibid* 839.

of the property rights of finders.[125] In *Lawrence v State of Tennessee*,[126] a barber was indicted for larceny of US$480 removed from a pocket-book accidentally left behind by one of his customers. The Supreme Court of Tennessee thought that, at the time of the appropriation, the pocket-book was in the constructive possession of its owner, and that larceny lay well on the facts.

There was still a third view, which laid its emphasis on the facts available to the defendant at the time of finding, and which appears to have been concerned with punishing dishonesty. With some refinement it would provide the rationale for the specific offence of larceny by finding, and it would also generate again the distinction between rightful and wrongful finding that had first been the product of 'the law of charity'. In *R v Lamb* the driver of a hackney coach was convicted of larceny of a trunk left there on the ground that he must have known who its owner was.[127] In an anonymous case of 1804, the defendant found a pocket-book on the highway and converted banknotes therein to his own use. Lawrence J held that a finder committed larceny if he converted the find and either he knew who its owner was, or there was some mark upon the goods by which the owner could be known.[128]

The case of 1804 was followed by Park J in *R v Pope*[129] and *R v Kerr*,[130] and the rule expressed in similar terms, but the difficulty with all of these cases is that none of them explains why the facts as they appeared to the defendant at the time of the alleged taking should have had any bearing on the more general and essential question whether there was a taking on those facts. In 1834, reflecting the contemporary concern to punish dishonesty, the Criminal Law Commissioners expressed the view that if a lost thing was taken not for the benefit of the loser, but with an intent from the first to appropriate it to one's own use, then this should be larceny.[131] A rationale began to emerge on this basis in *Merry v Green*.[132] That was another case of concealed goods, in which the plaintiff found a purse of money in the secret drawer of a bureau he bought at auction. Much of the argument in the proceedings[133] turned on whether the plaintiff, as a purchaser, had a colourable right to the contents of the bureau, and ultimately Parke B ordered a retrial to allow the jury to consider disputed evidence that the auctioneer had sold the bureau 'with contents'.[134] But assuming the defendant's case, ie that the

---

[125] These proprietary implications are discussed in Chapter 3.
[126] (1839) 20 Tenn 228.
[127] (1694) 2 East PC 664.
[128] OW Russell, *A Treatise on Crimes and Misdemeanours* (London, Butterworths, 1819) 1044; P & W, 181.
[129] (1834) 6 Car & P 346.
[130] (1837) 8 Car & P 176.
[131] *First Report from the Royal Commission on Criminal Law* (1834) 18. The report is reprinted in P Ford and G Ford (eds), *British Parliamentary Papers* (Shannon, Irish University Press, 1971).
[132] (1841) 7 M & W 623.
[133] Which were proceedings in trespass for assault and false imprisonment relating to the plaintiff's detention on suspicion of larceny: *ibid* 624.
[134] *Ibid* 631.

plaintiff had express notice that he did not have title to contents, the learned judge thought that the plaintiff's appropriation was larceny.[135] First, the justification was expressed in terms of constructive possession that had echoes both of *The Carrier's Case* and *R v Pear*. So we read that, although the sale at auction gave the plaintiff a property in the bureau, it did not give him lawful possession of the contents.[136] Later, we find more or less a rehearsal of the dictum of Lawrence J from the anonymous case of 1804:[137]

> if the finder knows who the owner of the lost chattel is, or if, from any mark upon it, or the circumstances under which it is found, the owner could be reasonably ascertained, then the fraudulent conversion, *animo furandi*, constitutes a larceny.[138]

Although this rule had been applied in cases before *Merry*, Parke B's reproduction of it is remarkable because he expressly based it on a shift of emphasis in the law of larceny. His Lordship noted the 'old rule' of Coke that there could be no larceny of lost goods,[139] but said that it had been qualified by modern 'limitations', one of which was the proposition of Lawrence J. Of course, as yet, none of the authorities relying on this proposition had attempted to reconcile it with the necessity of a trespassory taking.[140] Parke B put the matter thus:

> It is said that the offence cannot be larceny, unless the taking would be a trespass, and that is true; but if the finder, from the circumstances of the case, must have known who was the owner, and instead of keeping the chattel for him, means from the first to appropriate it to his own use, he does not acquire it by a rightful title, and the true owner might maintain trespass.[141]

---

[135] Notwithstanding the opinion of the Lord Chief Justice at the trial (*ibid* 626–7, 630) and a strong argument from counsel. The latter relied heavily on *Cartwright v Green*, where, as we have seen, Lord Eldon held the defendant had broken open a part of the bureau which he was not entitled to touch for the purposes of repair. In the instant case counsel pressed to the contrary that, since the plaintiff had the property in the bureau, he was entitled to open any part of it, and could not be guilty of trespass in so doing: *ibid* 629.

[136] *Ibid* 631. On its own terms the argument depended on absences of intention on the part of both vendor and plaintiff, being respectively the intentions to sell and receive the contents. The resulting possessory construction comes close to that used to explain the hackney coach cases, and the lost/mislaid cases emanating from *Lawrence v State* in the United States. It would be interesting to dwell on it, not least because it appears directly in conflict with some of the modern authorities on the acquisition of rights to lost goods by an occupier of land, where often it is no bar to acquisition that the occupier has no knowledge of the existence of the thing in which he acquires a property right: *Waverly BC v Fletcher* [1996] QB 334. But for present purposes, the second of Parke B's responses was more influential in shaping the law of larceny well into the twentieth century.

[137] No citation occurs of the case itself, but the reporter notes a reference to the first edition of *Russell on Crimes* where it seems the only record of the case is to be found: (1841) 7 M & W 623, 632, citing Russell, above n 128 at 1044. Wright also notes the case, but equally attributes its report to *Russell*: P & W, 181.

[138] (1841) 7 M & W 623, 631–2.

[139] *Ibid* 631.

[140] Parke B thought that Lawrence J's dictum accounted for the decisions in *Wynne's Case* and *Cartwright v Green*: (1841) 7 M & W 623, 632. The better view, however, as we have seen, is that in those cases the respective judges found a taking by analogy to the doctrine of breaking bulk.

[141] (1841) 7 M & W 623, 632.

The finder, who must have known the identity of the owner at the time he took up the goods, did not acquire them rightfully. Parke B offered no expansion of the idea of rightfulness here employed, but by its very mention it recalls the 'law of charity' in trespass. It might have been expressed by saying, as in *Pear*, that there was no change of possession when a finder took with an awareness of the owner, and this continuity of possession is further explained by presuming that the loser did not consent to any acquisition of his goods by one who would convert them to his own use.[142] But each of these is in some respects a fiction, and however we should choose to explain it, the ultimate aim of Parke B's explanation is to delineate the circumstances in which taking a lost chattel will be lawful. It will be remembered that by the early seventeenth century, the view was established that where someone took goods 'before they are lost', trespass lay against him.[143] In the civil cases, the question so raised was answered by examining whether the plaintiff's goods were really in any danger of perishing at the time they were taken. From the decision in *Merry*, it seemed that this question would be addressed in larceny, not by investigating dangers to the goods, but by examining whether or not the defendant knew the identity of the owner at the time of the taking.

The rule on larceny by finding was refined by the seven judges of the Exchequer Chamber in the leading case of *R v Thurborn*.[144] First, it confirmed a general rule that for a putative finder to escape a charge of larceny it was essential that the goods should be 'actually' or 'presumably lost', in the sense that they were taken in such a place or under such circumstances that the taker would reasonably presume the loser to have abandoned them, or at least not to know where to find them:

> if a horse is found feeding on an open common or on the side of a public road, or a watch found, apparently hidden, in a hay-stack, the taking of these would be larceny, because the taker had no right to presume that the owner did not know where to find them.[145]

Thus, it would always be larceny to take and intend to convert goods which were not actually or presumably lost. Where goods were actually or presumably lost, everything else turned on the defendant's beliefs at the time of the taking. If from the facts as they appeared to him,[146] he really believed that the owner could not be found, then he was not guilty of larceny, even if he took with an intent to convert the goods; but if he really did believe that the owner could be found, then he

---

[142] This latter, at least in part, was Tay's explanation: Tay, above n 43 at 227.

[143] *Isaack v Clark* (1614) 2 Bulst 306, 312.

[144] (1849) 2 Car & K 831.

[145] *Ibid* 837. It is worth noting that no specific authority for this proposition was cited by the court. We must suppose that it followed from the 'law of charity' that there could be no trespass where the goods taken were not 'really lost'.

[146] '[T]he guilt of the accused must depend on the circumstances as they appear to him': *ibid* 833.

was guilty of larceny, and it was no defence to say that the goods were actually or presumably lost:

> [I]f a man find goods that have been actually lost, or are reasonably supposed by him to have been lost, and appropriates them with intent to take the entire dominion over them, really believing, when he takes them, that the owner cannot be found, it is not larceny. But, if he has taken them with like intent, though lost or reasonably supposed to be lost, but reasonably believing that the owner can be found, it is larceny.[147]

On the facts of *Thurborn* itself, the defendant found a £10 note which had been accidentally dropped in the street. This first taking was held no larceny because although the note was 'really lost', there was no mark on it nor other means of identifying the owner, and nothing to suggest that the defendant believed that the owner could be found.[148] The day after taking the note, the defendant had learned the identity of the owner and the circumstances of the accidental loss, but proceeded nonetheless to change and convert it. The court held that this still was no larceny, for inasmuch as the first taking was lawful, a subsequent conversion could be no larceny.[149]

*Thurborn* attracted a good deal of criticism in the years immediately following its decision.[150] No doubt this was due (at least in part) to the curiosity that on the facts of the case itself the proposition of law given by the Exchequer judges served to acquit an initially lawful possessor of a subsequent dishonest conversion, which was exactly the sort of mischief the criminal law had been trying to avoid with centuries of evolution from *The Carrier's Case* onwards.[151] Nonetheless, the effect of the decision was substantially preserved by the Larceny Act 1916, which defined the expression 'takes' to include obtaining possession 'by finding, where at the time of the finding the finder believes that the owner can be discovered by taking reasonable steps'.[152] The substance of this rule has been preserved in the modern law of theft by the provisions of the Theft Act 1968,[153] although interestingly that statute makes the finder's belief relevant to a different constituent element of criminal liability. Section 2(1)(c), which provides that a person is not dishonest if he appropriates the property in the belief that the person to whom the property belongs cannot be discovered by taking

---

[147] *Ibid* 839–40.

[148] *Ibid* 840.

[149] *Ibid* 839–40.

[150] By 1866 the editor of *Russell on Crimes* asserted that the case had 'met with very general disapprobation among criminal lawyers, and has been often questioned since': CS Greaves (ed), *Russell on Crimes and Misdemeanours* 4th edn (London, Stevens & Sons, 1866) vol II, 180 fn (t).

[151] It is worth noting that *Thurborn* led to a spate of overturned convictions. See *R v Yorke* (1849) 2 Car & K 841; *R v Thristle* (1849) 2 Car & K 842 and 843; *R v Preston* (1851) 2 Den 353; *R v Christopher* (1858) 8 Cox CC 91; *R v Glyde* (1868) LR 1 CCR 139; *R v Gardner* (1862) Le & Ca 243; *R v Matthews* (1873) 12 Cox CC 489.

[152] Larceny Act 1916, s 1(2)(i)(d).

[153] D Ormerod (ed), *Smith and Hogan Criminal Law* 11th edn (Oxford, Oxford University Press, 2005) 694–5.

reasonable steps, was 'obviously intended to preserve the substance of the common law rule relating to finding'.[154] So now it seems that the facts of finding are relevant to the *mens rea* of the accused, but without yet exploring the reasons for that switch in emphasis we can at least conclude that, from the late seventeenth century onwards, they have served to defend an accused on the ground that he lacks some constituent element of criminal liability.[155]

## Armory v Delamirie

These three strands of the legal history of finding must inform the context of the decision in *Armory v Delamirie*,[156] perhaps the most famous case involving a finder. In 1722, the fiction of finding governed proceedings in trover and 'the law of charity' seemed to offer a substantive defence, whilst on the authority of *Lamb* the view will have been beginning to emerge that it could be larceny to take discovered goods. *Armory*, however, would later be taken as establishing a fourth proposition, about the kind of right acquired by a finder in the object of her find. A finder of goods would be said to have a general right to those goods against all the world save the true owner.

The facts of *Armory* are thought to be well known, though the reality is that we do not know very much about the relevant events. A chimney sweep's boy found a jewel ring. The half-page report tells us nothing about the location or other circumstances of this find,[157] but concentrates on what happened next. The boy took the ring to a local goldsmith 'to know what it was'. Possibly the boy was intending to sell the ring; possibly he planned to have it valued and keep it for himself; possibly he genuinely wanted to know what it was and thought that a goldsmith might help him make enquiries for the owner. To the extent that the first two are true, there is every chance that the boy was a thief, but the report is silent on his intentions. We do know that on arrival at the shop, the boy delivered the ring to the goldsmith's apprentice 'who, under the pretence of weighing it, took out the stones and called the master to let him know that it came to three halfpence'. The master offered this sum to the boy. The offer was refused. The boy insisted on having the ring returned to him, perhaps because he knew he was being defrauded, perhaps because his first concern was to have the ring irrespective of its value. Whichever, we know that the apprentice returned only the empty ring socket to the boy, and that subsequently the boy

---

[154] D Ormerod and DW Williams (eds), *Smith's Law of Theft* 9th edn (Oxford, Oxford University Press, 2007) 2.282.
[155] See further Chapters 3 and 7.
[156] (1722) 1 Stra 505.
[157] A point to which we return in Chapter 3.

recovered damages in trover to the value of the 'best jewels' that could have been set in the socket.[158]

We have already rehearsed the famous ruling of Pratt CJKB.[159] Nearly 130 years later in *Bridges v Hawkesworth*, this dictum would be taken as establishing 'the general right of the finder to any article which has been lost, as against all the world, but the true owner'.[160] However, it is important to note that there is not enough in *Armory* to suggest the enunciation of some principle specifically applicable to *finders*. It is the last phrase of Pratt CJ's dictum that contains the essence of the decision. *Armory* is about the ability of the boy to maintain trover. By 1722 it was already well established that trover lay at the suit of various classes of non-owner where they had been in possession of the converted goods.[161] So it was that a pledgee could maintain trover;[162] and likewise a sheriff,[163] a carrier,[164] a bailee at will,[165] a factor and a trustee.[166]

The better view of *Armory v Delamirie* is that it extends this list to include finders, or to be yet more accurate, that it confirms the right of a finder to bring trover as is the case with other non-owning possessors. Indeed, until the middle of the nineteenth century it seems that *Armory* was understood in this way. It was applied in *Webb v Fox* to allow an uncertified bankrupt to maintain trover for goods acquired by him since his bankruptcy;[167] in *Sutton v Buck* in favour of the possessor of a ship under a failed transfer;[168] in *Borne v Fosbrooke* to allow the plaintiff to recover goods 'given' to her by her aunt, even though there had not been sufficient delivery to effect a legal gift owing to the rules of matrimonial property;[169] and in *Elliott v Kemp* it was used by counsel to support the general proposition that 'against a wrongdoer, the actual possessor of any chattel may maintain an action for it'.[170] Only in *Bridges* do we first find dicta suggesting that *Armory* was about the rights of *finders*. It cannot so have been confined in the mind of Pratt CJ. And this, of course, is why his judgment makes no mention of the circumstances of the find, the facts of its

---

[158] (1722) 1 Stra 505.

[159] See *Introduction* above.

[160] (1851) 15 Jur 1079, 1082 (Patteson J).

[161] Though not, necessarily, *by reason* of that possession: see further Chapter 5.

[162] *Ratcliff v Davies* (1611) Cro Jac 244.

[163] *Wilbraham v Snow* (1670) 1 Mod 30; 2 Wms Saund 47.

[164] *Arnold v Jefferson* (1697) 1 Ld Raym 275.

[165] *Templeman v Case* (1712) 10 Mod 24.

[166] See generally the notes to *Wilbraham v Snow* in Saunders' report: (1670) 2 Wms Saund 47 fn (h).

[167] (1797) 7 TR 391.

[168] (1810) Taunt 302, though the case is equivocally explained by some of the judges on the ground that the plaintiff was the bailee of the owner and could set up a claim though him: (1810) Taunt 302, 309–10, opinions of Lawrence and Chambre JJ.

[169] (1865) 18 CBNS 515.

[170] (1840) 7 M & W 306, 307, though on the facts of this case the court concluded that the proposition was not relevant because the plaintiff had never been in possession of the goods in question: (1840) 7 M & W 306, 312 (Parke B).

loss, or the boy's intentions. None of these are relevant to his ability to bring trover against the goldsmith. Thus, although it has become the 'jural icon' of finders' rights,[171] *Armory* was not intended to confine the rights of the boy to the facts of his finding, or to create any discrete propositions or laws about finders to be understood separately from the more general learning on trover and conversion.

---

[171] S Roberts, 'More Lost Than Found' (1982) 45 *MLR* 683.

# 2

# The Possessor of Land Cases

In 1851, a new kind of dispute made its way from the county court to an appeal at the Queen's Bench. The case was called *Bridges v Hawkesworth*.[1] Its judgment purported to confirm 'the general right of a finder to any article which has been lost as against all the world except the true owner'.[2]

Flanked chronologically by developments significant to the liability of finders,[3] *Bridges* exemplifies the dominant factual matrix in modern cases about a finder's rights. It is a dispute between a possessor of land (on the facts of *Bridges*, an occupier of premises) and a visitor to that land. The visitor discovers something there, the existence of which was not known to the possessor of land, and so 'finds' something in that sense. The possessor of land does not claim the thing as owner, but because the thing has been found on his land he considers himself better entitled to it than the finder. For his own part, the finder disputes this claim, relying on *Armory v Delamirie* to argue that he is entitled to the find as against all but the true owner.

The modern orthodoxy holds that resolution of these disputes depends on a factual distinction made according to the circumstances in which the goods were found.[4] Where goods have been found buried in or otherwise attached to land, the possessor of land always has a better right than a finder.[5] Where goods have been found unattached on the surface of land, the finder will have a better right unless the possessor of land can prove a manifest intention to control the land and anything that might be lying unattached thereon.[6] Despite its continued acceptance in recent cases, there is no coherent basis for this in/on land distinction, and judicial attempts to account for it appear weak and strained. Here it will be argued that lying behind the distinction is a concept of possession that is theoretically consistent and workable in practice. When possession is brought to the fore, perceived doctrinal difficulties in the cases entirely disappear. The mistake in the most recent decisions has been to ignore this possessory concept and emphasise instead only the facts of the distinction.

---

[1] (1851) 15 Jur 1079.
[2] *Ibid* 1082 (Patteson J).
[3] *R v Thurborn* (1849) 2 Car & K 831; Common Law Procedure Act 1852: see Chapter 1.
[4] *EPL*, 4.420; Palmer, *Bailment*, 1437–9.
[5] *Waverly Borough Council v Fletcher* [1996] QB 334 (CA).
[6] *Parker v British Airways Board* [1982] 1 QB 1004 (CA).

An important caveat, not often remarked, is that the modern formulation of possession in the common law post-dates *Bridges v Hawkesworth*. This case was decided on an entirely different ground, having more to do with an absence of liability in the defendant occupier than his failure to establish a right on the facts of possession. To be clear about its influence on the common law we need first to be clear about its ratio. For this reason, this chapter begins with an analysis of *Bridges* and the closely related decisions in *R v Rowe*[7] and *Elwes v Briggs Gas Co*.[8] It moves on then to chart the emergence of a theory of possession in the common law, which theory best accounts for the law governing disputes between a finder and a possessor of land.

## The Beginning: Right Follows Liability

To the modern lawyer looking back, *Elwes v Brigg Gas Co* and *Bridges v Hawkesworth* are easily complementary. They are contrasting sides of the in/on land distinction, and might be taken respectively as the earliest authority for each limb of that distinction. Moreover, the result in each coincides exactly with the decisions in *Waverly Borough Council v Fletcher* and *Parker v British Airways Board*, which now are taken as the leading cases (respectively) on the in/on land distinction. However, at the date of judgment in *Elwes*, we can be certain that its connection with *Bridges* was not perceived, or at least, not in these terms. Indeed, *Bridges* was not even cited by the court in *Elwes*.[9] Insofar as they could have been related in 1886, it would have been because each of the decisions could have been said to turn (though *Bridges* to a much greater extent) on a consideration of the duty owed by the possessor of land to the loser of the goods in question, which duty in both cases was conceived by analogy to the common law duties of innkeepers. We will explore this connection briefly below, but whatever its success, the main point of the present section is that, unlike the modern cases, *Bridges* and *Elwes* were not resolved by a general theory on possession in the common law.

Byfield & Hawkesworth was a bookshop on Charing Cross Road in London. In October 1847, the plaintiff (who was a commercial traveller) visited those premises on business. As he was leaving the shop, he picked up from the floor a parcel containing £65 in banknotes. The defendant was called to the shop by his shopkeeper. The plaintiff asked the defendant to keep the banknotes safely for their owner. The defendant agreed, and subsequently caused the find to be advertised in a newspaper, but no owner appeared. After three years, the plaintiff applied to the defendant for the return of the banknotes, offering to pay for their

---

[7] (1859) Bell 93.
[8] (1886) 33 Ch D 562.
[9] It had been cited by counsel for the plaintiff, though somewhat out of point: (1886) 33 Ch D 562, 564.

advertisement and to indemnify him against any future claim from their owner. When the defendant refused to return them, the plaintiff commenced proceedings in the county court. The court gave judgment for the defendant, but found as a matter of fact that by delivering the notes to the defendant, the plaintiff had not intended to waive any right he might have to them. The plaintiff appealed successfully to the Divisional Court of the Queen's Bench.

Remarkably given its 'posthumous career',[10] the judgment of the Divisional Court consists of only four paragraphs. Patteson J recorded that the notes had dropped 'by mere accident' on the floor of the shop and were 'manifestly lost' by someone, then cited *Armory v Delamirie* as establishing 'the general right of a finder to any article which has been lost as against all the world except the true owner'.[11] The learned judge did not doubt that this right would have accrued to the plaintiff if he had found the packet of banknotes outside the defendant's shop, and if such a right had accrued to him in the instant case, none of the events occurring thereafter (ie the delivery of the notes to the defendant and their advertisement) operated to divest it. So the only question for the court to decide was 'whether the circumstance of the notes being found inside the defendant's shop gives him, the defendant, the right to have them, as against the plaintiff who found them'.[12]

The court accepted that any right in the defendant must have accrued to him before the plaintiff took up the notes, 'for that finding could not give the defendant any right'.[13] The modern cases would resolve this question by looking at facts relating to the defendant's occupation of the premises, and to his intention to control objects found there. In *Bridges*, there was no consideration of these facts. Instead, the court relied on the fact that the owner of the banknotes had not deposited them intentionally with the defendant so as to make the latter liable for their safety. The relevant passage is in the following terms:

> If the discovery [of the banknotes by the plaintiff] had never been communicated to the defendant, could the real owner have had any cause of action against him because they were found in his house? Certainly not. The notes were never in the custody of the defendant, nor within the protection of his house, before they were found, as they would have been had they been intentionally deposited there.[14]

The phrase 'within the protection of his house' is a reference to the law on innkeepers. At common law, an innkeeper was strictly liable for the loss or damage of goods *infra hospitium* ('within the protection of his house'), and was not allowed to limit the extent of his liability.[15] He was recognised as holding a special property in goods *infra hospitium*, and could restrain wrongful interferences with those goods, but the right was consequent on the duty: because he was liable to his guest for

---

[10] AL Goodhart, 'Three Cases on Possession' (1927–29) 3 *Camb LJ* 195, 196.
[11] (1851) Jur 1079, 1082.
[12] *Ibid.*
[13] *Ibid.*
[14] *Ibid.*
[15] *Cayle's Case* (1583) 8 Co Rep 32a (KB); *Williams v Linnitt* [1951] 1 KB 565 (CA).

their safety, an innkeeper was given the right to protect goods against strangers. In argument in *Bridges*, Patteson J had noted the existence of the innkeeper's right.[16] Of course, the defendant in *Bridges* was not an innkeeper, and Patteson J recognised that he neither owed an innkeeper's duty nor held an innkeeper's right,[17] but the reference reveals the nature of the court's enquiry. If the defendant was to be regarded as having a right in the banknotes sufficient to sustain recovery against a stranger, there must exist first in the defendant a duty to the 'real owner' of the banknotes on which that right could be consequent. That the court considered that this duty was not owed is evident in the passage reproduced above, and inasmuch as this accounts for the absence of a right in the defendant, it also accounts for the court's decision.

The only real ambiguity[18] in *Bridges* concerns the facts that would have been sufficient for the court to find that the defendant owed a duty to the owner of the packet of banknotes. Clearly, Patteson J supposed that an intentional deposit would have been enough, though he left a doubt as what exactly he meant by 'intentional deposit'. As to this, it has been suggested that the language of the judge invokes a strict concept of bailment, and would have required a delivery to the defendant from the true owner, such that the former would have owed to the latter the duties of a bailee in a literal sense.[19] On the other hand, in several of the United States we find the more expansive proposition that where goods are intentionally removed from the custody of their owner, and later forgotten, a possessor of land owes a duty to keep them safely for that owner, and can recover them from a finder.[20] Alternatively, in the absence of an intentional deposit, it might have been enough that the defendant had assumed a duty to keep lost goods safely. In *R v Rowe*,[21] decided soon after *Bridges*, the Court for Crown Cases upheld a conviction for larceny of a quantity of iron taken from the bed of a canal. The defendant was a stranger to the canal company, and had discovered the iron at a time when the canal had been drained for cleaning. In finding that the company had sufficient possession to maintain a conviction for larceny, the court had evidence that the company's practice was to return discovered items to their owners where possible.[22] For that reason the court was able to press the analogy

---

[16] (1851) Jur 1079, 1080.

[17] *Ibid* 1081.

[18] Contrast the supposed difficulties evident in the mistreatment of this case by the commentators. See AL Goodhart, 'Three Cases on Possession' (1927–29) 3 *Camb LJ* 195, discussed below.

[19] AES Tay, '*Bridges v Hawkesworth* and the Early History of Finding' (1964) 8 *American Journal of Legal History* 223, 236.

[20] Thus, on facts superficially similar to *Bridges*, a barber recovered from his customer a pocketbook containing banknotes found by the customer on a table in the barber's shop: *McAvoy v Medina* (1866) 11 Allen (Mass) 548. In Massachusetts and other jurisdictions, *Bridges* is reconciled to *McAvoy* by developing a distinction between goods 'lost' and 'mislaid', the facts of intentional deposit (in the wide sense) being more or less sufficient to warrant the latter designation. We will return to this distinction in Chapter 3.

[21] (1859) Bell 93.

[22] *Ibid* 94.

with innkeepers and hold that the company's interest in the iron 'was of the same nature as that which a landlord has in goods left behind by a guest'.[23]

Whichever of these possibilities is to be preferred, it is clear that in *Bridges* the plaintiff was successful because the defendant did not owe any duty to the owner of the banknotes. For that reason, the court thought that he could not assert any right to the notes in priority to the right of the plaintiff. Patteson J did not consider any alternative source of right in the defendant. He certainly did not consider that such a right might arise in virtue of the facts of possession independently of any prior duty. It will be argued below that the mistake of latter-day commentators in describing or criticising *Bridges* has invariably been the assumption that the decision turned on possessory facts, and on a theory of possession which was not in fact present in the mind of the judges. To the extent that decisions in the modern cases depend on that latter theory, *Bridges* can never be reconciled to them absolutely, and it is meaningless to insist on (or equally to criticise) its continuing authority.

In *Elwes v Brigg Gas Co*,[24] the defendant company found a prehistoric canoe embedded some six feet below the surface of land let to it by the plaintiff, who was tenant for life in possession of the Elwes family estates. Apparently the boat had lain there for centuries, over time succumbing to burial by alluvial accretions and other 'natural causes', and remaining so buried until its discovery by the defendants.[25] This discovery occurred in the course of excavations permitted by the lease, but the plaintiff claimed the boat and demanded it from the defendants. The defendants refused to comply with this demand, and asserted that the boat belonged to them. Chitty J resolved the dispute by holding (a) that at the time of the creation of the lease the plaintiff had a property interest in the boat; (b) that nothing in the lease agreement operated to transfer the plaintiff's interest to the defendant; and that therefore (c) the plaintiff was entitled to delivery up of the boat.[26]

For our purposes, the interest in *Elwes* lies in the reasons given by Chitty J for attributing property in the boat to the plaintiff at the time of the creation of the lease. The judgment is complicated because it expresses three reasons for such attribution which vary according to a factual determination of the boat's nature. There had been much discussion of that issue in argument, counsel for the plaintiff suggesting alternatively that the boat could be considered as a movable chattel, or a chattel fixed to the soil, or as 'something in the nature of a mineral'.[27] Counsel favoured the latter option, seeking to avail of a clause in the lease which reserved all minerals to the plaintiff. Chitty J declined to decide the factual issue, because he thought each of the possible solutions entailed that the plaintiff was entitled to

---

[23] *Ibid* 95, Pollock CB giving the judgment of the court.

[24] (1886) LR 33 Ch D 562.

[25] The judgment acknowledges that this statement of fact was conjectural, but it was accepted by both parties: (1886) LR 33 Ch D 562, 566.

[26] (1886) LR 33 Ch D 562, 570.

[27] *Ibid* 563.

the boat at the time of the creation of the lease. If the boat was mineral, or fixed to the soil, it belonged to the tenant for life as part of his inheritance.[28] If it was a chattel, it belonged to him in virtue of his lawful possession of the land:

> Being entitled to the inheritance ... [the plaintiff] was in possession of the ground, not merely of the surface, but of everything that lay beneath the surface down to the centre of the earth, and consequently in possession of the boat.[29]

Thus, to the extent that the boat was to be considered a movable chattel, *Elwes* stands for the proposition that the plaintiff was entitled to the boat because he was in lawful possession of the land. The only authority given for this proposition was *R v Rowe*,[30] where as we have seen, the Court for Crown Cases held that the canal company had sufficient possession of the iron to maintain an indictment for larceny.[31] Chitty J made his judgment relatively on a comparison of the facts, holding that if 'the fact of iron having being left on the surface of the ground covered by water' was sufficient in law to give possession of the iron to the canal company as possessor of the land, a fortiori the fact that a chattel was embedded in soil was sufficient to give possession in law to the plaintiff as possessor of the land. However, the point was not considered that in *Rowe* the right of the canal company was conceived by analogy to the right of an innkeeper, insofar as the company had assumed a duty to return items found in the canal to their owner. There was no evidence of any equivalent duty in *Elwes*, and precisely its absence had accounted for the decision in *Bridges*. Had this been considered, *Elwes* might have been decided differently, at least insofar as the canoe was to be regarded as a chattel. Moreover, our law would have had a very different shape, resolving disputes between possessors of land and finders according to the imposition or assumption of a duty in possessors of land to keep discovered goods safely for their owner. As it was, shortly after its decision *Elwes* would be taken as establishing a general proposition that a possessor of land was also in possession of any thing buried in that land.[32] Whilst on a strict reading of the authorities the acquisition of such rights were always in consequence of duties owed to owners, soon they would be said to depend solely on the facts of possession, as a new theory emerged at common law.

---

[28] *Ibid* 568. In explaining the entitlement of the plaintiff to objects fixed to the soil reference was made to the maxim *fixatur solo, solo cedit* ('that which is fixed to the soil accedes to the soil'): *ibid* 567. This maxim is sometimes given as a complete rationale for the result in *Elwes* (see eg the opinion of Auld LJ in *Waverly BC v Fletcher* [1996] QB 334, 341), but that is to ignore the various strands of reasoning present in the mind of Chitty J, which vary according to the factual determination of the boat.

[29] (1886) 33 Ch D 562, 568.

[30] (1859) Bell 93.

[31] *Ibid* 95.

[32] P & W, 41.

# The Innovation: Right Follows Possession

In the years either side of *Elwes* were published two influential accounts of possession in the common law. Holmes' lecture on the subject appeared in print in 1881,[33] and seven years later came the book-length treatment of Pollock and Wright.[34] There are definite similarities between the two works, at least as far as their general conception of possession is concerned. Significantly, each conceived of possession as a set of facts, which facts were sufficient to generate an interest at law.[35] The permutations of the facts might be capable of infinite variation, but in essence they were facts of control, comprising physical and mental elements. So Holmes declared confidently that:

> To gain possession … a man must stand in a certain physical relation to the object and to the rest of world, and must have a certain intent.[36]

The precise nature of this physical relation and (perhaps even more so) this intent have never succumbed to satisfactory definition,[37] but the idea that they are separate requirements and that they must concur in order to generate a possessory right has generally been accepted. Indeed, so pervasive is the construction that one eminent judge recently remarked that:

> there has always, both in Roman law and in common law, been a requirement to show an intention to possess in addition to objective acts of physical possession.[38]

As an aside we might remark that if this proposition is true of English law, it is only because the elementary structure of possession was adopted rather uncritically from the Roman law.[39] Whilst it is true that the Roman texts stipulate the concurrent need for factual and mental elements in order to create legal possession (called *possessio*),[40] the import of that legal right bears very little resemblance to the right said to result at common law. In Roman law, the principal significance of the attribution of legal possession was that the possessor was

---

[33] OW Holmes, Jnr, *The Common Law* (Boston, MA, Little Brown, 1881).

[34] F Pollock and RS Wright, *An Essay on Possession in the Common Law* (Oxford, Clarendon Press, 1888).

[35] P & W, 28 *et seq*; Holmes, *CL*, 214–15.

[36] Holmes, *CL*, 206.

[37] OR Marshall, 'The Problem of Finding' (1949) 2 *Current Legal Problems* 68, 75; AP Bell, *Modern Law of Personal Property in England and Ireland* (London, Butterworths, 1989) 35–7; S Gleeson, *Personal Property Law* (London, FT Law & Tax, 1997) 25.

[38] *J A Pye (Oxford) Ltd v Graham* [2003] 1 AC 419, 435, per Lord Browne-Wilkinson.

[39] O Radley-Gardner, 'Civilised Squatting' (2005) 25 *OJLS* 727, 738, considering the use of the control/intention formula to resolve cases of adverse possession of land.

[40] D.13.7.37; D.41.2.1.20. Truthfully, the identification of these elements of possession in Roman law depends rather more on ex post facto rationalisations of the Roman texts than on any substantive evidence of Roman civil procedure. The chief rationaliser was Savigny, whose work is discussed briefly below. For an overview, see WW Buckland, *A Textbook on Roman Law* 2nd edn (Cambridge, Cambridge University Press, 1932) 197–202.

entitled to avail of a praetorian system of protection known as the possessory interdicts. These were a set of legal procedures which allowed the possessor an action to retain[41] or recover[42] possession of a thing as the circumstances of his case dictated, but access to these procedures was premised on the protection of the person of the possessor, rather than on the realisation of any right to the thing possessed. As Savigny said, a Roman citizen in possession of a thing did 'not thereby obtain any right to detention, but ... [had] the right of demanding that no-one shall else use force against him'.[43] To put the matter more simply again, the product of possessory facts were obligations rather than property rights. A Roman possessor was allowed to restrain violence, but he was not allowed to bring a *vindicatio* and thereby assert a proprietary right to the goods in question.[44] Without more, then, there was no cause to import the elementary structure of Roman *possessio* to the common law, where the argument would be that possessors enjoyed access to proceedings for trover, detinue and trespass identically with owners of goods.[45] Pollock's treatment is particularly contingent: he seems to have posited the *corpus/animus* formula solely in reliance on Savigny's treatment of the Roman rules, an English translation of which had appeared in 1848.[46] Holmes took the time to locate the work of Savigny and his contemporaries in the larger philosophical tradition of Immanuel Kant, which insists on the element of intention as being the mechanism by which the human will is engaged with the object possessed (and thus the reason for which possession is protected),[47] and which might, in that sense, provide a more general justification for positing an intention requirement. But Holmes almost certainly would have resisted the influence of that level of justification, being adamant that anything more than the immediately pragmatic was to be rejected as a ground for the protection of possession.[48]

Having accepted that at common law a right to goods could be generated by the coincidence of factual control and an intention to possess, both Holmes and

---

[41] As in the interdicts *uti possidetis* (land) and *utrubi* (movables), which could brought by a possessor to confirm his possession relative to his opponent: D.43.17.2.

[42] Where force had been used to take possession from the possessor, he could bring *utrubi* again for movables, and the interdicts *unde vi* and *unde armata* for the recovery of land. The last of these only applied where armed force had been used.

[43] FC von Savigny, *Treatise on Possession; or the Jus Possessionis of the Civil Law* (E Perry (trans), London, Sweet, 1848) 6–7.

[44] Of course, in Roman law possession might ripen into ownership by long use (*usucapio*), but for this to occur there were other stipulations to be satisfied in addition to *possessio*, including a general requirement of good faith, and *iusta causa*, which required that the taking of possession be the result of some transaction which was ordinarily a basis for lawful acquisition (sale, gift, succession, and so on). For this reason acquisition by *usucapio* was sharply distinguished from the interdictal protection afforded to a possessor: Savigny, above n 43 at 129.

[45] See Chapter 5 for the development of Pollock's argument on the rights of possessors.

[46] Above n 43.

[47] Holmes, *CL*, 206–13.

[48] *Ibid.*

Pollock applied this proposition to *Bridges v Hawkesworth*. Interestingly, they thought the case turned on different limbs of the test.[49] For Holmes, *Bridges* was about intent, or rather the lack of it. The defendant, ignorant of the existence of the packet of banknotes, 'could not have had the intent to appropriate it', and having invited members of the public in to his shop, 'could not have the intent to exclude them from it'.[50] For Pollock on the other hand, the case turned on an absence of physical control. Since the banknotes were found in a part of the shop frequented by customers, 'it is impossible to say that the shopkeeper has any possession in fact'.[51] It would have been an absolute answer to Holmes and Pollock to say that *Bridges* was decided because the court could find no duty in the defendant sufficient to give him consequentially a right to the banknotes against the plaintiff. Insofar as they suggested otherwise, the learned authors applied to the facts of *Bridges* a theory unknown to the common law in 1851, and not considered or invoked by the Divisional Court.

Much the same observation could be made in relation to *Elwes*. Chitty J was obviously familiar with Holmes' work, and cited it once,[52] but he did not discuss any theory of possession. Indeed, as we have seen, the learned judge relied analogically on *Rowe* to justify a judgment for the plaintiff lessor, at least insofar as it could be said that the boat had remained a movable chattel throughout the period of its burial. Overlooking this caveat, Pollock gave *Elwes* as holding much more generally that:

> The possession of land carries with it in general … possession of everything which is attached to or under that land, and, in the absence of a better title elsewhere, the right to possess it also.[53]

In explaining this proposition, Pollock rejected the view it was a flat rule of law. Instead, the possessor's right to objects buried in his land depended on the coincidence of physical control and intent. Thus it seemed:

> preferable to say that the legal possession rests on a real de facto possession, constituted by the occupier's general power and intent to exclude unauthorised interference.[54]

---

[49] See the criticisms of Goodhart, above n 18 at 198–201.

[50] The two kinds of intention given here reflect different conceptions of the intent required to generate a possessory right. The first is relevant if the intention required is an *animus domini* (an intention to acquire ownership), the second if the intention required is an *animus possidendi* (an intention to possess, which equates to an intention to exclude others). Holmes favoured the latter intention, and thought that where it existed in relation to a building or premises, it included an intention to exclude others from objects found on the premises: Holmes, *CL*, 222. We return to this below.

[51] P & W, 39.

[52] For the proposition that a trespasser could not have acquired possession of the boat because the act of digging it up would have involved waste and spoil of the plaintiff's inheritance: (1886) LR 33 Ch D 562, 568, citing Holmes, *CL*, 223 and *Blades v Higgs* (1865) 13 CBNS 844.

[53] P & W, 41.

[54] P & W, 41.

The term de facto was used by Pollock to connote possession in its ordinary sense, meaning 'effective occupation or control'.[55] Otherwise, the above proposition is linguistically similar to a passage in Holmes' lecture, though the passage was not cited by Pollock. In considering whether *Bridges* would have been decided differently if the notes had been found on the floor of a private house, Holmes had canvassed the view that an intention to control a specific thing was contained in any intention to exclude persons from the premises on which the thing was found, such that where the latter was present there was always the former.[56] Pollock was repeating this opinion, albeit in the differing context of objects buried in land. At any rate, the point is clear. Pollock's explanation of *Elwes*, like *Bridges*, was couched in terms of his general theory of possession, which was not expressly considered or invoked by the court.

## South Staffordshire Water Co v Sharman

If this grander possessory theory of Holmes and Pollock was not evident in the cases they first used to exemplify it, it took very little time for its tenets to be applied to the resolution of a similar dispute. In *South Staffs Water Co v Sharman*,[57] the plaintiffs were the holders in fee simple of the site of Minster Pool in Lichfield. They engaged contractors to clean the pool, and the report records that during that cleaning operation several objects were found. The defendant found two rings embedded in the mud at the bottom of the pool, but refused to deliver them on demand from the plaintiffs.[58] In proceedings for detinue, a county court judge found for the defendant on the strength of *Armory* and *Bridges*. On appeal to the Queen's Bench, counsel for the defendant conceded that if the plaintiffs could prove 'a de facto possession' they were entitled to the rings. Lord Russell of Killowen CJ reproduced the passages from Pollock given immediately above, and on them expressly based his judgment for the plaintiffs.[59] Having done so, he gave his own formulation of the possession theory:

> It is somewhat strange that there is no more direct authority on the question; but the general principle seems to me to be that where a person has possession of a house or land, with a manifest intention to exercise control over it and the things which may be upon or in it, then, if something is found on that land, whether by an employee of the

---

[55] P & W, 12. On Pollock's view such de facto possession was the ground of a legal right ('legal possession' or 'possession in law'), and depended on the coincidence of physical control and intent. See generally, P & W, 11–16.

[56] Holmes, *CL*, 222.

[57] [1896] 2 QB 44.

[58] It is worth noting that there was no suggestion that the defendant behaved dishonestly. Having refused the demand of the plaintiffs, he delivered the rings to the police to hold them for their owner. The legal proceedings arose after the police redelivered the rings to the defendant, having been unable to trace the owner: [1896] 2 QB 44.

[59] [1896] 2 QB 44, 47.

owner or by a stranger, the presumption is that the possession of the thing is in the owner of the locus in quo.[60]

Later, Lord Russell would receive criticism for aspects of this dictum,[61] but it is enormously significant. It represents the first occasion in the case law on which the issue between possessor of land and finder was brought down squarely to the former's ability to assert a prior right by virtue of the facts of possession. Moreover, it purported to have a reconciling effect. Lord Russell thought that the passage from Pollock not only accounted for his decision in the instant case, but also explained its distinction from *Bridges v Hawkesworth*.[62] Of course, this was an innovation. It need scarcely be repeated that *Bridges* was decided on an absence of duty in the defendant, and not on his failure to manifest an intention to control goods on his premises. Nonetheless, had no more been said, we might from this point have had a coherent law for resolving these disputes based on the possessor of land's ability in a given case to establish the possessory facts of control and intention. Unfortunately, Lord Russell added a further gloss on *Bridges*, stressing the public nature of the shop and hence the find.[63] Counsel for the plaintiffs had laid that emphasis in argument, rationalising the cases along a public/private divide in an attempt to distinguish *Bridges*, and so contend that the county court judge had been wrong to rely on it.[64] Thus, it was submitted that where goods were found in a public place, they belonged to the finder; but when goods were on 'private property', they belonged to owner of the land.[65] Having distinguished *Bridges* using the views of Pollock, Lord Russell need not have made any comment on this contention, or any further comment on *Bridges*. Yet, although his Lordship thought it rightly decided, he was content to opine that *Bridges* 'stands by itself,

---

[60] *Ibid.*

[61] Two criticisms are worth identifying. First, Goodhart doubted the need to confine the outcome of possessory facts to a *presumption*, thinking it difficult to conceive of a situation in which, if it was a presumption, it could be rebutted: Goodhart, above n 18 at 207. One possibility was that it could be rebutted by a landowner's lack of knowledge of the existence of the thing in question, but a rejection of this view is entailed by the decision in *Sharman* itself, which Lord Russell assumed was 'like the case ... where an article is found on private property, although the owners of that property are ignorant that it is there': [1896] 2 QB 44, 47. Secondly, it has on occasion been observed that the dictum goes beyond the passage of Pollock on which it relies insofar as it contemplates possession of things 'upon' land: Goodhart, above n 18 at 206; *City of London Corporation v Appleyard* [1963] 1 WLR 982, 987. The relevance of this observation could easily be dismissed by showing that Pollock's formulation itself echoed the view of Holmes given in a discussion of the 'upon' land find in *Bridges v Hawkesworth*, but in any case it would later be established by the Court of Appeal that proof of a manifest intention to control things unattached on land would suffice to generate a title to them in a possessor of land. See the discussion below of *Parker v British Airways Board* [1982] 1 QB 1004.

[62] This was merely asserted, and his Lordship did not offer any elaboration. Presumably on this view the claim failed in *Bridges* because the defendant had not manifested an intention to control the premises and objects which might found there. That was, roughly, Holmes' view: *CL*, 222.

[63] [1896] 2 QB 44, 47.

[64] [1896] 2 QB 44, 45. *Armory v Delamirie*, on which authority the county court judge had also relied, was dismissed by counsel as irrelevant to the instant dispute, since it proved only that a finder could maintain trover proceedings against a wrongdoer: [1896] 2 QB 44, 45.

[65] [1896] 2 QB 44, 45.

and on special grounds', inasmuch as 'the notes, being dropped in the public part of the shop, were never in the custody of the shopkeeper, or "within the protection of his house"'.[66]

After *Sharman*, the law suffers from this lack of clarity. The first judicial suggestion that in cases of this kind the right follows possession was clouded by an unnecessary publicity requirement, and the difficulty in applying the new theory to *Bridges*. The unsatisfactory state of law was reflected in academic commentary, which began the business of reconciling seemingly irreconcilable cases.[67] One of these commentaries much more than the others was to have lasting impact on the law, and, albeit unintentionally, offered an analytical suggestion that eventually would take finding problems away from the general theory of possession on which they had been said to depend.

# The Distraction: Evolution of the In/On Land Distinction

In 1929, Goodhart published a famous essay discussing *Bridges*, *Elwes* and *Sharman*.[68] The paper was critical, not necessarily of the decisions themselves, but of attempts to explain their ratios by propositions not present in the judgments. Having identified the pertinent criticisms,[69] Goodhart attempted to extract general principles from the three cases, and deduced the following:[70]

> 1. A man possesses everything which is attached to or under the land which he possesses ... 2. A man does not necessarily possess a thing which is lying unattached on the surface of his land, even though the thing is not possessed by some one else.[71]

In Goodhart's view, *Elwes* and *Sharman* were authorities for the first of these propositions, and *Bridges* was a precedent for the second 'even though the ratio decidendi of that case is uncertain'.[72] Of course, if the propositions were right,

---

[66] [1896] 2 QB 44, 47. In Chapter 6 we return to this public/private question, and consider its significance for the rights of finders and possessors of land.

[67] JH Williams and WM Crowdy (eds), *Goodeve's Modern Law of Personal Property* 3rd edn (London, Sweet and Maxwell, 1899) 14; RW Aigler, 'Rights of Finders' (1922–23) *21 Michigan Law Review* 664; JW Salmond, *Jurisprudence* 7th edn (London, Sweet and Maxwell, 1924) 304–5; R Moreland, 'The Rights of Finders of Lost Property' (1927) 16 *Kentucky Law Journal* 3; Goodhart, above n 18; JF Francis, 'Three Cases on Possession: Some Further Observations' (1928–29) 13 *St Louis Law Review* 11.

[68] Goodhart, above n 18.

[69] Many of these criticisms have already been identified where relevant above. For Goodhart's own overview, see his statement of six possible theories to explain *Bridges*: above n 18 at 202.

[70] The following principles assume that *Bridges* was correctly decided. See below for a discussion of Goodhart's view that it was not correctly decided.

[71] Above n 18 at 207.

[72] *Ibid* 207.

they necessitated a third rule to explain which unattached things the occupier of land possessed and which he did not, but that was an open question as far as Goodhart was concerned.[73] We will return to this below, but for now we must note that the above passage is significant because it is the first occasion in the literature where things 'attached to or under' land are juxtaposed in this way to things 'lying unattached on the surface'. It is absolutely clear that Goodhart himself would have rejected the use of this distinction as a basis for law. In the essay he acknowledged an obvious distinction in fact between the two situations: where goods were lying on the surface of land they could be picked up by a passer-by, but where they were buried in or attached to land, they could not be taken without some 'interference with the land itself'.[74] But Goodhart did not think that this distinction was 'of sufficient importance in principle to warrant separate rules as to possession'.[75] Indeed, the proposition about things lying unattached on land was only necessary if *Bridges v Hawkesworth* was correctly decided,[76] which Goodhart himself doubted.[77] We can be absolutely clear, then, that Goodhart distinguished attached and unattached things only as a method of summarising the outcomes of the existing decisions. He must have supposed the existence of a more general theory of possession that could explain them consistently.[78] Unfortunately, on the next occasion when a similar dispute came before a court, the emphasis would be laid on the attached/unattached distinction, and this rhetoric would greatly influence the development of the law.

---

[73] The penultimate paragraph of the paper lists three possibilities, according to whether the theory of Holmes, Pollock or Salmond was to be preferred. Thus, respectively: (a) 'a man possesses everything which is on his land from which he excludes the public'; or (b) 'an occupier of land possesses those things on his land of which he has de facto control'; or (c) 'an occupier of land possesses only those things on his land of which he has actual knowledge and which he intends to possess': above n 18 at 208.

[74] *Ibid* 207.

[75] *Ibid* 207.

[76] Had judgment there been given for the defendant, the second proposition could have held that a man 'possesses those things on his land which are not possessed by anyone else', and there would have been no need for any further rules to resolve disputes of this kind.

[77] Goodhart thought that only Pollock's explanation, ie that the defendant did not have control of the premises, could reasonably distinguish *Bridges* from the case of a thing being dropped in a private house. He disagreed with Pollock's conclusion on the facts, opining that the defendant did 'have the necessary control. The average customer who is honest does recognise that the shopkeeper has some claim or duty in relation to the thing lost by turning it over to him for safekeeping': above n 18 at 202. Of course, the reference to a shopkeeper's duty also gives another argument against the decision in *Bridges*. Goodhart could have suggested that Patteson J was wrong to hold that the defendant owed no duty to the owner of the banknotes. It is submitted that this would have been a stronger argument. Insofar as Goodhart gives an answer to *Bridges* based on the theory of Pollock, he is himself guilty of analysing the case on grounds not to be found in the judgment, which is exactly the mischief his essay hoped to avoid.

[78] The final paragraph specifically disclaims any attempt in the essay to outline a general theory of possession, but Goodhart clearly supposed that the three cases would be relevant to that enquiry. They had been chosen 'because so much of the learning on the subject is concerned with them': above n 18 at 208.

Giving judgment in *Hannah v Peel*,[79] Birkett J thought that the law to be applied was 'very uncertain', and characterised the authorities as a set of 'conflicting propositions'.[80] The defendant was the owner of a house which he had never himself occupied, and which at the material time had been requisitioned for the use of the armed forces. The plaintiff was a lance corporal of the Royal Artillery stationed at the house. He found a brooch in a crevice on the top of a window frame in a bedroom of the house used as a sick bay. Initially, he kept the brooch and said nothing of the find, but a few months later he reported the matter to his commanding officer, and then, at the latter's request, delivered the brooch to the police. Unfruitful searches for the owner were made, and after two years, despite receiving it from the plaintiff, the police delivered the brooch to the defendant. The defendant sold the brooch for £66.[81] He offered a reward to the plaintiff, but this was declined, the plaintiff maintaining throughout a right to keep the brooch against all but the true owner. At the trial, in proceedings for trover and detinue, Birkett J purported to follow *Bridges*, and gave judgment for the plaintiff.

The opinion of Birkett J is heavily dependent on Goodhart. Although that essay is formally cited only once (for the proposition, ultimately rejected by Birkett J, that *Bridges* was wrongly decided), the judgment discusses only *Bridges*, *Elwes* and *Sharman*, rehearsing the relevant theories and criticisms in precisely the language used by Goodhart. In the penultimate paragraph of the judgment, we find Goodhart's summary of the general principles to be drawn from these three cases, though again no reference is made to his essay. Thus, Birkett J considered it:

> fairly clear from the authorities that a man possesses everything which is attached to or under his land. Secondly, it would appear to be the law from the authorities I have cited, and particularly from *Bridges v Hawkesworth*, that a man does not necessarily possess a thing which is lying unattached on the surface of his land even though the thing is not possessed by someone else. A difficulty however, arises, because the rule which governs things an occupier possesses as against those which he does not, has never been very clearly formulated in our law.[82]

The novelty in *Hannah* might have been an attempt to formulate this missing dividing line for possessed unattached things. As it was, Birkett J thought it sufficient to remark that the defendant had never been in actual possession of the premises, and for that reason could lay no claim to the brooch.[83] The learned judge thought that he was 'following' *Bridges* in reaching this conclusion, but, as we have seen, absence of control over the premises was not part of the ratio in that case. In effect, what *Hannah v Peel* decides is that *possession* of land, as opposed

---

[79] [1945] 1 KB 509.

[80] [1945] 1 KB 509, 513.

[81] To a firm based in London, who resold it the following month for £88: [1945] 1 KB 509, 510.

[82] [1945] 1 KB 509, 520.

[83] 'The defendant was never physically in possession of these premises at any time. It is clear that the brooch was never his, in the ordinary acceptation of that term, in that he had the prior possession': [1945] 1 KB 509, 521.

to ownership or occupation, is a necessary prerequisite to any claim against a finder of goods, at least where the claimant has not otherwise established some title to the find, for example, by delivery or assumed duty. In other words, actual possession of land is the only way of proving that 'general power and intent to exclude unauthorised interference' given by Pollock as the justification for a claim to unknown goods. To this extent, Birkett J qualifies the dictum of Lord Russell in *Sharman*, where the presumption was that possession of discovered articles was in the '*owner* of the locus in quo'.[84]

The judgment in *Hannah* incorporated Goodhart's statement of the general principles to be drawn from the cases, and kept *Bridges* alive by claiming to 'follow' it, thereby rejecting the view that it had been wrongly decided. This structure of the law received further judicial support shortly afterwards in *Hibbert v McKiernan*.[85] This case might have been taken as resolving the doubt over the criteria to determine those unattached things possessed by a possessor of land. Certainly there is evidence of the view, first expressed in *Sharman* and later to be confirmed by the Court of Appeal in *Parker v British Airways Board*, that in order to acquire possession of goods lying unattached on his land, a possessor of land must manifest an intention to control that land and those things which may be upon it. *Hibbert* was an appeal against a conviction of larceny. The appellant had taken lost golf balls from a links course in Cheshire. The trial justices referred to *Bridges*, *Elwes*, *Sharman* and *Hannah*, and concluded that (a) at the time they were taken the golf balls were lying unattached on the golf links; (b) a possessor of land does not *necessarily* own objects lying unattached on his land; (c) given (b), there must be some circumstances in which a possessor of land *does* and some circumstances in which he *does not* own objects lying unattached on his land; and therefore (d) to satisfy a court that a possessor of land does own objects lying unattached on his land requires more evidence than the mere fact that the objects were lying unattached on that land. The only other evidence available to the court in the instant case was that a police officer had been present on the course with the special duty of warding off or apprehending persons taking golf balls from the links, in consequence of which the appellant had been apprehended. The trial justices thought that this was enough to hold that the members of the club were in possession of the golf balls at the time they were taken, because it was 'evidence of an intention by the club to exercise control over those golf balls'.[86]

The justices stopped short of expressing the basis of their resolution as a general proposition, although in its search for evidence of an intention to control

---

[84] [1986] 2 QB 44, 47 (emphasis added). The dicta are not necessarily inconsistent. In the earlier part of his statement of general principle, Lord Russell had identified the relevant fact scenario as 'that where a person has possession of house or land'. Had his mind been drawn to the question it seems likely that to avail of Pollock's 'larger intent' his Lordship would have insisted that a landowner be in actual possession of that land.

[85] [1948] 2 KB 142

[86] *Ibid* 144.

goods on land it echoes the view of Lord Russell CJ in *Sharman*, and to that extent the possession theories of Holmes and Pollock on which we have said that decision to depend. I have argued fully elsewhere that the judgments of the Divisional Court should be read as endorsing a similar position.[87] Both Humphreys and Pritchard JJ laid emphasis on the club owners' intention to control lost golf balls lying on their land, as manifested by the police officer on special duty.[88] Lord Goddard CJ made his judgment ostensibly on the authority of *Rowe*, but also emphasised the dishonest conduct of the appellant, apparently suggesting at one stage that this dishonesty was a source of the club owner's property in golf balls.[89] Perhaps because of this reliance on wrongful conduct, and the tendency of his Lordship's judgment to suggest that the case turned on a general proposition of criminal law, *Hibbert* has never been taken as having any settling influence on the law. Ironically, discounting a recent decision on virtually identical facts,[90] it appears to be the only case in English law where a possessor of land has been held better entitled than a subsequent taker to goods lying unattached on the surface of his land.[91]

The year after *Hibbert* was reported, the Chief Justice of the Ontario High Court considered the cases and concluded that 'British law cannot yet be said to be settled'.[92] The conclusion is evidenced by contemporaneous judgments, which contain mixed rationales and struggle to achieve any conceptual clarity. Another Ontario judge dismissed the contention that lost goods always belonged to the owner of private premises by observing a distinction in the cases between 'articles attached to or under land' and those 'on the surface of land or in a building thereon',[93] but ultimately preferred to distinguish *Bridges* and *Hannah* from *Elwes* and *Sharman* insofar as in the former cases the possessor of land did not know of the existence of the goods in question.[94] In *City of London Corporation v Appleyard*, McNair J recognised 'many fine possible points of distinction' between

---

[87] R Hickey, 'Stealing Abandoned Goods: Possessory Title in Proceedings for Theft' (2006) *Legal Studies* 584.

[88] [1948] 2 KB 142, 151, 152.

[89] For criticism see Chapter 6.

[90] *R v Rostron* [2003] EWCA Crim 2206, [2003] All ER (D) 269.

[91] Though note also the *Button 'B' Pennies Case* (1947) *The Solicitor*, vol 14, no 3, 50, discussed by Marshall, above n 37 at 68. There, the defendant was convicted of larceny of coins recovered from 42 phone booths by pressing the eponymous coin-reject button. In *The Solicitor* the case is explained on the basis of a bailment between those who inserted coins in the phone box and the Postmaster-General, allowing property to be laid in the latter for the purposes of an indictment for larceny. Marshall argues the case could equally have been decided on the basis that the Postmaster-General had the necessary factual control of the coins, and had manifested an intention 'to exclude people from entering the phone booth for an unlawful, speculative purpose': (1949) 2 *Current Legal Problems* 68, 82.

[92] *Bird v Fort Frances* (1949) 2 DLR 791, 793 (McRuer CJHC). No claim was raised by the possessor of land to a box of money found by a young boy, and the cases were considered only to throw 'indirect light' on the question whether a finder's right should be qualified where he was also a wrongdoer. We return to this aspect of *Bird*, and to this question generally, in Chapter 6.

[93] *Grafstein v Holme and Freeman* (1958) 12 DLR 727, 733 (Ontario Court of Appeal) per LeBel JA, giving the judgment of the Court.

[94] (1958) 12 DLR 727, 737.

goods found 'upon', 'under' and 'embedded' in land,[95] but declined to define precisely any of those points because he felt the case before him was so clearly covered by *Sharman* that 'no purpose would be served by any lengthy examination of the finer problems involved'.[96] Thus, the learned judge decided that a safe in a wall formed part of premises, such that the possessor of the premises was also in possession of the safe and its contents (a wooden box containing £5,728 in banknotes) and could resist a claim by a finder though ignorant of the existence of the safe. However, it is by no means clear that possession of a safe (or any receptacle) should also include possession of its contents. McNair J had resisted counsel's attempt to press such a distinction,[97] but he could have taken the point on the authority of *Merry v Green*,[98] where Parke B held that to pass title by delivery to the contents of a bureau it was necessary that it should have been expressly sold 'with contents'.[99] Had this argument not so swiftly been rejected, McNair J could not so easily have considered the box of money to be part of the premises, and might have said more on the finer points of the distinction between goods found in and on land. As it was, nearly a decade later a Law Reform Committee report on conversion repeated the view that the law was in an unsatisfactory state,[100] and it continued to be said that the principal difficulty occurred where goods were found lying unattached on land.[101]

## *Parker v British Airways Board*

In 1982, the Court of Appeal had its first opportunity to consider a dispute between a possessor of land and a finder. In *Parker v British Airways Board*,[102] the plaintiff found a gold bracelet on the floor of an airport executive lounge operated and occupied by the defendants. Donaldson LJ was conscious that the English rules of precedent meant that technically there was no decision binding on the court, and took the opportunity to offer a restatement of the law well beyond the facts immediately before him.[103] Giving the leading judgment, his Lordship described the dispute as a contest of 'conflicting rights'. The plaintiff relied on 'the ancient

---

[95] [1963] 1 WLR 982, 986.

[96] *Ibid* 986.

[97] *Ibid* 987, though he thought the submission 'rather faintly' argued.

[98] (1841) 7 M & W 623.

[99] For a discussion of *Merry* see Chapter 1. In the later case of *Moffatt v Kazana* [1969] 2 QB 152, Wrangham J resisted the contention that the conveyance of a house also passed title to a box of money hidden in the chimney-breast.

[100] Law Reform Committee, *Eighteenth Report (Conversion and Detinue)*, Cmnd 4774 (1971).

[101] *Kowal v Ellis* (1977) 76 DLR (3d) 546, 547.

[102] [1982] 1 QB 1004.

[103] The judgment purports to offer a complete restatement of the applicable rules, which are set out at length and then 'applied' to the facts of the instant case: [1982] 1 QB 1004, 1017–18. We will rehearse these here only insofar as they have a bearing on the nature of the possessory facts to be proved by one who claims title to goods lying unattached on his land. Other aspects of the restatement are dealt with elsewhere in this work, especially in Chapters 4, 6 and 7.

common law rule that the act of finding a chattel which has been lost and taking control of it gives the finder rights with respect to that chattel'.[104] The defendants claimed on the basis that as occupiers of the lounge they had rights to the bracelet which existed before the plaintiff found it, even though they were not aware of its existence before he had delivered to them.[105] As to the latter, Donaldson LJ's judgment disclosed the distinction between goods found in or attached to land and those found upon it.[106] He took it to be reasonably well settled that a possessor of land had rights superior than a finder to goods found in or attached to land, giving *Elwes* and *Sharman* as authority.[107] As for objects found on land, he accepted Lord Russell's 'statement of the general principle',[108] formulating it as follows:

> An occupier of a building has rights superior to those of a finder over chattels upon or in, but not attached to, that building if, but only if, before the chattel is found, he has manifested an intention to exercise control over the building and the things which may be upon it or in it.[109]

Applying this proposition to the facts of the case, Donaldson LJ concluded that the defendants had not sufficiently manifested an intention to control lost objects found in the executive lounge.[110] Whilst he acknowledged the right of the defendants to control entry to the lounge and restrict access to all but certain classes of passenger, and also referenced their undoubted intent to exclude specific items, such as guns and bombs, this kind of control was not relevant to their intention to control lost items.[111] Neither was the provision to staff of instructions for dealing with lost property, at least insofar as these had not been published to users of the lounge.[112] The result was an unhelpfully negative explanation of the manifest intention requirement. We are not told what is necessary to establish it, except that the conduct of the defendants in the instant case did not suffice. Precisely the same misfortune occurred a few years later in the New Zealand case of *Tamworth Industries Ltd v Attorney-General*.[113] In deciding that the police had a sufficient possessory title to retain monies found and seized on land even after the relevant statutory authority had expired, the High Court was not satisfied that the possessor of land had sufficiently manifested the intention required to prove an earlier possession than the police.[114] It is clear that relevant factors in the decision included the ease of access which members of the public had to the premises, and

---

[104] [1982] 1 QB 1004, 1008. No older authority was given for this proposition than *Armory v Delamirie* (1722) 1 Stra 505.
[105] [1982] 1 QB 1004, 1008.
[106] *Ibid* 1010, 1018. See also the judgment of Sir David Cairns, at 1021.
[107] *Ibid* 1010.
[108] *Ibid* 1014.
[109] *Ibid* 1018.
[110] *Ibid.*
[111] *Ibid.*
[112] [1982] 1 QB 1004, 1019.
[113] [1991] 3 NZLR 616.
[114] *Ibid* 624.

the general disrepair of the building,[115] but again there is no formulation of any general test for manifest intention. Thus, although *Parker* might now be taken as the leading case where goods are found on the land of another, little has been done to settle the evidential difficulty first articulated by Goodhart some 80 years ago.

## The Mistake: Right Follows Circumstance of Find

Apart from the higher appellate level of the decision, and the largely unnecessary restatement of the rules governing disputes of this kind, we might consider *Parker* to contain little of novelty. Indeed, the judgment has been criticised for relying too heavily on lengthy citation and containing 'rather little that could pass for conventional legal analysis'.[116] Insofar as is relevant it repeats in virtually identical terms the dictum of Lord Russell CJ on which it is said to depend, and it offers no conclusive answer to the essential question identified by Goodhart and in the cases, ie to which goods lying unattached on his land does a possessor of land have a claim? However, there is a difference in *Parker*. When Lord Russell offered his dictum in *Sharman*, he gave it as a complete solution to disputes between finders and possessors of land: he drew no distinction between things found on land and things found attached to it. That observation was first made by Goodhart, but he was clear that it should not be taken as the basis for different rules on possession. These were to be settled by whatever more general theory of possession was to be found in the common law, a question which Goodhart avowedly made no attempt to answer. In *Parker*, however, are the first signs of a modern trend to take the distinction itself as the basis of the applicable rules, and so hold that the factual circumstance of the find dictates the allocation of rights between the parties. This trend begins when Donaldson LJ offers two independent policy justifications for the apparent rule that a possessor of land will always have a better right than a finder to goods found attached to his land:

> The rationale of this rule is probably either that the chattel is to be treated as an integral part of the realty as against all but the true owner and so incapable of being lost or that the 'finder' has to do something to the realty in order to get at or detach the chattel and, if he is not thereby to become a trespasser, will have to justify his actions by reference to some form of licence by the occupier. In all likely circumstances that licence will give the occupier a superior right to that of the finder.[117]

These are new rationales, and there is little hint of either of them in any of the earlier cases. It is tempting to resist them by observing that each is flawed in some measure,[118] but that is not the present point. Whatever the success of the

---

[115]  *Ibid* 623.
[116]  S Roberts, 'More Lost Than Found' (1982) 45 *MLR* 683, 685.
[117]  [1982] 1 QB 1004, 1010.
[118]  The point is taken below.

justifications on their own terms, that they are proffered at all serves to suggest that the 'in land' proposition is an independent rule of law requiring its own justification. It distances this proposition from the possessory theory of Pollock and Holmes on which it depends, and distinguishes the proposition about goods 'lying unattached' on land. Consequently, it reinforces the view that disputes of this kind turn on the application of 'conflicting' rules and principles, and perpetuates the unsatisfactory nature of our law.

This new attempt at justification is even more readily apparent in *Waverly Borough Council v Fletcher*.[119] There, the Court of Appeal allowed the plaintiff council to recover a medieval gold brooch found buried some nine inches below the surface of its land (a public park). Counsel for the defendant vigorously resisted the contention that the applicable test to resolve the dispute was 'whether the article was found in or on the land'.[120] Such a test was 'arbitrary and leads to absurd results'.[121] That was also the view of the judge at first instance, who 'could see no reason in common sense why the better possessory claim should depend on whether an object was found on or in ground'.[122] Giving judgment, however, Auld LJ[123] thought that the authorities 'accepted as established law the distinction to be made between articles found in and on land', and considered the defendant's counsel 'undaunted' by the weight of that authority.[124] He also thought that the cases disclosed 'a number of sound and practical reasons for the distinction',[125] though none of these is very convincing.

First, he repeated Donaldson LJ's justifications for the 'in land' rule in the passage set out above, neither of which is completely satisfactory. The idea that a given thing can be treated as part of land for some purposes (ie claims by subsequent possessors) but not others (ie claims by true owners) is not intellectually satisfying,[126] but it does seem to have some legal credence,[127] and it is part of the justification in *Elwes*, at least to the extent that the canoe was to be considered part of the soil during the currency of its burial, and not a movable chattel.[128]

---

[119] [1996] QB 334 (CA).

[120] *Ibid* 337.

[121] *Ibid*.

[122] *Ibid* 345 (Auld LJ paraphrasing, or at best repeating without formal quotation, the view of Judge Fawcus, sitting as a judge of the Queen's Bench).

[123] With whom Ward LJ and Sir Thomas Bingham MR agreed: *ibid* 350.

[124] *Ibid* 344.

[125] *Ibid* 345.

[126] In the event that something accedes to realty it would seem preferable to say that it loses its individual character, at least for so long as it remains annexed. This proposition would make impossible any claim by the 'true owner' during the accession. Compare the argument of counsel for the defence in *Waverly*: [1996] QB 334, 345; and see generally B McFarlane, *The Structure of Property Law* (Oxford, Hart Publishing, 2008) 157–8.

[127] *Wake v Hall* (1883) 8 App Cas 195; *Simmons v Midford* [1969] 2 Ch 415.

[128] This, of course, is the first irony with the argument that the 'in land' rule is justified insofar as goods attached to land are to be treated as part of the realty. It seeks to justify a rule said to stem from Chitty J's conclusion in *Elwes* that the canoe was a chattel with authorities used by the learned judge to answer the case that it was not a chattel but part of the soil.

However, even if the general principle is correct, Donaldson LJ's formula still supposes that goods must be 'lost' before a finder can acquire any rights therein, which is doubtful.[129] As to the second justification, even if we were to get past the requisite implication that a licence to excavate confers title on the possessor of land to goods found in the course of those excavations,[130] for its completeness the dictum relies on the further assumption that a finder will acquire no rights when he has no licence, ie when he is a trespasser, which is an assumption contrary to all common law authority.[131]

Auld LJ's second justification was that 'removal of an object in or attached to land would normally involve interference with the land and may damage it'. This proposition is more promising, and is persuasive when it is connected to a more general theory of possession. In argument in *Waverly*, counsel for the defence had rejected the existence of a flat rule giving title to attached things to the possessor of land, preferring the view that in every case the latter establishes his claim on the possessory facts of control and intention.[132] It might well have been answered that the possessor of land's intention to exclude interference with his land discharged that latter requirement, which in effect was the view of Pollock. But in Auld LJ's judgment this connection is not apparent, and the interference with land statement appears as a flat proposition disconnected from any theory of possession. In these terms, the short answer to it is that the law of trespass to land exists to resist interference with land and compensate the possessor of land. Without more, the occurrence of such a wrong has nothing to say about the allocation of property rights in discovered goods.

The third justification is the least persuasive. This purports to distinguish things found in and on land according to the likelihood that the owner of the lost thing will return to claim it, an entirely speculative fact totally inappropriate to the resolution of a proprietary dispute. It contends that 'in the case of an object in the ground its original owner is unlikely in most cases to be there to claim it' whereas an unattached object 'is likely in most cases to have been recently lost, and the true owner may well claim it'.[133] An initial observation against this contention is that difficult litigation results in cases where things are found unattached on land, even when they appear to have been recently lost, *precisely*

---

[129] The argument in Chapter 3 is that English law discloses no requirement of 'loss' as a prerequisite to the acquisition of right by a finder.

[130] In cases where a finder has had permission to dig on the land of a rival claimant, the disputes have been settled either because (a) the possessor of land had a property interest in the goods before the grant of permission, such that the grant itself was irrelevant to the question of title (*Elwes v Brigg Gas Co* (1886) LR 33 Ch D 562, 568), or; (b) the agreement between the parties provided expressly for some reservation of discovered articles to the grantor (*City of London Corporation v Appleyard* [1963] 1 WLR 982, 989–90).

[131] See Chapter 6. In *Parker*, Donaldson LJ had supposed that a trespassing finder acquired no rights to the object of his find, but this opinion depended on a misunderstanding of *Hibbert*. Nonetheless, his Lordship's view on trespassing finders probably accounts for his second justification.

[132] [1996] QB 334, 337.

[133] *Ibid* 345.

*because* the 'true owner' has made no claim. *Parker* provides an obvious example. More worrying still is that the proposition substitutes for detailed rules on the acquisition of title a series of over-sweeping generalisations which the court has no competency to assess. But quite apart from these, on the facts of the decided authorities the contention is manifestly false. In *Sharman*, nothing turned on the recency of the loss, which equivocally could have been days or years before the find, and yet Auld LJ considered the rings 'just on the "in" side of the borderline between objects found in and on land'. In *Hannah*, there was no evidence at all of how the brooch came to be in the window crevice, nor the money in its hiding places in *Appleyard* and *Tamworth*. To this extent, likelihood of recovery is simply not relevant to the resolution of these disputes.

The only attraction in the third justification is that it seems to aim at an overall policy justification for the law relating to finders. Auld LJ spoke of the need to look for a 'substitute owner' in cases where the real owner was unlikely to be found. As we shall see later, there is a line of authority at US state common law which attempts to resolve disputes between possessors of land and finders according to which of them (generally) is in the better position to facilitate a reunion between owner and lost object, and it seems possible that Auld LJ thought that the in/on land distinction executed that general policy.[134] But insofar as it exhibits a preference for a possessor of land as a substitute owner, this statement of policy rests on the misconceived assumption that a possessor of land is always in a better position than a finder to secure the return of a lost item to its loser. This assumption is not borne out on the facts of the litigated disputes, where often the finders took steps to notify the competent authorities. Indeed, in *Waverly* itself, the finder's first action was to deliver the brooch to the coroner for a determination as to whether it was treasure.[135]

There is little of persuasion in any of these 'sound and practical' reasons for distinguishing goods found in and on land. In a final flourish, Auld LJ remarked that 'the distinction is now long and well established', which is precisely the problem. It was never intended that disputes between possessors of land and finders be resolved on the basis of such a distinction per se. Goodhart had offered the observation only as a summary of the three decided cases, and did not think it a sufficient basis of law. The great mistake in subsequent cases, and especially in *Parker* and *Waverly*, has been to treat the distinction as the determining cause of rights acquisition. This trend is evident too in some of the books.[136] The result

---

[134] Note the observation that there was 'no compelling reason why [an unattached object] should pass into the possession of the landowner': [1996] QB 334, 345.

[135] See also *Bridges* (notes advertised and claimed by finder after three years); *Sharman* (rings delivered to the police and advertised); *Hannah* (brooch delivered to the police and advertised); *Parker* (bracelet delivered to defendant's employee and advertised).

[136] 'The dominant position now seems to be that for articles found *in* the land, the better claim is that of the possessor of land, though for things found *on* the land, the finder has the better claim unless the possessor of the land has manifested an intention to control things found on it': *EPL*, 4.420 (original emphasis), though it is noted that there is no satisfactory explanation for the distinction.

is that the law on disputes of this kind looks arbitrary. It seems like a discrete set of rules or principles, qualifying or amending a supposed 'general rule' in *Armory* according to circumstances which disclose no good reason for any distinction. It would be much better if we removed our emphasis from the in/on circumstances of a find and laid it again on the ordinary facts of possession, and the parties' relative abilities to establish them.

# The Answer: Evidentiary Concessions to Proof of Possession

It is interesting to compare Donaldson LJ's judgment in *Parker* to that of Eveleigh LJ. The latter made no mention of the in/on land distinction, but instead emphasised only the facts of possession:

> for the defendants to succeed it must be shown that they had possession of the bracelet at the time when the plaintiff found it and took it into his possession. Whatever the difficulties which surround the concept of possession in English law, the two elements of control and *animus possidendi* must co-exist.[137]

On this view, the 'on land' rule is a function of this general possessory principle, and the difficulty in the cases is about the level of proof required to discharge the requirement of intention. Eveleigh LJ reproduced Lord Russell's dictum in *Sharman*, and regarded the learned Chief Justice as holding that a possessor of land must 'prove that his intention was obvious',[138] that, in effect, being the meaning of 'manifest'.[139] There was the usual possessory caveat that what was necessary to do this would vary according the circumstances of a given case,[140] but additionally two examples of situations when the requirement would 'almost invariably' be satisfied, ie where goods were discovered on the floor of a private house; and where they were discovered on the floor of a bank vault.[141] In each of these cases it was the firmness of the occupier's control of the premises that accounted for the obviousness of the intention. Thus, Eveleigh LJ went so far as to hold that these

---

In *Personal Property Law*, Bridge notes it would have been preferable if the proposition about goods attached to land had been expressed as a function of a more general theory of possession, but then adds that 'it seems clear that a rule of law favours the occupier of land': 3rd edn (Oxford, Clarendon Press, 2003) 25. Also see *Clerk & Lindsell on Torts*, 17–49.

[137] [1982] 1 QB 1004, 1019.

[138] *Ibid* 1020.

[139] To this extent, Eveleigh LJ offered an analogy with the requirement to make clear to a visitor the terms of entry on to premises: 'A person permitted upon the property of another must respect the lawful claims of the occupier as the terms upon which he is allowed to enter, but it is only right that those claims or terms should be made clear': *ibid* 1020.

[140] *Ibid.*

[141] *Ibid.*

apparently distinct possessory facts were inversely related: 'the firmer the control, the less will be the need to demonstrate independently the *animus possidendi*'.[142]

The penultimate paragraph of Donaldson LJ's judgment indicated the same inversely proportionate relationship between control and intention, but did so conversely. Where a possessor of land had manifested an 'intention to exercise a very high degree of control', that intention could compensate for a very weak degree of physical control.[143] Rather confusingly, Donaldson LJ also used a bank vault to exemplify his contention, but this time the vault was open and a bracelet was found loose on the floor such that it could easily be taken. The point was that the obvious intention to control things in a bank vault operated to establish the bank's right, even though in real terms the level of physical control was slight.

This inverse variance of the apparently discrete facts of possession is the answer to disputes between a possessor of land and a finder, for inasmuch as it helps to explain the level of intention that must be manifested by the former if he is to oust the claim of the latter to goods found unattached on his land, it also explains his claim to goods found buried in that land. Conceivably we might approach the 'in land' rule from either end of the formula. We might say that a possessor of land has such firm control over objects beneath the surface of that land that he is relieved from the burden of establishing independently a manifest intention to possess them. That course, however, involves laying emphasis on the possessor of land's control of the lost objects themselves, whereas in the dicta in *Parker*, not to mention the theories derived from Holmes and Pollock, *control of the land* has been the significant factor. Thus, it seems preferable to say that the possessor of land's right to attached goods arises because his intention to exclude interference with the land is so obvious as to speak for itself. This in effect was Pollock's view, which, it will be recalled, elected to rest possession of attached goods on 'a real de facto possession, constituted by the occupier's general power and intent to exclude unauthorised interference'.[144] As such, consistently with *Hannah v Peel*, to establish his claim to articles found buried in his land, a possessor of land need only adduce evidence of his factual control of the land.

Construed this way, there is no difference per se in goods found in or attached to land, but only differences in what a possessor of land will be required to prove in order to establish possession of them. The 'in land' rule is not a flat proposition of law, but rather an example of a situation in which a possessor of land is relieved from the burden of proving a manifest intention to control things which might be found on his land. This explanation lays the emphasis in these cases as Holmes and Pollock intended, as did Lord Russell in *Sharman*, ie on the ordinary facts of possession. It removes the arbitrary reliance on the circumstances of the find all too evident in modern commentary, and lends a degree of simplicity and

---

[142] *Ibid.*
[143] [1982] 1 QB 1004, 1019.
[144] P & W, 41, considering *Elwes*.

coherence to cases which have long been thought to contain 'a really difficult question of law'.[145] Put shortly, disputes between possessors of land and finders are to be resolved according to which of the parties can show a prior right by virtue of possession. This always depends on the possessor of land's ability to oust the claim of the finder by proving the twin possessory elements of control and intention, but sometimes we remove from him the burden of proving the latter because it is so obvious as to speak for itself. The apparent rule giving a possessor of land a better right to goods attached to his land is no more than the most widely recognised example of this evidentiary concession.

Of course, our decision to accept this explanation of the in/on land distinction, and thus of the cases, depends on our acceptance of the general theory of possession which underlies it. It seems now to be generally agreed that at common law a property right to goods is generated on the concurrence in a given person of a certain physical control of the goods and a certain intention to possess them. As we have seen, this theory seems to have been borrowed uncritically from the Roman law and incorporated in common law jurisprudence first by Holmes and then by Pollock, and no doubt could be resisted in some measure, were we so inclined, on the ground of its shaky foundations.[146] But for now it will be enough to observe that, whatever the outcome of the larger question on possession, the modern theory will never do as an explanation of *Bridges v Hawkesworth*, which was decided on an altogether different ground. On its own terms, *Bridges* was a coherent decision, but it cannot be made to depend on a theory which did not exist in the common law at the time it was decided. Of course, an intentional deposit from true owner to possessor of land would still be enough to trump the claim of a finder if the same facts were to come before a court today. But the law has changed since 1851, and offers now another ground for the resolution of these disputes which makes the rights of the parties turn on their relative abilities to establish the facts of possession.

*Bridges* will remain significant in our legal history as the case which first featured the facts of a dispute between a possessor of land and a finder, and as that which purported to elevate the incremental extension of trover liability in *Armory* to the 'general right of the finder to any article which has been lost, as against all the world, except the true owner'.[147] In subsequent cases, this right has been judged against the claims of possessors of land, and despite perceived difficulties in the law it seems clear now that the judgment in *Armory* requires substantial qualification. The finder of goods has such property as will enable him to keep it against everyone save those who can establish a prior possession. This much has been accepted before now, but the commensurability of the rights of finders and prior possessors brings to focus a correlative proposition which has not yet fully been

---

[145] *Hibbert v McKiernan* [1942] 2 KB 142, 149 (Lord Goddard CJ).

[146] This matter is addressed further in Chapter 5, where we consider the general argument that possession is a source of property rights.

[147] (1851) 15 Jur 1079, 1082.

explored: the finder's right is a consequence of her possession. The simplicity and apparent obviousness of this contention belies its expansive explanatory power. Once it is accepted, there is no need to regard finders as a special case outside the normally applicable rules of possession. The goal of the next two chapters is to substantiate this claim by arguing respectively (a) that the facts of finding (ie of loss, absence of control, subsequent discovery) have no bearing on the generation of right in the finder except insofar as they offer evidence of her possession; and (b) that the finder owes no special obligations to the loser of goods such as would distinguish her from the general class of possessors.

# 3

# The Significance of the Facts of Loss

In Chapter 2 we considered the dominant factual matrix in modern finding disputes. A finder discovers some item on the land or premises of another, and the possessor of the land and the finder each claim the object in question. Saliently in each case there is a discovery of an object the existence of which previously was unknown to either party, and neither party sets up a claim as owner of the object. Outside this core, however, there are manifold nuances of fact that conceivably might justify distinctions. In *Bridges*, the packet of banknotes was taken to have been 'accidentally dropped' on the shop floor and was 'manifestly lost'. So it was held with the bracelet in *Parker*, although it is not impossible to suppose that there the bracelet had first been removed intentionally and placed, say, on a table, only later to be nudged to the floor by accident. In *Elwes*, the canoe had lain embedded for centuries, and little was known about how it came to be there. Perhaps it had been intentionally abandoned, maybe even jettisoned in the course of a troubled voyage;[1] perhaps it had been left for safe-keeping with some intention to return to it; perhaps even its existence had been forgotten. The last certainly could have been true of the quantities of money discovered in *Appleyard*, *Moffatt* and *Tamworth*, although in each of these cases the money must initially have been placed intentionally in the place where it was discovered, and in *Tamworth* there was additionally the suspicion that the banknotes represented the proceeds of crime. As for the rings in *Sharman*, it is easy to believe they had been lost accidentally,[2] though perhaps more romantically we might suppose they had been cast into the water as the result of some quarrel.

Consistently with academic commentary on finders,[3] we might rationalise these various factual possibilities to four general categories. First, we might say that in some cases goods have been 'lost'. In the US literature, 'lost' property is that which

---

[1] There was evidence before the court in *Elwes* that the boat had been found within a few feet of the River Ancholme, leaving open the suggestion that it was abandoned in the course of a voyage: (1886) LR 33 Ch D 562.

[2] A walkway was created around Minster Pool in 1772, which remains with some additions today: see the website of Lichfield District Council at www.lichfielddc.gov.uk/.

[3] See generally WB Raushenbush, *Brown on Personal Property* 3rd edn (Chicago, IL, Callaghan & Co, 1975) 29–30; RW Aigler, 'Rights of Finders' (1922–23) 21 *Michigan Law Review* 664; R Moreland, 'The Rights of Finders of Lost Property' (1927) 16 *Kentucky Law Journal* 3; Anon, 'Comment on Lost, Mislaid, and Abandoned Property' (1939) 8 *Fordham Law Review* 222.

'has passed out of the owner's possession unintentionally and involuntarily', as where a coin falls through a hole in my pocket and on to the ground.[4] The banknotes in *Bridges* and the bracelet in *Parker* could be considered 'lost', at least to the extent that their loser knew nothing of their separation from his control.[5] Secondly, goods might be 'mislaid'. Unlike lost goods, initially these are removed intentionally from the custody of their holder, but later are forgotten,[6] as where I put down my umbrella while I pay for a coffee, but leave forgetting to lift it again. Thirdly, goods might be 'hidden', that is, intentionally placed somewhere for the purpose of concealment, whatever the motivation for such concealment. Insofar as the intention is that the goods remain concealed, the hider intends that they remain out of his custody, though he does not intend to divest himself of any property in the goods. Where that latter divesting intention is present, we might categorise the goods in question as 'abandoned', as did the successive courts the golf balls stolen by Mr Hibbert.

The criteria governing each of these categories relate to various intentions (or imputed intentions) on the part of the owner of the goods in question, or more accurately, on the part of the person from whose custody those goods were removed prior to their discovery. There seem to be three relevant intentions, the presence or absence of which in various combinations accounts for the designation of goods. They are (a) an initial intention to remove the goods from immediate physical custody; (b) an intention that, once removed, the goods remain out of custody; and (c) an intention to divest any property interest in the goods. We might summarise the various permutations as shown in Table 3.1.

**Table 3.1: Permutations of owner's intentions**

|  | Intention to remove goods from custody | Intention for goods to remain out of custody | Intention to divest property in goods |
|---|---|---|---|
| Lost | ✗ | ✗ | ✗ |
| Mislaid | ✓ | ✗ | ✗ |
| Hidden | ✓ | ✓ | ✗ |
| Abandoned | ✓ | ✓ | ✓ |

[4] 1 Am Jur 2d, *Abandoned, Lost, and Unclaimed Property* (1962) § 12; Anon, 'Comment on Lost, Mislaid, and Abandoned Property' (1939) 8 *Fordham Law Review* 222, 223. This Comment has been described more recently as 'one of the best guides to the traditional rules and leading cases on the subject': RH Helmholz, 'Equitable Division and the Law of Finders' (1983–84) 52 *Fordham Law Review* 313.

[5] Note that the commentaries seem to oscillate between the language of intention and awareness when describing this kind of voluntary or involuntary conduct. So A might be said to have 'lost' goods if he *does not intend* to part with their custody, or if he *is not aware* that they have left his presence.

[6] 1 Am Jur 2d, *Abandoned, Lost, and Unclaimed Property* (1962) § 14.

In the United States, this classification of goods has been extremely influential in determining the nature and extent of a finder's right in the object of her find. In England, it has not enjoyed this same influence, and whilst on various occasions it has been invoked by a court,[7] it will be argued here that our reliance on the facts of possession makes it unnecessary to use the classification to resolve disputes about entitlement to discovered goods. The better view is that questions of right in these cases depend not on the facts of loss or the consequent designation of discovered goods, but solely on the relative abilities of the parties to any dispute to establish the possessory facts of control and intention. That is not to say that the facts of loss are never relevant to English legal proceedings. On the contrary, they might serve to confirm or deny a criminal or civil liability, and this function is considered below. The point is just that they do not bear on the acquisition of right by a finder, or to put the matter another way, the facts of loss do not have any proprietary significance in English law. Insofar as this is true, this chapter concludes by suggesting that 'finding' cases should not be regarded as *sui generis*, but are a manifestation of the operation of more general rules on possession.

# The Relevance of Loss and Mislaying

## US State Common Law: Categorisation Designates Right

In the United States, most state jurisdictions recognise a distinction at common law between goods which have been lost and goods which have been mislaid.[8] In cases involving finders and possessors of land, this distinction has been used expressly to determine the rights of the parties. Traditionally, a finder acquires a property interest only in goods categorised as 'lost'. Generally the state courts have felt bound in this respect by *Armory v Delamirie*,[9] and the rights of a finder are rehearsed in similar terms. So the finder of lost goods acquires a property in them good against the whole world, save the true owner.[10] Of course, this view rests on an artificially narrow reading of *Armory*, where there was nothing in the judgment to suggest that its application was confined to goods which were

---

[7] Note especially the following dictum of Donaldson LJ in *Parker* [1982] QB 1004, 1017: 'The finder of a chattel acquires no rights over it unless (a) it has been abandoned or lost and (b) he takes it into his care and control'.

[8] Anon, 'Comment on Lost, Mislaid, and Abandoned Property' (1939) 8 *Fordham Law Review* 222.

[9] (1722) 1 Stra 505; *Durfee v Jones* (1877) 11 RI 588; *Batteiger v Pennsylvania Company*, 64 Pa Super 195, 198 (1916). On the accepted authority of *Armory* in the United States, see Raushenbush, above n 3 at 24; B Burke, *Property* 2nd edn (New York, Aspen Publishers, 2004) 31; B Burke *et al* (eds), *Fundamentals of Property* 2nd edn (Newark, NJ, LexisNexis, 2004) 24.

[10] *Danielson v Roberts*, 44 Ore 108 (1904).

'lost' in this sense,[11] but it has prevailed nonetheless. An instructive case is *Bowen v Sullivan*.[12] The plaintiff was visiting the premises of the defendants (a paper mill) and she discovered two 50 dollar bills lying on the floor in an envelope. On a promise that he would return them to her, the plaintiff handed the notes to one of the defendants to determine whether they were genuine, but the defendant refused to return them and subsequently the defendants converted the notes to their own use. Factually the case bears some similarity to *Parker*. The plaintiff was lawfully on the defendants' premises, honest enough initially to turn over her find, diligent enough to secure a promise of its return, and equally subjected to a subsequent conversion of the find by the defendants in breach of their undertaking to return it. As we have seen, *Parker* was decided according to the relative facts of possession between the parties. The finder had a better right because the defendant board had not sufficiently manifested an intention to control the premises and objects which might have been found there. In *Bowen*, the matter was settled because the court was satisfied that the banknotes were lost. The trial judge directed the jury that 'if the bank-notes were lost property and the plaintiff … found them, it does not matter where she found them; they belong to her as against every person but the loser, or real owner'.[13] The jury found for the plaintiff, and the verdict was upheld on appeal.

Whilst the better view of English law does not emphasise the place of the find as a determining factor in itself,[14] still our courts are bound to consider the facts of possession and control of premises, and in that sense the location of the find can make a difference. That those facts were not taken or considered in *Bowen* illustrates the divergence of English and US state law on this question.[15] Moreover, the pervasiveness of the US rule is highlighted inasmuch as on occasion a finder has been able to recover 'lost' goods even against one with an apparently prior possessory interest.[16] In *Danielson v Roberts*, for example, two young brothers succeeded in recovering US$7,000 in gold coins which they had found buried in the defendant's land.[17] In England, even then, the defendant certainly would have been able to resist the boys' claim.[18]

In contrast to lost goods, on the US view the finder of mislaid goods does not normally acquire any rights therein. Indeed, the general wisdom is that the

---

[11] In effect the US courts are not following *Armory*, but its rehearsal in *Bridges v Hawkesworth*, where Patteson J took it as establishing 'the general right of the finder to any article which has been lost': 15 Jur 1079, 1082 (1851).

[12] 62 Ind 281 (1878) (Supreme Court of Indiana).

[13] 62 Ind 281, 284 (1878).

[14] See further Chapter 6.

[15] See also *Loucks v Gallogly*, 1 Misc 22 (1892) (50 dollars lying on a desk in the National Exchange Bank of Albany were not lost, so that their finder could maintain no claim against the defendant teller).

[16] To this extent the US state courts treat *Armory* literally and allow a finder to recover against all save the true owner. Aigler is alive to this erroneous use of *Armory*: above n 3 at 667.

[17] 44 Ore 108 (1904). Also *Roberson v Ellis*, 58 Ore 219 (1911).

[18] *South Staffordshire Water Co v Sharman* [1896] 2 QB 44.

discovery of mislaid goods does not amount to a 'finding' at all. As is said in the leading US treatise, *Brown on Personal Property*:

> To intentionally place an article down and then go away, forgetting it, has often been held not a losing of it; thus the discoverer of the article is not a 'finder' and does not have a finders' rights.[19]

In *McAvoy v Medina*,[20] the plaintiff customer discovered a pocket-book containing banknotes on a table in the defendant's barber shop. He gave it to the defendant, telling him to return it to the owner if he should come looking for it, and otherwise to advertise it, which the defendant promised to do. Subsequently, the plaintiff made three demands for the money, and eventually sued the defendant for its recovery. It was agreed that the pocket-book had been placed on the table by a transient customer of the defendant and left there accidentally, and also that it had first been seen and taken up by the plaintiff.[21] On these facts, the Supreme Judicial Court of Massachusetts upheld a ruling for the defendant. The pocket-book was 'not to be treated as lost property in that sense in which a finder has a valid claim'.[22] The plaintiff did not by discovering and picking up the pocket-book acquire any original right therein, and neither did the subsequent conduct of the defendant in receiving and holding the pocket-book create any right in the plaintiff.[23] Therefore, the plaintiff could maintain no action against the defendant.

It will be apparent that the facts of *McAvoy* closely resemble those of *Bridges v Hawkesworth*,[24] where, of course, the opposite result was reached. *Bridges* was cited in *Medina*, but not followed because the court felt constrained by a Tennessee authority we shall discuss shortly.[25] The divergence of these cases, and the divergence of *Bridges* from the later English authorities, means in effect that the authorities disclose three possible means of resolving disputes between possessors of land and finders, according to whether (a) the possessor of land has a prior possessory interest to the finder; (b) the possessor of land is under a legal liability to the loser of goods, and has a right in consequence of that duty; or (c) the goods in question have been lost or mislaid. It might be enough to dismiss the relevance in English law of this latter method by showing simply that it is not exhibited in the cases, but before we do this, and to make stronger our general argument in favour of possession, it will be helpful to show that there are indications in the US literature that the use of the loss/mislaid distinction to resolve these disputes is regarded as unsatisfactory.

---

[19] Raushenbush, above n 3 at 29.
[20] 11 Allen (Mass) 548 (1866).
[21] *Ibid*.
[22] *Ibid* 549.
[23] *Ibid* 549.
[24] (1851) 21 LJQB 75.
[25] See 11 Allen (Mass) 548, 549 (1866).

First, authoritatively the provenance of the distinction at US state common law is to be doubted. In *Medina*, as we noted above, the Massachusetts court chose to disregard *Bridges* because it felt constrained by the ruling of the Supreme Court of Tennessee in *Lawrence v State*.[26] That was another case about a pocket-book left by a customer on a table in a barber shop, but the proceedings were criminal. A barber was indicted for grand larceny of US$480 accidentally left in the shop by one of his patrons. When the customer returned to the shop after realising his loss, the barber denied all knowledge of the money. The state Supreme Court upheld his conviction. In Tennessee law at that time, as elsewhere in the United States, it was axiomatic that there could be no larceny of lost goods.[27] The offence required an immediate trespassory interference with goods, which could never be present when the goods taken were out of the custody of their owner, and thus could never be present when lost goods were discovered. Counsel for the defence pressed that, for this reason, there was no larceny on the facts of *Lawrence*. The Court answered:

> the pocket book, under the circumstances proved, was not lost, nor could the defend-
> ant be called a finder. The pocket book was left, not lost ... If I place my watch or
> pocket-book under my pillow in a bed chamber, or upon a table or bureau, I may leave
> them behind me indeed, but if that be all, I cannot be said with propriety to have lost
> them. To lose is not to place or put any thing carefully and voluntarily in the place you
> intend and then forget it, it is casually and involuntarily to part from the possession; and
> the thing is then usually found in a place or under circumstances to prove to the finder
> that the owner's will was not employed in placing it there. To place a pocket book, there-
> fore, upon a table, and to omit or forget to take it away, is not to lose it in the sense in
> which the authorities referred to speak of lost property; and we are of opinion, therefore,
> that there was no error in the charge of the court in reference to the facts in this case,
> and we affirm the judgment.[28]

This reasoning was made without reference to any authority, and its novelty results in *Lawrence* being credited as a leading decision on the lost/mislaid distinction.[29] But it ought to be clear that the Massachusetts court did some violence in applying it to the facts of *Medina*. *Lawrence* concerned a dispute between the owner/loser of a pocket-book and a subsequent possessor. It was not a contest between two non-owning possessors, as was *Medina*. Moreover, the significance in *Lawrence* of the ruling that the goods were not lost was that it made safe the defendant's criminal conviction. From here it is a large step to *Medina*, where deeming the goods not lost allowed the court to ignore *Bridges* and posit a new rule giving title to mislaid goods to the occupier of the land on which they were found. The better view is that *Lawrence* was applicable to the facts of *Medina* only to the extent that

---

[26] *Lawrence v State of Tennessee*, 20 Tenn 228 (1839).

[27] *Porter v State of Tennessee*, Martin & Yer 226 (1827); citing the first edition of *Russell on Crime*, 1034.

[28] 20 Tenn 228, 229–30 (1839) (Reese J for the court).

[29] Anon, 'Comment on Lost, Mislaid, and Abandoned Property' (1939) 8 *Fordham Law Review* 222, 233.

it confirmed that a finder or occupier would be answerable in larceny for any dishonest conversion of goods discovered,[30] and without more it had nothing to say about the property rights of these parties inter se.

Secondly, even if we accept in principle that disputes of this kind can be resolved according to the factual classification of goods as lost and mislaid, the distinction is difficult to apply. By definition the problem only arises when an owner of goods makes no claim to them, and so the court lacks direct evidence of the intentions of the person on whose intentions the distinction is said to rest. Consequently, the determination in a given case of whether goods are lost or mislaid is made on largely speculative inferences of fact, and often on flat presumptions. So, for example, where goods are found in the street, or a similarly public place, they 'may be presumed to be lost because their situation would indicate that the owners had involuntarily parted with the possession'.[31] By contrast, where they are found concealed or hidden there is a presumption that they were parted with initially voluntarily so as not to be lost.[32] In the absence of an operative presumption, inferences are drawn from the circumstances of the case, including the nature of the premises and surroundings,[33] and in particular the situation of the found item. Where something was found on a table-top the likelihood was that it had been intentionally placed and thus mislaid, whereas if it was discovered on the floor it was probably lost.[34] There is nothing satisfactory about using such a vague and imprecise methodology to resolve disputes about title to personal property. It would not be difficult in fact or supposition for a mislaid pocket-book to be nudged inadvertently from its place on a counter to the floor, and yet with this the lost/mislaid distinction is transgressed and the rights of the parties alternatively resolved. It seems impossible to believe that basic rights to goods should be determined in such a speculative manner.

Thirdly, inasmuch as the state courts continued to affirm the lost/mislaid distinction well into the twentieth century,[35] the cases contain mixed rationales and thus admit of equivocal explanation. A good example is *Foulke v New York Consolidated Railroad Co*,[36] where the defendant, as operator of an underground railway service, was held to have sufficient interest in a package left unattended in one of its carriages to maintain a prosecution for petty larceny against the plaintiff finder.[37] The judgment records that the package[38] had been mislaid rather than lost, and confirms as sound the rule distinguishing these respective

---

[30] Compare *People of New York v M'Garren*, 17 Wend 460 (1837).
[31] *Loucks v Gallogly*, 1 Misc 22, 26 (1892) (County Court of New York).
[32] *Schley v Couch*, 155 Tex 195 (Supreme Court of Texas).
[33] *Hamaker v Blanchard*, Pa 377, 379 (1879) (Supreme Court of Pennsylvania).
[34] *Loucks v Gallogly*, 1 Misc 22, 25–26 (1892).
[35] *Jackson v Steinberg* 186 Ore 129 (1948).
[36] 228 NY 269 (1920) (Court of Appeals of New York).
[37] The plaintiff was seeking damages for malicious prosecution and unlawful imprisonment.
[38] Which on later examination was found to contain a loaf of bread: 228 NY 269, 273 (1920). The plaintiff had been arrested and released on bail of US$500: 228 NY 269, 273 (1920).

factual situations,[39] but ostensibly the court found for the defendant because it had assumed a duty to keep safely the goods of passengers:

> After the passenger owner had left the car, forgetting to take the package with him, the plaintiff knew the package was not lost property. It or the custody of it did not belong to him then any more than it did while its owner was in the car. He saw and knew the owner had forgotten it, had left it by mistake. It then had become in the custody and the potential actual possession of the defendant. It was the right of the defendant and its duty to become as to it and its owner a gratuitous bailee. It was its right and duty to possess and use the care of a gratuitous bailee for the safekeeping of the package until the owner should call for it.[40]

Insofar as it rests the defendant's right to the package on the duty he owed to its owner, the judgment in *Foulke* accords with *Bridges v Hawkesworth*. But in England the decision in *Bridges* has been superseded by developments in the general theory of possession, and there is also some evidence of these developments in the US cases. In *Foster v Fidelity Safe Deposit Co*,[41] the court found that the defendant company had a better right than a finder to a packet of banknotes discovered on its premises because it was in possession of them at the time of their discovery. However, the judgment proceeded to discuss a line of cases from *Medina*. The court held that the banknotes were mislaid; affirmed the traditional lost/mislaid distinction;[42] and thereby conflated two discrete methods of resolving disputes, ie possession and the lost/mislaid distinction.[43] But the prior possession rationale has also been applied to cases of lost goods, so that, as in England, a finder's rights will not avail against a possessor of land who can establish a prior possessory right. In *Ferguson v Ray*,[44] the Supreme Court of Oregon followed *South Staffs Water Co v Sharman* to hold that a quantity of quartz crystal found buried in the defendant's land was in his possession against the claim of a finder.[45] Again, though, the judgment is equally consistent with the view that, because it had been buried and thus parted with voluntarily, the quartz was not 'lost', and therefore the finder had no right to it.[46] Indeed, we might go further

[39] *Ibid* 273–4.

[40] *Ibid* 274.

[41] 264 Mo 89 (1915) (Supreme Court of Missouri, though apart from introductory and concluding paragraphs the judgment consists in citations from the preceding judgment in the Kansas City Court of Appeals).

[42] 264 Mo 89, 96–102 (1915). The concluding paragraph applies the common law distinction to a Missouri statute governing the prescriptive rights of finders, confining its remit to the discovery of 'lost' goods: 264 Mo 89, 102–3 (1915).

[43] 'Plaintiff, to sustain himself, must show that he found money which was lost. Property in the possession of another cannot be found, in the sense of the law of lost property, for the reason that it is not lost': 264 Mo 89, 95 (1915) (Bond J). There is also evidence of the duty rationale at 96.

[44] 44 Ore 557 (1904). Generally, the authority of *South Staffs Water Co v Sharman* is accepted in this regard: see R Moreland 'The Rights of Finders of Lost Property' (1927) 26 *Kentucky Law Journal* 3, 9–10.

[45] 44 Ore 557, 567–68 (1904).

[46] *Ibid* 565.

still and designate a further category of found goods, ie 'embedded goods',[47] title to which is given to the possessor of land in priority to the finder on the basis of a flat rule. Nonetheless, whichever of these solutions is to be preferred, the presence in the cases of such mixed rationales is a confusing influence in state common law, and adds a further layer of complexity to the already difficult lost/mislaid distinction.

In recognition of the difficulties in their application, the recent trend has been to supplement the common law rules with legislation.[48] In 1958, the state of New York imposed on finders the statutory obligation within 10 days of the find to return found goods to their owner or report and deposit them with the police.[49] Significantly, the legislation sought to override the lost/mislaid distinction, and, unless the contrary could be proved, its provision applied to all goods that were found, irrespective of their factual classification:

> Since neither the finder nor the police can determine whether found property is, on the one hand, lost or mislaid property or, on the other hand, is actually abandoned property, waived property, treasure trove, or possibly in none of these categories, all found property is presumed to be 'lost property', and the presumption is made conclusive unless it is established, in an action commenced within six months after the date of the finding, that the property is not lost property.[50]

This is not quite an abolition of the lost/mislaid distinction, but it does at least seem to abolish the speculative role of courts, inasmuch as it is for a litigant to prove, rather than for a court to designate, whether goods are lost, mislaid, and so on. However, legislation has not in every case proved to be an answer, and although the lost/mislaid distinction has been discredited, the common law rules continue to be engaged in modern dispute resolution.[51] In *Kahr v Markland*,[52] a quantity of silver belonging to the plaintiffs but accidentally mixed up in a bag of clothes they donated to a charity shop was held to be lost property,[53] so that a transferee of the silver from the charity shop did not receive full title to it within the provisions of the Uniform Commercial Code. Section 2-403(2) of that Code provided to merchants a power to transfer, in goods entrusted to them, all the rights of the entruster. By section 2-403(3), 'entrust' included any delivery, and

---

[47] L Izuel, 'Property Owners' Constructive Possession of Treasure Trove: Rethinking the Finders' Keepers Rule' (1990–91) 38 *UCLA Law Review* 1659, 1672–3.

[48] See further Chapter 7, where legislative provision in the United States is considered in greater detail.

[49] New York Personal Property Law § 252.1; *Saritejdiam v Excess Insurance*, 971 F.2d 910, 915 (1992), US Court of Appeals for the Second Circuit.

[50] Recommendation of the Law Revision Commission, reported in *McKinney's 1958 Session Laws of New York* (Brooklyn, NY, Edward Thompson Co, 1958) 1702.

[51] Generally, it seems that in most states the common law concepts of 'lost' and 'mislaid' remain operative. Where it exists, legislation has been used to connote the consequences of finding lost or mislaid property, not to provide new definitions for the concepts themselves: 1 Am Jur 2d, *Abandoned, Lost, and Unclaimed Property* (1962) § 2.

[52] 187 Ill App 3d 603 (1987).

[53] *Ibid* 608.

any acquiescence in retention of possession by the merchant, and so prima facie on the facts of the case the charity had power to pass the plaintiffs full title to the silver. But the Fourth District Appellate Court of Illinois thought that the provisions of the Code were not intended to apply to lost property, and allowed the plaintiffs to replevy the silver.[54] The lost/mislaid distinction has also recently served courts considering a US$250,000 liability under a contract of insurance,[55] the right to claim enemy property discovered in wartime,[56] and convictions from courts martial.[57] In this regard it continues to feature as a methodology by which US courts, state and federal, determine the rights of finders to discovered goods.

## English Common Law: Classification Influences Liability

In English law, *Armory v Delamirie* gives a first clue that the classification of dis-covered goods does not affect the allocation of rights in them. Whilst this case has been taken as establishing the general right of a finder to keep the object of his find against all but the true owner, the report tells us nothing about the circumstances of the find. That the boy was a chimney sweep (and that the report records this fact) has sometimes led to the assumption that he found the jewel in the course of his employment, and perhaps in a chimney flue. If the latter was correct, it might support equivocally an inference of loss, hiding or abandonment, but at any rate we are guessing. The irresistible conclusion is that the boy's acquisition of right in *Armory* did not depend at all on the circumstances in which the jewel was removed from the custody of its former possessor. This makes it rather surprising that in *Parker*, Donaldson LJ should insist that a finder acquires no rights in the object of her find 'unless it has been abandoned or lost'.[58]

The cases considered in Chapter 2 generally support the view that the facts of loss do not determine the acquisition of property rights in English law. Although these disputes have involved the discovery of differently classified goods, they have been decided in the same manner and without reference to the classification. Let us take as examples the following fact situations relating to discovered goods:

(a)  lost: *Parker*, bracelet accidentally dropped on lounge floor;
(b)  mislaid: *Hannah*, brooch removed and left on window frame;[59]
(c)  hidden: *Appleyard*, cash stored in safe and forgotten;
(d)  abandoned: *Hibbert*, golf balls erroneously driven and relinquished.

---

[54] *Ibid* 609, relying on R Anderson, *Uniform Commercial Code* 3rd edn (Rochester, NY, Lawyers Co-operative Publishing Co, 1983) 584.
[55] *Saritejdiam v Excess Insurance*, 971 F.2d 910 (1992).
[56] *Morrison v United States*, 492 F.2d 1219 (1974).
[57] *United States v Meeks*, 32 MJ 1033 (1991); *United States v Weiderkehr*, 33 MJ 539 (1991).
[58] [1982] QB 1004, 1017.
[59] 'If ever a piece of property was mislaid, this brooch was': ER Cohen, 'The Finders Cases Revisited' (1970) 48 *Texas Law Review* 1001, 1013 fn 21.

An obvious objection to this statement is that probably in each case the goods in question admit of equivocal classifications. The bracelet in *Parker* might just as easily have been mislaid or abandoned; the brooch in *Hannah* might have been deliberately hidden or abandoned; the cash in *Appleyard* might have been mislaid or abandoned; and the golf balls in *Hibbert* could have been considered lost.[60] Setting this aside, we have seen in the previous chapter that the best explanation of these cases is that they have been decided on the relative possessory claims of the parties. In *Parker*, the defendant board had not sufficiently manifested an intention to control the departure lounge and objects which might be found there. In *Hannah*, the defendant had never been in possession of the requisitioned house, and therefore could not establish possession of objects which might be found there. In *Appleyard*, the safe and its contents were part of the demised premises, and the lessee had a better right than a subsequent finder. In *Hibbert*, the members of the golf club had established possession of the golf balls through their act of posting on the course a policeman with the special duty of preventing the dishonest removal of golf balls. Insofar as each decision employs the facts of possession as a mechanism to resolve its dispute, irrespective of the designation of the goods in question or the circumstances in which they were removed from the custody of their owner, it seems plain that these circumstances do not operate on a finder's acquisition of rights in the object of her find.

None of this entails, of course, that the fact that certain goods were lost or mislaid has *no* relevance in English law; just that it has no relevance to the acquisition of right by a finder. The facts might be relevant to her civil and criminal liabilities. In Chapter 1, we saw that for a putative finder to escape a charge of larceny it was essential that the goods should be 'actually' or 'presumably lost'.[61] No one would be allowed to evade a charge of larceny simply by pleading that she found the goods in question:[62] the pretence of finding was no excuse.[63] Thus, it became a common practice for judges to deny a defence of finding by holding that the goods taken were not 'really lost'. So, in *R v Pierce*,[64] the employee of a railway company was convicted of larceny of a dressing case accidentally left in a railway carriage. Williams J thought it was 'absurd' to suggest that the defendant was a finder, and that there was 'no pretence for treating this as a case of lost property'.[65] Likewise in *R v West*,[66] a pocket-book left on the defendant's market

---

[60] Indeed, in *Hibbert*, Humphreys J expressed some disagreement with the opinion that the balls were abandoned, finding 'nothing in the facts of the case as stated to support such an inference': [1948] 2 KB 142, 151.

[61] *R v Thurborn* (1849) 2 Car & K 831, 837.

[62] See the argument of counsel in *R v Reed* (1843) Car & M 306, 307.

[63] East 2 PC 664.

[64] (1852) Cox CC 117.

[65] (1852) Cox CC 117, 119.

[66] (1854) Dears 401.

stall was not lost, so that it was larceny for her feloniously to convert it. Jervis CJ thought that there was 'a clear distinction between property lost and merely mislaid, put down and left by mistake as in this case'.[67] The reason was that where goods had been mislaid, the circumstances would enable the owner of the chattel 'to know the place where he had left it' such that he 'would naturally return for it'.[68] *Pierce* and *West* were cited in *Lawrence v State of Tennessee*, and to that extent were instrumental in the development of the US lost/mislaid distinction. In England, their authority was confirmed in the courts,[69] though a later case laid the emphasis not on the facts of loss or mislaying but on the rationale underlying the distinction. In *R v Moore*, Cockburn CJ referred to *Thurborn* and opined that it was larceny feloniously to convert found goods unless 'the circumstances of the finding are such that the finder is warranted in believing that the goods are lost, or that the owner could not be found'.[70] On this view, consistently with the statement of the law in *Thurborn*, cases like *Pierce* and *West* were cases where the finder was not justified in believing that the owner could not be found, because the circumstances showed he was likely to return to claim the goods.[71] Thus, in English law the facts of loss were relevant to the extent that where genuinely present they denied the possibility of a criminal conviction, and the facts of mislaying relevant to the extent that they precluded any belief by a defendant that goods were lost.

# The Relevance of Hiding

In one aspect of English law, hiding historically was the antithesis of loss and abandonment,[72] and directly influenced a finder's acquisition of title to certain chattels. From the twelfth century, it was a stipulation of our law of treasure trove that, additionally to the requirement that they be composed of gold or silver,[73]

---

[67] *Ibid* 404.

[68] *Ibid*. See also *R v Pope* (1834) 6 Car & P 346.

[69] *R v Dixon* (1855) Dears 580, 585 (Parke B).

[70] (1861) Le & Ca 1, 7–8.

[71] Wright adds a further distinction, differentiating the cases according to whether (a) the owner knows where to find his goods; or (b) 'although mislaid by the owner' the thing in question remains in the vicinity of his house, as where jewels are dropped in a garden (*R v Peters* (1843) 1 Car & K 245): P & W, 186. It is doubtful that the US cases would use the term 'mislaid' to cover all cases of the latter. In *Peters*, for example, it is clear that the jewels were dropped accidentally. For present purposes, however, it is enough to note that in each of these classes of case Wright considered that there was only 'a colourable but not real loss or finding': P & W, 180.

[72] W Martin, 'Treasure Trove and the British Museum' (1904) 20 *LQR* 27, 32.

[73] In the *Overton (Farms)* case the Court of Appeal held that an item must be composed of a 'substantial amount' of gold or silver to be deemed treasure trove at common law: *Attorney-General of the Duchy of Lancaster v G E Overton (Farms) Ltd* [1982] 2 Ch 277, 291 (Lord Denning MR).

goods must have been hidden by their owner if they were to be classed as treasure.[74] Thus wrote Coke:

> Treasure trove is when any gold or silver, in coin, plate or bullyon hath been of ancient time hidden; wheresoever it be found, whereof no person can prove any property, it doth belong to the king.[75]

If goods claimed as treasure had been lost or abandoned, rather than hidden, it was settled that for that reason they were not treasure; the Crown had no title to them; and they were subject to the ordinary rights of finder.[76] Of course, the matter of determining whether goods had been hidden was beset by obvious difficulties. By definition, a determination of whether goods had been lost, hidden or abandoned entailed a determination of the intentions of an unknown person.[77] Since these facts were impossible to discern, the question was settled by inferences and presumptions. Courts 'must presume the intention to hide or to abandon from the relevant surrounding circumstances, and the motives that usually influence persons acting under such circumstances, according to the ordinary dictates of human nature'.[78] In particular, where the goods claimed as treasure were especially valuable, or had been discovered buried in ground, or had otherwise been safely concealed, the Crown benefited from a presumption that they had been hidden.[79]

To the extent that the facts of hiding confirmed or denied the Crown's title to objects claimed as treasure trove, they bore on the finder's position. A finder could never have a better right than the Crown to a gold or silver thing which had been hidden; but if that same thing alternatively had not been hidden, the finder's claim would defeat that of the Crown.[80] In modern law, the impact of this proposition

---

[74] For a short overview see J Carman, *Valuing Ancient Things* (Leicester, University Press, 1996) 46–7. Bracton referred to goods 'forgotten' rather than hidden: Bracton, f 120.

[75] 3 Co Inst 132; *Attorney-General of the Duchy of Lancaster v G E Overton (Farms) Ltd* [1982] Ch 277, 288. Likewise, Blackstone thought the treasure designation to apply to goods found 'hidden in the earth, or other private place': 1 Bl Comm, Ch 8; and Chitty spoke of things 'concealed': J Chitty, *Prerogatives of the Crown* (London, Butterworths, 1820) 152.

[76] '[I]f he that laid [a thing claimed as treasure] be known or afterwards discovered, the owner and not the King is entitled to it; this prerogative right only applying in the absence of an owner to claim the property. If the owner, instead of hiding the treasure, casually lost it, or purposely parted with it, in such a manner that it is evident he intended to abandon the property altogether, and did not purpose to resume it on another occasion, as if he threw it on the ground, or other public place, or in the sea, the first finder is entitled to the property, as against every one but the owner, and the King's prerogative does not in this respect obtain. So that it is the hiding, and not the abandonment, of the property that entitles the King to it': Chitty, above n 75 at 152–3.

[77] *Attorney-General v Trustees of the British Museum* [1903] 2 Ch 598, 609 (Farwell J); C MacMillan 'Burying Treasure Trove' (1996) *New Law Journal* 1346. Palmer described the restriction of treasure to hidden goods as a 'wholly anachronistic impediment': 'Treasure Trove and the Protection of Antiquities' (1981) 44 *MLR* 178, 182.

[78] [1903] 2 Ch 598, 609 (Farwell J).

[79] M Bridge, *Personal Property Law* 3rd edn (Oxford, Clarendon Press, 2003) 25.

[80] Although it would of course be subject to the claims of other prior possessors, including the possessor of the land on which the putative treasure was found.

largely has been resisted by the Treasure Act 1996, the terms of which provide a new statutory definition of treasure[81] which does not include the requirement of hiding except insofar as it is stipulated that treasure includes those things that would have been treasure trove at common law.[82] Even so, it is important to note that at common law, the facts of hiding served only to confirm or deny the existence in a third party of a better interest than a finder. Although some of the commentaries spoke of putative treasures 'belonging' to a finder where they had been lost or abandoned, but not where they had been hidden,[83] there is no reason to suppose that the kind of right acquired by the finder was different in each case. It is just that where such goods had been hidden, there also existed a better right in the Crown.

Apart from this function as an element of the Crown's prerogative claim to treasure, the facts of hiding do not seem significant at common law. At least it is true that, when goods which are not treasure have been found hidden, the hiding has not seemed to operate on the resolution of any dispute. In *Moffatt v Kazana*,[84] *Bird v Fort Frances*,[85] *City of London v Appleyard*[86] and *Tamworth Industries v Attorney General*,[87] entitlement disputes to hidden goods were all resolved according to the relative possessory priorities of the parties, and no court laid emphasis on the fact the goods were hidden. Hiding, then, was relevant in English law to the extent that it was a constituent element of the Crown's claim to treasure trove, but otherwise seems not to be relevant.

# The Relevance of Abandonment

Where goods are cast out of custody with an intention that any property interest in them be divested, there is dubious authority to suggest that the relinquent thereby succeeds in terminating his property in the goods.[88] If this is right, then abandonment operates as a kind of converse correlative to hiding. Whereas the facts of hiding had the potential to confirm the presence of a better right than the finder (albeit in the limited sphere of goods classed as treasure trove), the facts of abandonment potentially confirm the absence of a better right.

---

[81] See s 1 for the definition of treasure. The long title of the Act declares that its purpose is 'to abolish treasure trove and to make fresh provision in relation to treasure'.

[82] Treasure Act 1996, s 1(1)(c).

[83] See eg Martin, above n 72 at 32.

[84] [1969] 2 WLR 152.

[85] [1949] 2 DLR 791.

[86] [1963] 1 WLR 982.

[87] [1991] 3 NZLR 616.

[88] In English law this proposition can be traced to Bracton (vol II, f 8, f 41 b), though that work relied rather uncritically on the texts of the Roman law, and especially J Inst II.1.47.

As it happens, English law has never resolved with any certainty the question whether divesting abandonment is possible at common law, and the modern commentaries are chequered.[89] Yet even if we were to allow the possibility, the fact of abandonment would not necessarily have great significance for the rights of finders. In the first place, to the extent that her right is possessory, the finder's claim will necessarily be subordinate to those of other prior possessors, as where the possessor of land establishes a claim in the manner discussed in Chapter 2. If on given facts any such prior right can be established, the finder's claim will be defeated and it will not help her to rely on the abandonment. Correlatively, she need not rely on the facts of abandonment to defeat the claim of a subsequent possessor: her prior possession is enough. This was well illustrated in a US case where a jury had affirmed the plaintiff's title as a finder to certain gold coins.[90] The defendant complained on appeal that the jury had not been directed to consider that the goods might have been abandoned, and not lost. The court replied that it could not concern the defendant whether the plaintiff proved 'a qualified property by means of the rules relating to ... lost property' or 'an absolute ownership through the discovery of abandoned property'.[91] In either case, the right generated would be sufficient to allow the plaintiff's recovery from the defendant, who was a stranger to the coins with no title.

Thus, if divesting abandonment is possible at common law, the facts of abandonment serve to confirm the absence of *one of* the prior rights that could defeat the rights of a finder. However, as with loss and mislaying, abandonment might additionally be relevant to the liabilities of a finder. This is particularly clear in the criminal law, where abandonment can be said to operate in one of two ways. If divesting abandonment is possible, where present it goes to the *actus reus* of theft. Since theft requires the dishonest appropriation of property belonging to another,[92] it can never be theft to take goods in which no proprietary interest is

---

[89] The editors of *Crossley Vaines* reject altogether the possibility of divesting abandonment, citing *Hayne's Case* (1614) 12 Co Rep 113 for the general proposition that, 'once owned, a thing remains owned': ELG Tyler and NE Palmer (eds), *Crossley Vaines Personal Property* 5th edn (London, Butterworths, 1973) 427. *English Private Law* acknowledges the controversy, but finds more persuasive the school of thought against abandonment: *EPL*, 4.503–4.505. On the other hand, the latest edition of Goode's *Commercial Law* gives abandonment as one of six means by which ownership of goods may be terminated: R Goode, *Commercial Law* 3rd edn (London, LexisNexis UK, 2004) 38. Likewise, Bridge seems content to assume the possibility, though he does think the law 'obscure and difficult to relate to modern conditions': *Personal Property Law* (Oxford, Clarendon Press, 2003) 22–3. The strongest arguments in support of divesting abandonment have come from Hudson. Central to his argument is the contention that in two of the fields where allegations of abandonment are most pertinent, namely theft and wreck, 'the courts seem clearly to have recognised the efficacy of divesting abandonment', albeit subject to rigorous limitations and restrictions: A Hudson, 'Abandonment' in NE Palmer and E McKendrick (eds), *Interests in Goods* 2nd edn (London, LLP, 1998) 618; 'Is Divesting Abandonment Possible at Common Law?' (1984) 100 *LQR* 110.

[90] *Roberson v Ellis*, 58 Ore 219 (1911).

[91] 58 Ore 219, 224 (1911) (Burnett J).

[92] Theft Act 1968, s 1. On the meaning of 'belonging to another' see Theft Act 1968, s 5, and generally D Ormerod (ed), *Smith and Hogan on Criminal Law* 11th edn (Oxford, OUP, 2005) 674–92; ATH

subsisting at the time of the taking.[93] It follows, theoretically, that the finder of abandoned goods cannot be a thief.[94] Moreover, even if divesting abandonment is not possible, the facts of abandonment are yet relevant to criminal liability in a second sense. In *Ellerman Wilson Line v Webster*,[95] Lord Goddard CJ (with whom Byrne and Parker JJ agreed) seems to have considered abandonment relevant to the *mens rea* of the accused, rather than to the *actus reus*. So his Lordship thought:

> it was open to the learned magistrate (we cannot say that it was not open ...) to come to the conclusion that the man had no felonious intent, because if the property had been abandoned you cannot be charged with stealing abandoned property.[96]

In the same vein was the earlier case of *R v White*,[97] where a conviction for larceny of a quantity of pig iron taken from the premises of a canal company was overturned because there had not been a specific direction to the jury on the relevance of an allegation of abandonment. Counsel for the defence viewed this as a proprietary matter, contending that the prosecution had never proved that the property lay in the canal company.[98] The Court of Criminal Appeal agreed that there had not been a sufficient direction to the jury, and that there was evidence consistent with the iron having been abandoned by its owner, but thought the matter relevant to the beliefs of the defendant:

> If the property had been abandoned, the person charged has a right to have the jury directed that if he took it really believing that it was abandoned, he is not guilty of larceny.[99]

The effect of these passages in *Ellerman* and *White* (both of which were larceny cases) seems to have been preserved in the modern law of theft. Generally, it has been suggested that section 2(1)(c) of the Theft Act 1968 (which provides that a person is not dishonest if he appropriates the property in the belief that the person to whom the property belongs cannot be discovered by taking

---

Smith, *Property Offences* (London, Sweet and Maxwell, 1994) ch 4. A similar requirement obtained in the law of larceny: Larceny Act 1916, s 1(2)(iii); *Russell on Crime*, vol II, 889.

[93] In the words of JC Smith, 'if property belongs to no one, it cannot be stolen. If property has been abandoned there can be no theft of it': *The Law of Theft* 8th edn (London, Butterworths, 1997) 37.

[94] And the proposition is theoretical only, because in practice criminal courts have been extremely reluctant to conclude in fact that goods have been abandoned: see eg *R v Reed* (1843) Car & M 306, 308; *R v Peters* (1843) 1 Car & K 245, 247; *R v Edwards and Stacey* (1877) Cox CC 384, 385; *Williams v Phillips* (1957) 41 Cr App Rep 5. There are a few cases where the courts have concluded reluctantly that goods have been abandoned (*Ellerman Wilson Line v Webster* [1952] 1 Lloyd's LL Rep 179; *Hibbert v McKiernan* [1948] 2 KB 142; *Rostron* [2003] EWCA Crim 2206), but in the current state of the law of theft such occasions are likely to be few, because the conclusion that goods have been abandoned disrupts the ability of the prosecution to lay property in 'persons unknown' when framing an indictment: see generally R Hickey, 'Stealing Abandoned Goods' (2006) 26 *Legal Studies* 584.

[95] [1952] 1 Lloyd's LL Rep 179.

[96] [1952] 1 Lloyd's LL Rep 179, 180.

[97] (1912) 6 Cr App Rep 266.

[98] *Ibid.*

[99] *Ibid* 268.

reasonable steps) was 'obviously intended to preserve the substance of the common law rule relating to finding', even though the Act itself makes no express mention of finding.[100] There is also more specific evidence in the modern cases that the facts of abandonment go to *mens rea*. In *R v Small*,[101] the defendant was charged with theft of a car, but argued that he found it 'dumped' on a kerb, with a flat tyre and battery, a broken windscreen and an empty petrol tank. His appeal against conviction was allowed because the jury should have been directed to consider, consistently with the leading case of *Ghosh*:[102] (1) whether according to the standards of reasonable and honest people, what the defendant did was dishonest by those standards; and (2) if so, whether the defendant must have realised that what he was doing was dishonest by those standards.[103] Everything in the case turned on this determination of the accused's state of mind, and it was this determination to which the allegation of abandonment was pertinent.

Thus, the facts of abandonment are relevant to finders in two respects. First, they might confirm the absence of one prior competitive right. The significance of this proposition is at least limited by the vulnerability of the finder's right to other prior possessory rights, and at worst is non-existent in the face of the impossibility of divesting abandonment at common law, a matter which itself has never authoritatively been settled. Whichever is the case, the facts of abandonment will still be relevant to the criminal liability of a finder, since it is possible that one who takes abandoned goods is not dishonest.

# The Significance of 'Finding'

So we have seen that the facts of loss, mislaying, hiding and abandonment are not immediately relevant to the acquisition of right by a finder. Clearing this ground brings us back to the statement of salient fact with which we began this chapter. In the factual matrix which dominates the modern law on finders, there is in every case the discovery of some item the existence of which previously was unknown both to the finder and to the possessor of land. In the cases where a finder has been successful,[104] she has been successful because the possessor of land could show no prior right.[105] To put the matter another way, the finder has won

---

[100] *Smith and Hogan*, above n 92 at 694–5. In this regard, note the opinion of Smith that 'if the taker believes there is no owner, he cannot believe that the owner can be discovered by taking reasonable steps': JC Smith, 'Title to Discovered Antiquities: Theft and Possessory Title' in *Title to Finds and Discovered Antiquities*, seminar proceedings of the Institute of Art and Law, 3 October 1995, reading 4, 2.

[101] (1988) 86 Cr App Rep 170.

[102] (1982) 75 Cr App Rep 154.

[103] (1988) 86 Cr App Rep 170, 173–4.

[104] ie *Bridges, Hannah, Bird, Parker*.

[105] Although, as we have seen, in *Bridges* that lack of title was explained on a different ground than in the other cases.

when the possessor of land has not been in possession of the discovered object. When *that* possession has been shown, the possessor of land has always been the victor.[106]

Stating the cases thus accords with a proposition to be found in Pollock's work. In considering *Bridges v Hawkesworth*, the learned author offered the opinion that 'the finder's right starts from the absence of any de facto control at the moment of finding'.[107] Yet even this view adds an unnecessary gloss on the acquisition of right by a finder. Historically, there might have been good reasons for laying legal emphasis on the fact that certain goods were not in the immediate control or custody of anyone at the time they were taken. It was no trespass to take up such goods, and, until the late seventeenth century, neither was it larceny.[108] However, in the modern law each of these propositions has been eroded. As for the criminal element, in the development of the offence of larceny by finding, the law steadily evaded the objection that there could be no larceny where there was not also a physical taking, by construing as a taking the assumption of goods by a finder where she believed that the owner could be discovered by taking reasonable steps.[109] Indeed, as larceny neared the end of its legal life, its connection with physical interference had disappeared altogether, as the courts considered it an offence against ownership, even to the point of being content in framing an indictment to lay the property in 'persons unknown'.[110] This trend has continued in the modern law of theft, where ordinarily questions of title are treated as self-evident and not at issue. A court need only be satisfied that goods allegedly stolen were *owned* by *someone* at the time they were taken and the title element of the offence will be satisfied.[111] In the case of evidential doubt, the prosecution retains the ability to lay the property in persons unknown.[112] The result is that theft is ever more an offence against ownership, greatly distanced from its roots in the classical form of larceny as a trespassory interference with possession. Similarly, civil liabilities for dealings with goods are framed by the modern courts as interferences with rights. In Chapter 4 we will see that the best modern construction of the tort of conversion regards it as the wrong of asserting a right to goods which is inconsistent with the rights of the owner or other

---

[106] *Elwes, Sharman, Appleyard, Waverly. Hibbert* would also do as a supporting authority.

[107] P & W, 40.

[108] Chapter 1.

[109] *R v Thurborn* (1849) 2 Car & K 831.

[110] Such were the opinions of Lord Goddard CJ and Humphreys J in *Hibbert v McKiernan*, each being satisfied that as long as the goods belonged to someone at the time they were taken, the identity of the immediately prior possessor was not relevant to the prosecution: [1948] 2 KB 142, 149, 151–2. For an argument to the contrary, insisting that proof of the identity of the prior possessor was a crucial element of a larceny prosecution, see J Edwards, 'Possession and Larceny' (1950) 3 *Current Legal Problems* 127.

[111] ATH Smith, *Property Offences* (London, Sweet and Maxwell, 1994) ch 4, 2-17a, citing *R v Joiner* (1910) 4 Cr App Rep 64, *Noon v Smith* [1964] 1 WLR 1450 and *Hibbert v McKiernan* [1948] 2 KB 142.

[112] Smith, above n 111 at 2-17d.

person entitled to possession.[113] Conversion is about interference with title, not about interference with custody.

These modern rights-based constructions diminish the conceptual value of facts like 'loss' and 'absence of custody'. Indeed, one judge has expressed the view that 'nothing can be said to be lost in the literal sense if it continues to exist even though its owner may be unknown or because it has been unknowingly mis-placed'.[114] In each of these cases the salient point is that the right of the owner endures the physical separation of his goods from his custody,[115] and grounds a civil or criminal liability in respect of any subsequently inconsistent assertion of right to them. We could frame this to deal with Pollock's contention by saying that goods howsoever displaced always remain in the possession of their owner, so that legally speaking they are always in his control,[116] but that would be a fic-tion. The better view is that these legal contests which historically have turned on the facts of custody are really contests involving competing claims of right. As long as this is so, ideas of physical loss and separation are conceptually redundant in English law.

Notice, then, that this leaves us a final comment on the meaning of finding. The facts of loss, mislaying, hiding, abandoning and finding are only relevant to the extent that they serve to establish the generation of a property right in a finder. Inasmuch as in English law the generation of this right is consequent on the facts of possession, these stated facts of loss are relevant to the extent that they prove that a finder has been in physical control of the found goods with an intention to possess them. Beyond this, the facts of finding have no significance, and there is nothing yet to suggest that finding is a *sui generis* event operating to generate property rights at common law.

---

[113] *Kuwait Airways Corporation v Iraqi Airways Co (Nos 4 and 5)* [2002] 2 AC 883, 1104.

[114] *Webb v Ireland* [1988] ILRM 565, 600 (Walsh J).

[115] 'A man who loses anything does not thereby lose his property in it': *R v Reed* (1843) Car & M 306, 308 (Coleridge J).

[116] HW Elphinstone and JW Clark (eds), *Goodeve's Modern Law of Personal Property* 2nd edn (London, Sweet and Maxwell, 1892) 15.

# 4

# The Obligations of a Finder

A nother possible reason to distinguish finders from possessors generally is that from time to time finders have been said to owe obligations to losers of goods. Perhaps surprisingly, this matter has never been resolved in English law; indeed, it has only been considered very occasionally. When the contention has been made, it has taken one of two principal forms. First, it has been said that obligations exist specific to the finder, which arise in virtue of the facts of finding. Secondly, it has been said that a finder is to be treated as a bailee for the loser, owing obligations in virtue of that status. In this chapter each of these contentions is doubted, and it is argued that the better view is that a finder owes no special obligations to the loser of goods. On the other hand, insofar as the property rights of the loser withstand the involuntary loss of a chattel, a finder will certainly be subject to those general duties of the law of obligations[1] that serve to protect the proprietary interests of the loser.[2] Their impact on the finder is considered briefly, at this stage only to emphasise that they do not reproduce the content of the supposed specific obligations. The chapter concludes by suggesting that attempts to propose such obligations have been motivated by public policy concerns. This introduces the important issue of the policy aims of the law of finds, and reveals a position on the relation between policy and doctrine which will frame the remaining chapters of this work.

## Specifically Imposed Obligations

*Parker v British Airways Board*[3] is often taken as establishing that finders owe duties to losers of goods. This is not surprising. As we saw in Chapter 2, conscious that

---

[1] Principally the torts of conversion and negligence, and the law of unjust enrichment, all of which are discussed further below. Of a course, a dishonest finder might also occasion criminal responsibility as a thief: Theft Act 1968, especially s 2(1)(c), which contemplates expressly the case of finding. We return to the theft provisions in Chapter 7.

[2] 'An article may be lost. In this case the owner still retains his property in the thing, but he has lost the possession of it ... If therefore another person should find the article lost, he will have no right to convert it to his own use, but must on demand deliver it up to the rightful owner, in whom the property is already vested. If he should refuse to do so, such refusal will argue that he claims it as his own, and will accordingly be evidence of a conversion of the thing to his own use': J Williams, *Principles of the Law of Real Property* (London, H Sweet, 1848) 22.

[3] [1982] 1 QB 1004.

technically the Court of Appeal was not bound by any prior decision, Donaldson LJ purported to restate 'the general principles or rules of law' applicable to finding scenarios and reduced them to a series of discrete propositions.[4] One of these propositions included the view that a finder owed certain duties to the owner of discovered goods:

> A person having a finder's rights has an obligation to take such measures as in all the circumstances are reasonable to acquaint the true owner of the finding and present whereabouts of the chattel and to care for it meanwhile.[5]

It might be better to regard this statement as imposing two separate obligations on the acquisitive finder.[6] First is the obligation to take care of the goods. Since it is an obligation for *reasonable* care, it is safe to assume that it aims at the ordinary standards of the tort of negligence, though possibly it was envisaged that the finder should bear the burden of showing that the duty has been satisfied. In other words, perhaps it is for the finder to prove that she took care of the goods, not for the loser to establish that the finder has been negligent in damaging or losing them.[7] Second is the obligation to acquaint the loser with what has happened. This has as its aim only that the loser learns of the discovery of his goods and their location. It does not expressly contemplate that the finder will return the goods to the loser. So the finder might discharge her obligation by delivering the goods to the police or to the occupier of the place where they were found.[8]

This opinion of Donaldson LJ is by far the most unequivocal statement of a finder's obligations in English law. Similar observations are found in the judgment of Coke CJ in *Isaack v Clark*,[9] but these were made in the context of considering whether a finder could escape liability for trover by proving that she had dispossessed herself of the goods in question, and thus appear only as a gloss on the view that a finder was bound to restore goods to their owner if the latter demanded them from her. Moreover, *Isaack* was not a dispute about finders. The plaintiff sought recovery of a bag of money he had delivered to the defendant

---

[4] [1982] 1 QB 1004, 1017.

[5] *Ibid* 1017. Donaldson LJ would have imposed similar obligations on a possessor of land, at least in those cases where the latter had manifested an intention to control objects that 'may be upon or in' his land. Additionally the possessor of land was said to be under the 'obligation to take such measures as in all the circumstances are reasonable to ensure that lost chattels are found': [1982] 1 QB 1004, 1018.

[6] It is important to note that no rights or obligations arise simply by the act of finding, that is, by mere discovery of an item: 'If a man comes upon an object, he has no duty to pick it up. He may leave it where he finds it. For not intermeddling, he has no liability to the owner of the chattel and acquires no rights with respect to it' (Sullivan JA in *Kowal v Ellis* (1977) 76 DLR (3d) 546). It follows that for the generation of these rights and duties, the finder must at least reduce the item into his physical control: see Donaldson LJ in *Parker* [1982] QB 1004, 1009.

[7] Compare *Morris v CW Martins & Sons Ltd* [1966] 1 QB 716 (CA), discussed below.

[8] [1982] QB 1004, 1017–18 (Donaldson LJ).

[9] (1614) 1 Bulst 306, 312. Here we read of a finder of goods: 'at the first it is in his election, whether he will take them or not into his custody, but when he hath them, one only hath then right unto them, and therefore he ought to keep them safely; if a man therefore which findes goods, if he be wise, he will then search out the right owner of them, and so deliver them unto him…'.

to stay the execution of an order levying the goods of the pledgee of a judgment debtor. The comments on finding (and on the finder's obligations in particular) were only relevant to the extent that they cast light on the general question whether a refusal to redeliver on demand was without more a conversion.[10] We could make similarly restrictive comments about *Parker*. Although it was a dispute drawn from the facts of finding, the issue of the claimant's duty towards the loser of the bracelet was not at stake. The case turned on the relative rights of the parties. The defendants' claim failed because they had not made out the necessary possessory title by manifesting an intention to control chattels that might be lying upon their premises.[11] In these circumstances, the court thought it impossible for the defendants to assert a right to the bracelet in priority to that of the claimant, and so the claimant was entitled to the value of the bracelet.[12] Inasmuch as this conclusion holds true irrespective of any duties owed by either party to the loser of the bracelet, the statement of those obligations is obiter.

Serving to emphasise this last comment is that, of the three judges presiding in *Parker*, only Donaldson LJ turned his mind to the question of a finder's obligations. His Lordship did not cite any authority for the proposition offered, though he was much impressed with the Canadian case of *Kowal v Ellis*,[13] which seems to hold that a finder owes obligations as bailee of the loser. Beyond lengthy citations from that case, there was no attempt at any discussion or synthesis of the existing law such as would lead to a coherent position on the obligations of a finder. Although it is abundantly clear that Donaldson LJ supposed the existence of these obligations at common law, his proposition must rank as the barest statement of principle, and there is little within *Parker* to support it. Indeed, his treatment of the issue accords with four more general deficiencies in the proposition that at common law specific duties are imposed on a finder. First, there are very few direct authorities on the matter, and no case that holds unequivocally that a finder owes the kind of obligations contemplated in *Parker*. Secondly, the vast majority of litigated finding disputes are cases between finders and non-owning possessors, to which the obligations of a finder to a loser are not immediately relevant. Thirdly, in most of the reported finding disputes, finders have behaved reasonably or honestly and have not needed to have their conduct

---

[10] This was the live issue, and at that time it was a matter of some disagreement between the courts. To deem a refusal to redeliver (which was nonfeasance) a conversion was to conflate detinue (which lay to remedy that kind of nonfeasance) and trover (which was premised on misfeasance). In 1595, the (recently formed) Exchequer Chamber was prepared to allow a claimant to elect between the two remedies: *Eason v Newman* (1595) Cro Eliz 495 (though there was a forceful dissent from Popham CJ). Initially the King's Bench seems to have been equally liberal, but the Common Pleas was against it, preferring to adhere properly to the form of the actions. In *Isaack v Clark*, the King's Bench squared the circle, acknowledging a formal distinction between detinue and conversion, but expressing a method of proving conversion notwithstanding evidence of nonfeasance only. The device was to treat demand and refusal as 'evidence of conversion': (1614) 2 Bulst 306, 310 (Dodderidge J), 314 (Coke CJ).

[11] [1982] 1 QB 1004, 1018–19.

[12] *Ibid* 1019.

[13] (1977) 76 DLR (3d) 546, discussed below.

regulated by positive obligations. And fourthly, in the absence of any more direct authorities, English courts have tended to rely rather uncritically on the idea that a finder is a bailee to justify the supposition that she owes obligations, without really subjecting that idea to proper scrutiny. We will turn briefly to consider each of these deficiencies.

## Absence of Direct Authority

There seems to be only one reported decision in English law in which a loser of goods has relied on the obligations of a finder in framing his action,[14] and even this is equivocal. In *Newman v Bourne and Hollingsworth*,[15] the claimant accidentally left her diamond brooch in the defendants' shop. It was handed to the shopkeeper by another of the defendants' employees, and the shopkeeper put it in his desk for safe-keeping. When the claimant returned to claim the brooch, it was not in the desk, and a further search did not yield its discovery. At the trial, the judge held that the defendants 'had not exercised that degree of care which was due from one who had found an article and assumed possession of it'.[16] However, this holding and the remainder of the judgment are consistent with the view that the claimant's action lay for breach of a general tortious duty of negligence and not for breach of any obligation owed in virtue of the defendants' status as finders. The Divisional Court upheld the decision at first instance, but the judgments are confined to a consideration of the meaning of 'gross negligence', with some further remarks on vicarious liability, and they do not discuss expressly the nature of the obligation in question.[17]

*Newman* apart, there is no sign of the actionability of deficient conduct on the part of the finder, and no general authority to suggest that the common law imposes specific obligations on a finder. Undoubtedly part of the problem is the relative paucity of litigated disputes between finders and losers of goods,[18] but occasionally the courts have missed useful opportunities to comment on or clarify the position. For example, in *Moffatt v Kazana*[19] the defendant found a biscuit tin containing about £2,000 in £1 notes hidden in the chimney flue of a bungalow conveyed to him by the claimant. The court was satisfied that the claimant had hidden the notes and had forgotten about them. Having done nothing to divest himself of the property in them, he remained their owner and could recover their value. In that sense, the case was straightforward and could be disposed of shortly.

---

[14] Palmer, *Bailment*, 1467, suggests that there are 'few' cases of this nature, but does not identify any. Palmer discusses at this point only the New Zealand decision of *Helson v McKenzies* [1950] NZLR 878, but sets it aside as not raising the issue.

[15] (1915) TLR 209.

[16] *Ibid.*

[17] *Ibid* 210.

[18] Generally, it is conceded that the case law on finding and other possessory concepts is scarce (see eg, the opinion of D Riesman, 'Possession and the Law of Finders' (1939) *Harv LR* 1105).

[19] [1969] 2 QB 152.

Nonetheless, there was a chance for the court to comment on the obligations owed to the claimant in the interim. Counsel for the defence argued that the sale of the moneys to the defendant should be implied in the conveyance of the bungalow.[20] If such a conveyance were not implied, he suggested, an impasse might be reached between claimants and defendants in the situation where the defendant refused to redeliver a chattel to the claimant:

> Suppose that [the defendant] had said to [the claimant], 'I do not claim this tin box at all, it is not mine; I dare say it is yours, but in no circumstances am I going to allow you upon my land. Still less am I going to allow you to burrow about in the false flue of the bungalow, possibly damaging the flue, and in those circumstances the tin box remains where it is'.[21]

This argument was aimed squarely at the conduct required of a finder who discovers lost property in his custody. Wrangham J thought it raised 'difficulties which [counsel for the claimant] was never able wholly satisfactorily to answer'. Conceivably it could have been answered in a number of ways. It could have been answered by arguing that the common law imposed on a finder a specific obligation to redeliver lost goods to an identified owner. It could have been answered by arguing that a refusal to deliver goods in such circumstances amounted to a conversion.[22] It could even have been answered by arguing that the finder, by notifying the loser, had done all that was required of him,[23] such that there was a genuine impasse between loser and finder and a gap in the loser's protection. But beyond the flat assertion of its difficulty, the court did not engage with the argument of counsel, missing a rare opportunity to comment on the obligations of a finder in a case where these were sensibly pertinent to the outcome. At best then, it is doubtful that at common law specific obligations of the kind envisaged in *Parker* are imposed on an acquisitive finder. Certainly there is no case in English law that decides unequivocally the existence of these obligations.

## Loser of Goods is a Background Consideration

As we have seen, in the 150 years since *Bridges v Hawkesworth*,[24] the vast majority of finding cases have adjudicated the position between non-owning possessors and finders.[25] In almost none of these cases has there been express discussion of

---

[20] And he did so notwithstanding Law of Property Act 1925, s 62, which provides 'in effect that a conveyance of land does not include a conveyance of chattels': [1969] 2 QB 152, 156 (Wrangham J).

[21] [1969] 2 QB 152, 156–7. The quotation is Wrangham J's rehearsal of the argument of counsel.

[22] Probably it does: see *Howard E Perry & Co v British Railway Board* [1980] 1 WLR 1375, though compare *British Economical Lamp Co v Empire Mile End* (1913) 29 TLR 386 and *Capital Finance v Bray* [1964] 1 WLR 323.

[23] The conduct suggested by counsel does seem to satisfy a literal reading of the acquaintance obligation as proposed in *Parker*.

[24] (1851) 15 Jur 1079.

[25] See Chapter 2; Palmer, *Bailment*, 1419.

the finder or possessor of land's obligations. Disputes are resolved according to the relative rights of claimant and defendant, and this of course is the reason why most of the finding decisions are silent on the obligations on a finder. The relativity of title disputes allows (indeed, requires) a court to treat the loser of goods as a background consideration.[26] The court must adjudicate the competing claims of the parties to the dispute, and as such, unless the loser is one of those parties,[27] his interest in the goods is not a proper matter for the court's consideration.

This was very clearly illustrated in the judgment of the High Court of Ontario in *Bird v Fort Frances*.[28] A young boy found a quantity of banknotes underneath a pool room on private property, and he claimed their value from the municipality of Fort Frances, with whom the notes had been deposited following their seizure by the police. Again the contest turned on the relative rights of the boy and the police (and particularly on the extent to which the right of the former would be limited by any wrongdoing or felonious activity on his part),[29] but additionally the municipality sought to resist the boy's claim on the basis that it had received a demand for return of the monies from the owner of the premises on which they were found. At the trial, McRuer CJHC refused to consider this element of the defence, unless the owner of the premises was prepared to make his claim formally and at the consequent risk of costs. With that, the matter was dropped, and the judgment reveals clearly the disjunctive and relative approach to dispute resolution that governs title disputes to personal property:

> Whatever the rights of the [owner of the premises] may be, they cannot be considered or disposed of in this action as framed.[30]

Precisely the same core principle is at work in the English finding cases. Unless the loser of goods is a party to the proceedings, then the merits of any claim he might have should not be considered by the court. Necessarily, this forces the loser to the background of the claim and offers a reason why our courts have been slow to consider the obligations that might be owed to him. Put very simply, many of these disputes can be decided without reference to the loser of goods, who should be left to pursue any claim in later proceedings.

## Honesty of Litigants

A further (though coincidental) reason for the lack of judicial authority in this area is that a great many of the litigated finding disputes concern finders who were considered by the courts to have behaved commendably or honestly.

---

[26] S Roberts, 'More Lost than Found' (1982) 45 *MLR* 683, 686.
[27] Whether directly, or as a result of being joined as a defendant under the *ius tertii* provisions of Torts (Interference with Goods) Act (1977), s 8.
[28] (1949) 2 DLR 791.
[29] See Chapter 6 for discussion of this aspect of the case.
[30] (1949) 2 DLR 791, 793.

In other words, the reported disputes concern finders who did not need to have their conduct regulated by positive obligations. In *Waverly*, the defendant reported his find to the coroner in the belief that it might be treasure.[31] In *Hannah*, the soldier on duty reported the find of a brooch to his commanding officer and to the police as soon as he believed the brooch to be of value.[32] In *Bridges*, the claimant caused the banknotes to be stored by the defendant and caused the loss to be advertised, and claimed them himself only on the expiry of three years after the date of the find, having offered an indemnity for expenses to the defendant.[33] In *Parker* itself, Donaldson LJ thought that the claimant finder 'acted as one would have hoped and expected [him] to act'.[34]

Perhaps in circumstances such as these the courts have been so confident that the finder has done all that her duty requires of her that they have not needed to express formally the existence of that duty or its content. Of course, we would then expect the contrary to be true in cases where the finder's behaviour has been unmeritorious or dishonest, but here such complaints have largely been made in the different context of theft proceedings,[35] have been considered irrelevant to the issues at hand,[36] or have simply been ignored.[37]

## Uncritical Reliance on Bailment

In *Parker*, Donaldson LJ reproduced lengthy citations from the Canadian case of *Kowal v Ellis*.[38] *Kowal* was decided on facts very similar to *Parker*, and in the absence of any more direct authority, Donaldson LJ seems to have allowed the judgment to influence his comments on a finder's duty. The plaintiff took possession of a pump lying unattached on land belonging to the defendant. The defendant took the pump from the plaintiff, but the latter recovered damages in detinue. An appeal against this judgment was dismissed by the Manitoba Court of Appeal. Sullivan JA clearly contemplated that the plaintiff incurred obligations to the owner of the pump:

> [When] a person finds a chattel and takes possession of it, then he immediately becomes responsible to the owner of the chattel to take reasonable care of it and, in my view, to make reasonable efforts to locate the owner.[39]

---

[31] [1996] QB 334, 338–9. *Waverly* was decided before the Treasure Act 1996 came into force, though it is worth noting that Mr Fletcher's actions would have satisfied the reporting duty required of him by that enactment: Treasure Act 1996, s 8.

[32] [1945] 1 KB 509, 510.

[33] (1851) 15 Jur 1079, 1080.

[34] [1982] QB 1004, 1007.

[35] *Hibbert v McKiernan* [1948] 2 KB 142; *Rostron* [2003] EWCA Crim 2206; [2003] All ER (D) 269.

[36] *Bird v Fort Frances* (1949) 2 DLR 791.

[37] A famous example, often overlooked, is perhaps *Armory v Delamirie* (1722) 1 Stra 505. There is a good chance the chimney sweep's boy was a thief intending to keep the jewel for himself, but in the half-page report the matter is not discussed, and the boy is awarded damages to the value of the most expensive jewel that could have been set in the socket.

[38] (1977) 76 DLR (3d) 546.

[39] *Ibid* 548.

It is also clear that the court considered these obligations to have arisen from the creation of a bailment between the owner of the pump and the finder. The plaintiff, when he took possession of the pump, acquired a special property in it arising out of his relationship to the unknown owner:

> The relationship was one of bailment and, like any other bailee, the plaintiff has become entitled to sue in trover or, as here, detinue anyone who has interfered with his right of possession, save only the true owner or someone claiming through or on behalf of the true owner.[40]

Accordingly, Sullivan JA considered that, for the defendant to succeed, he would have needed to show that he was a 'prior bailee' of the chattel, with all the rights and obligations of a bailee.[41] To this extent, the judgment is consistent with an accurate reading of *Bridges v Hawkesworth*, but there are then two differences. The first is that, where Patteson J would have required an intentional deposit to ground the existence of a bailment, for Sullivan JA it was the defendant's ignorance of the existence of the pump that explained why he owed no duty to its owner.[42] Secondly, the judgment refers to the case law post-*Bridges*, and speaks of the acquisition of possession. In effect, it confuses the two distinct lines of reasoning identified in Chapter 2, which alternatively resolve disputes according to (a) the duties owed by a claimant to the loser of goods; or (b) a claimant's ability to establish a right in virtue of the facts of possession. Although the headnote in *Kowal* summarises the decision in terms of the former, there is enough in the judgment to indicate that it could be resolved on the latter. The second line of the judgment characterised the case as a dispute over 'the right to possession of a chattel';[43] *Armory v Delamirie* was said to encapsulate 'in a nutshell' the law applicable to the facts before him;[44] and citing *Bridges v Hawkesworth* and *Hannah v Peel*, Sullivan JA stated the conclusion in the case thus:

> It follows that the plaintiff is entitled to possession of the pump, unless the defendant asserts and proves a title to the pump superior to that of the plaintiff.[45]

Without more, this formulation is consistent with our analysis of the cases in Chapter 2, and the view that disputes of this kind are to be resolved according to the relative rights of the immediate parties. *Kowal* is complicated only to the extent that it invokes additionally the outmoded bailment analysis drawn from *Bridges v Hawkesworth*. Clearly, however, the bailment concept is operative only to the extent that it is required to generate the necessary possessory right in a successful claimant. Inasmuch as the cases cited in the judgment disclose another method of generating that right, ie possession, the bailment concept is technically

---

[40] *Ibid*, reproduced in *Parker* [1982] QB 1004, 1015.
[41] (1977) 76 DLR (3d) 546, 549.
[42] *Ibid*.
[43] (1977) 76 DLR (3d) 546, 547.
[44] *Ibid* 548.
[45] *Ibid*.

redundant in *Kowal*. And since the statement of a finder's obligations depends on the premise that she is a bailee, in a like manner their proposition adds nothing to the resolution of the case.

It follows that *Kowal v Ellis* cannot be used as an authority for the imposition of specific obligations on a finder. Its statement of a finder's duty is only valid to the extent that its more general premise is true, ie that a finder of goods is also a bailee of the same for their loser. This is nowhere discussed in *Parker*. We will turn next to consider it, but thus far it ought to be clear that at common law there is virtually nothing to suggest that a finder owes to a loser of goods the kind of obligations contemplated by Donaldson LJ. Certainly there is no direct authority that settles the matter and very little else in the case law that could be taken as providing support for the existence of obligations specifically imposed on finders.

# The Finder as Bailee

Palmer describes the equation of bailee and finder as 'partial and imperfect'.[46] His great work on bailment has a chapter devoted to 'finders and other unrequested keepers', which begins by suggesting that finding 'represents one of the more questionable forms of bailment'.[47] It is questionable because the fact scenario of finding does not neatly align to that of bailment, such that there are a number of identifiable difficulties. In the first place, there is no contract, agreement or delivery between loser and finder, as there would normally be between bailor and bailee. This is not a fatal objection, especially as (we shall see shortly) modern authorities have preferred to define bailment as depending only on the voluntary assumption of possession of the goods of another, and not on that transfer of possession from bailor to bailee contemplated by the literal case.[48] However, there are difficulties yet. A finder has no bailor in the literal sense, and perhaps no means of identifying his bailor. There is no relation that informs the content of the finder's bailment, and some of the terms that the courts would require of the finder seem difficult to reproduce in a conventional bailment scenario.[49] Moreover, an ordinary bailee is at common law estopped from denying his bailor's title.[50] A finder, by contrast, is permitted time to investigate the claims of putative losers and can require those claims to be substantiated.[51]

---

[46] Palmer, *Bailment*, 1418.

[47] *Ibid* 1418.

[48] *Morris v CW Martin & Sons Ltd* [1966] 1 QB 716 (CA); *Gilchrist Watt and Sanderson Pty Ltd v York Products Pty Ltd* [1970] 3 All ER 825 (PC).

[49] Palmer, commenting on *Parker*, notes that it would be difficult to imagine any situation in which it would be necessary (or doctrinally legitimate) to impose upon a conventional bailee the positive obligation to take steps to reunite bailed goods with their true owner: *Bailment*, 1421.

[50] *Ibid* 265 *et seq.*

[51] *Isaack v Clark* (1615) 2 Bulstr 306; *Clayton v Le Roy* [1911] 2 KB 1031, 1051.

Despite these kinds of evident difficulty, Palmer does think that there is 'strong modern authority' for the equation of finder and bailee.[52] His principal argument in this regard suggests that finders are bailees because and insofar as they owe obligations to the loser:

> [T]he absence of any relation, either direct or indirect, to identify the terms on which the finder assumes possession … suggests that finders are bailees only to the limited extent that the custodial rights and obligations of both classes of possessor are … in substance the same.[53]

In the context of our discussion in the previous section, this argument is difficult. It makes for circular reasoning. In *Kowal*, Sullivan JA thought that a finder owed obligations because she was a bailee. According to Palmer, the finder is a bailee because she owes obligations. The problem is exacerbated inasmuch as two of the 'strong authorities' used by Palmer to support his contention are *Parker* and *Kowal*,[54] neither of which, as we have seen, will do as an authority for this argument. The other suggested authorities are *Morris v CW Martin & Sons Ltd*[55] and *Gilchrist Watt and Sanderson Pty Ltd v York Products Pty Ltd*.[56] Each of these was a case of sub-bailment, and the judgments concerned the liabilities incurred by a sub-bailee to his principal.

In *Morris*, the claimant owned a mink stole and wanted to have it cleaned. She took it to a furrier. He did not offer cleaning services, but with the claimant's permission he sent the stole to the defendants, a large and well-known cleaning company. While the fur was in the defendants' care, it was stolen by one of their employees, though without any negligence on the part of the defendants. The question in the appeal concerned the liability of the defendants to the claimant for this loss. Lord Denning MR identified it even more precisely as 'the important question of how far a master is liable for theft or dishonesty by one of his servants'.[57] Relying on a passage from Pollock and Wright, his Lordship held that a sub-bailee for reward owed to the principal all the duties of a bailee for reward, and hence in the instant case the defendants were answerable to the claimant unless they could show that the loss occurred without fault on the part of the defendants or their servants.[58]

Plainly, a finder is not a bailee for reward. *Morris* was not a case about finding, nor one in which the circumstances of finding were immediately relevant. Nonetheless, Diplock LJ is credited as providing an authoritative view on the idea that finders might be bailees.[59] But his Lordship mentioned finding only

---

[52] Palmer, *Bailment*, 1467.
[53] *Ibid* 1420; and see also 32–6 and 1418.
[54] *Ibid* 1465 fn 64 and accompanying text.
[55] [1966] 1 QB 716 (CA).
[56] [1970] 3 All ER 825 (PC).
[57] [1966] 1 QB 716, 723.
[58] *Ibid* 725.
[59] Palmer, *Bailment*, 33.

very briefly (indeed, in only three words) and assumed rather than proved that finders provide an example of a bailment arising otherwise than by contract or agreement:

> While most cases of bailment today are accompanied by a contractual relationship between bailee and bailor which may modify or extend the common law duties of the parties that would otherwise arise from the mere fact of bailment, this is not necessarily so—as witness gratuitous bailment or bailment by finding.[60]

Diplock LJ's real mission here is to characterise bailment generally as a set of obligations voluntarily assumed by lawfully taking into one's custody goods belonging to another. The obligations of a finder are only relevant to the extent that they arise because of a bailment relationship existing between finder and loser, the existence of which is assumed rather than argued or evidenced. Neither Lord Denning MR nor Salmon LJ mentioned the case of the finder at all, and this being so, it seems better to discount *Morris* as authority for the proposition that finders are bailees.

*Gilchrist Watt* follows the same course. The defendants were ships' agents and stevedores and had in their custody two cases of clocks for delivery to the claimants. One of the cases was lost by the defendants' failure to exercise reasonable care. Lord Pearson, relying on *Morris*, held that defendants as sub-bailees were given and took possession of the goods for the purpose of looking after them and delivering them to the claimants.[61] In so doing they assumed an obligation to the claimants 'to exercise due care for the safety of the goods, although there was no contractual relation or attornment' between them.[62]

In the course of this judgment, Lord Pearson referred to some finding cases, including *Newman v Bourne & Hollingsworth*,[63] which his Lordship took as an unequivocal authority for the existence of finder-obligations. Even allowing for the deficiency in that supposition, it is clear that the existence of such obligations was relevant only as analogical support to the argument at stake, which was to overcome the absence of a contract between claimants and defendants by characterising bailment as a set of duties voluntarily assumed by taking possession of the goods of another. To argue, as his Lordship did, that taking possession following a finding 'involves an assumption of responsibility for the safe keeping of the goods'[64] plainly supports the more general conclusion on bailment. The problem is that there is no authority at common law to support the premise that finders of goods assume a responsibility for their care. As things stand, this circle is unbroken. More recent cases on sub-bailment continue to use the finding cases as exemplary of a general principle that an assumption of possession also involves

---

[60] [1966] 1 QB 716, 732.
[61] [1970] 3 All ER 825, 829.
[62] *Ibid.*
[63] (1915) TLR 209.
[64] [1970] 3 All ER 825. This passage is cited by Palmer, *Bailment*, 34.

an assumption of responsibility, which grounds the existence of obligations.[65] Meanwhile, in the finding cases, judges use bailment literature to assume (hypothetically) that finders are kept in check by bailment obligations. These arguments are as weak as each other. Moreover, they are dealt a blow inasmuch as there was a case as recently as 1965 in which a finder was held not to be a bailee. In *Thompson v Nixon*,[66] the defendant found a bag of rabbit feeding pellets and took them in the belief that he could find their owner by taking reasonable steps. Several hours later, the appellant formed the dishonest intention of keeping the pellets for himself. Since the initial taking was not trespassory, larceny would not lie,[67] unless it could be shown that the defendant was a bailee.[68] The Court of Appeal rejected any argument to this effect, quashing the defendant's conviction. Authoritatively, a finder was not a bailee.

We need not make too much of *Thompson v Nixon*. It is clear that the Court of Appeal reached the decision in the case with some reluctance and felt constrained by earlier authority on the definition of larceny.[69] Nonetheless, the decision hints at longstanding doubt over the status of finders as bailees.[70] Taken together with the difficulty in aligning their obligations, and the circular analogical reasoning offered by the sub-bailment cases, there is little to suggest that the equation of finder and bailee is permissible at common law, and thus little to suggest that the concept of bailment can be used to justify the existence of finder-obligations. Of course, were we to accept the general conceptual view, canvassed in *Morris*, *Gilchrist Watt*, and elsewhere, that bailment involves and results from the voluntary assumption of possession of the goods of another, then of course finders are bailees inasmuch as they are possessors. A consideration of that thesis is beyond the scope of this work, but its recognition and adoption would serve to confirm rather than deny our general contention that finders are to be treated as ordinary possessors, and finding is not a *sui generis* event operating to generate property rights at common law.

---

[65] *The Pioneer Container* [1994] 2 AC 324 (PC); *East West Corporation v DKBS* [2003] 2 All ER 700.

[66] [1965] 2 All ER 741; T Hadden, 'Larceny by Finding: How Not to Reform the Law' (1965) *CLJ* 173.

[67] *R v Thurborn* (1849) 2 Car & K 831; generally Chapter 1.

[68] Larceny Act 1916, s 1(1) offers a general exception to the requirement of wrongful taking and expressly provides that a bailee may be guilty of stealing if he converts goods to his own use. See generally JP McCutcheon, *The Larceny Act 1916* (Dublin, Round Hall Press, 1989) 35–6.

[69] Particularly *Matthews* (1873) 12 Cox CC 491. Given that it was dealing with a matter involving the liberty of the subject, the court preferred to leave questions as to the justification of the larceny rules to Parliament: see [1965] 2 All ER 741, 742–3 (Sachs J).

[70] Indeed, ATH Smith suggests their non-equivalence when he observes that the creation of the offence 'larceny by finding' in the Larceny Act 1916, s 1(2)(i)(d) was needed to close a loophole in the law after general recognition that bailees could be prosecuted for larceny: *Property Offences* (London, Sweet and Maxwell, 1994) 9.

# Liability Under General Duties

Whilst it is to be doubted that English law imposes positive obligations on finders, whether as bailees or otherwise, it is certain that a finder will be subject to those general duties of the law of obligations that serve to protect interests in property. Thus, depending on the facts of her conduct, any finder risks engaging a tortious liability in conversion or negligence, and possibly also a liability for unjust enrichment. We will return to the tort of conversion in a later chapter, because its existence is crucial to the credibility of the law of finds from a policy perspective.[71] Now we observe only that these various general duties without more do not obligate a finder to perform the conduct envisaged in *Parker*.

## Conversion

Whilst in theory it was not formally dominant until the abolition of detinue in 1977,[72] for centuries conversion has been the primary vehicle for tortious protection against interferences with goods. Its emergence and development from the old form of trover is reasonably clear,[73] yet consistently it has attracted criticism for being a vague and poorly-defined wrong.[74] Increasingly, though, there is a trend towards general agreement about its salient features. In essence, conversion seeks to compensate a claimant for positive acts, done in relation to certain goods, which amount to a denial of his property in them. As it is put in *Clerk & Lindsell on Torts*, 'conversion is an act of deliberate dealing with a chattel in a manner inconsistent with another's right whereby that other is deprived of the use and possession of it'.[75] This formulation recently was approved by the House of Lords in the *Kuwait Airways* case,[76] in which, for conflict of laws purposes, their Lordships were afforded the opportunity to discuss conversion in English law. Lord Nicholls, accepting that the variety of circumstances in which a conversion could occur made framing a general definition nearly impossible, nonetheless identified three general features of the tort.[77] First, the defendant's conduct must be inconsistent with the rights of the owner (or of some other person entitled to possession). Secondly, the defendant's conduct must be deliberate, not accidental. And thirdly, the defendant's conduct must be so extensive an encroachment on the rights of

---

[71] See Chapter 7.
[72] As to which see generally S Douglas, 'The Abolition of Detinue' (2008) *Conv* 30.
[73] See Chapter 1.
[74] 'The word conversion is often used, but it is not very easy to understand what it means': Vaughan Williams LJ in *Clayton v Le Roy* [1911] 2 KB 1031, 1055. See also the oft-cited dictum of Bramwell LJ in *Hiort v L & NWR* (1879) 4 Ex D 188, 194.
[75] *Clerk and Lindsell on Torts*, 17.07.
[76] *Kuwait Airways Corporation v Iraqi Airways Co (Nos 4 and 5)* [2002] 2 AC 883.
[77] *Ibid* 1084.

the owner as to exclude him from use and possession of the goods.[78] Lord Steyn concurred that the essential feature of conversion was the denial of the claimant's title but put the matter more shortly: whenever a defendant manifests 'an assertion of rights or dominion over the goods which is inconsistent with the rights of the plaintiff', he converts the goods to his own use.[79]

A finder might commit conversion in any number of ways. Obviously, if she deliberately consumes or destroys the object of her find she will be liable for conversion,[80] and equally so if she transfers it away by sale or by gift.[81] It is probably also conversion if a finder makes any use of the object of her find, notwithstanding that this use is temporary or even trivial. In *Petre v Heneage*[82] it was conversion to wear a pearl necklace belonging to someone else, and similar conclusions have been reached about transitory, non-destructive uses of horses[83] and cars.[84] At the other end of the spectrum, in the absence of positive conduct, a finder will again be answerable in conversion if she refuses to redeliver found goods on the demand of the loser.[85] Of course, she might make a temporary refusal to allow her to verify the claim of any demandant, but if she is satisfied that the goods belong to him she must answer for their value.[86]

---

[78] The contrast here is with lesser acts of interference in which a defendant, say, damages goods without excluding the claimant from their possession. Such claims can give rise to claims for trespass or negligence, but they are not conversion. This preserves distinctions between the scope of the 'property torts' at common law and prevents conversion from being used as an all-purpose tort for the compensation of interference with goods.

[79] [2002] 2 AC 883, 1104.

[80] *Richardson v Atkinson* (1723) 1 Stra 576; *Clerk and Lindsell*, 17.29.

[81] *Martindale v Smith* (1841) 1 QB 389; *Clerk and Lindsell*, 17.15. Note that it seems an offer to sell, without more, is not enough: *Marcq v Christie Manson & Woods Ltd* [2004] QB 286.

[82] (1701) 12 Mod 519.

[83] *Rolle's Abridgement*, 'Action sur la case', 5, cited in *Clerk and Lindsell*, 17.11. In *Vandrink and Archer's Case* (1591) 1 Leon 221, 223, we also read this opinion of Windham J: 'for if a man find my horse, and rides upon him, or hereby he becomes lame, or otherwise by excessive travel misuseth him, so as my horse is the worse thereby; he may be ready to deliver me my horse, and yet this action will ly, for such an abusing of the horse is a conversion to his own use'. In *Walgrave v Ogden* (1591) 1 Leon 223, the justices of the Common Bench were unanimously of the opinion that the plaintiff could not have trover where the substance of the declaration was negligent keeping of goods found (in that case butter which had turned sour). Walmesley J illustrated the rule by opining that trover would not lie 'if a man find my goods and suffereth them to be eaten by moths', but thought it would be otherwise 'if he weareth my garments ... for the wearing is a conversion': (1591) 1 Leon 223.

[84] *Aitken Agencies Ltd v Richardson* [1967] NZLR 65.

[85] *Isaack v Clark* (1614) 1 Bulst 306, though, as we noted earlier, technically a refusal to redeliver was only evidence of conversion, and accordingly liability on this footing was considered 'conversion by construction of law': *Alexander v Southley* (1821) 5 B & A 247, 248 (Abbott CJKB). Salmond thought the label 'constructive conversion' paid too much respect to the borderlines of old forms of action, and preferred to explain the recognition of this kind of liability as an extension of the scope of conversion over the terrain of detinue: JW Salmond, 'Observations on Trover and Conversion' (1905) 21 *LQR* 43. However, it seems that modern courts will still require a claimant to prove an unequivocal refusal to redeliver goods if he is to succeed in establishing the defendant's liability in conversion in this way, and thus it remains correct to distinguish conversion from the old law on detinue by saying that the former requires commission of a 'definite act': see *Schwarzchild v Harrods Ltd* [2008] All ER (D) 299 (QB).

[86] *Clayton v Le Roy* [1911] 2 KB 1031 (CA).

Between these extremes, there is some middle ground. In the absence of a demand for redelivery, if the finder does not make use of her find, it seems that she does not convert it. It is not conversion merely to store goods, or to keep them without some positive act of withholding.[87] Correlatively, there is no responsibility to seek out a loser, or to acquaint him of his loss in the manner suggested by Donaldson LJ, and the tort of conversion does not reproduce the content of that supposed obligation. If a finder takes goods, brings them home, and leaves them in a cupboard, happy to return them to the loser should he come looking for them, but otherwise making no effort to reacquaint him of their whereabouts, she commits no conversion. On the face of it, this seems an extraordinary proposition. We shall see later that its significance is tempered by other aspects of law,[88] but there is no doubt that as a proposition of the tort of conversion it is consistent with authority. In *Capital Finance v Bray* we read that 'there is no obligation on a person who has another person's goods to return them to him, except by contract'.[89] A finder has no contract with a loser, and therefore no liability to return goods to him. Moreover, in *Capital Finance* the defendant knew who the owners were and how to find them. The defendant retained a car taken on a hire-purchase agreement from the plaintiffs even after the agreement had been wrongfully terminated by the plaintiffs. The plaintiffs wanted the defendant to deliver the car to them at his own expense. The defendant refused to make the delivery, but was not liable for conversion. He was bound to let the plaintiffs have the car if they came to collect it, but not bound to seek them out or deliver it.[90] If there is no liability in these circumstances, where a background transactional relationship exists between the parties, a fortiori there is no liability on the storing finder, who might have significantly lower prospects of tracing the loser of goods.

As to the second of the obligations proposed in *Parker*, ie the duty to take care of an item in the meantime, it has long been clear that conversion is not an appropriate mechanism for regulating the behaviour of finders in this respect. This was the view of Coke CJ in *Isaack v Clark*, who denied that trover would lie for 'ill and negligent keeping' of goods, which was nonfeasance, since trover required misfeasance.[91] The modern formulation of conversion, as is apparent from the judgments of their Lordships in *Kuwait Airways*,[92] remains entirely consistent with the view that liability in conversion is premised on an act of positive withholding.

---

[87] *Barclays Mercantile Finance Ltd v Sibec Developments* [1992] 1 WLR 1253, 1257–8 (Millett J); *Clayton v Le Roy* [1911] 2 KB 1031, 1052 (Farwell LJ). This insistence on a positive act of wrongdoing as the basis of liability in conversion is consistent with the opinion of their Lordships in *Kuwait Airways*.

[88] Specifically the rules relating to theft: see Chapter 7.

[89] [1963] 1 WLR 323, 328 (Lord Denning MR). See also 330 (Harman LJ).

[90] '[The defendant] was under no obligation to take the goods to [the plaintiff]. He could leave the goods at his house until the owner came to collect them. He would not be guilty of any unlawful detention unless, when the owner came to collect them, he prevented him taking possession of them': [1963] 1 WLR 323, 328.

[91] (1614) 2 Bulst 306, 312.

[92] Above n 76.

Accordingly, conversion does not reproduce the content of the second proposed obligation.

In general, then, it can be seen that conversion wholly fails to obligate finders to perform the conduct desired of them by Donaldson LJ. That said, there are certain provisions related to conversion which can work to the advantage of the loser of goods. Paradoxically, this advantage begins with the provision of an apparent benefit to the finder. Section 3(2) of the Limitation Act 1980 provides for a claimant's title to goods to be extinguished six years from the date of accrual of a right of action related to a conversion. This gives the finder an incentive to convert the goods (rather than store them and do nothing) inasmuch as it gives her the possibility of holding an indefeasible title on the expiry of the limitation period. In a later chapter we will show that, when combined with certain provisions related to the law of theft, this incentive to convert actually entails of the finder some effort to trace the loser by reasonable steps. So whilst as a matter of law it is clear that the tort of conversion does not *obligate* a finder to perform such conduct, it does provide a strong incentive to that end. This argument is fully developed in Chapter 7.

## Negligence

*Newman v Bourne and Hollingsworth*[93] is an authority for the proposition that a finder will be liable for losing or damaging a chattel if that loss or damage was caused by her negligence. This will go some way to meeting Donaldson LJ's assertion that finders are under an obligation to take care of lost items, yet the duties might not be symmetrical. A general duty in negligence places the burden of proving breach of that duty on the claimant, in this case the loser.[94] On the other hand, if the finder owed a specific duty to the loser to take care of lost items, it seems arguable that the burden is on the finder to show that she was *not negligent* in causing any loss to the claimant.[95] So a finder is always answerable to a loser for negligence, but the loser's case is more difficult to make if he must rely only on the general law of negligence.

## Unjust Enrichment

There are two kinds of difficulty with the suggestion that a loser might base a claim against a finder on unjust enrichment. The first is a general doctrinal question about whether such a liability can arise at all on the facts of finding, though so far as they go the authorities offer some support for the view that it can. The second is a question about what difference, if any, it would make to the

---

[93] (1915) TLR 209.
[94] *Clerk and Lindsell on Torts*, 8-149.
[95] Compare *Sorrell v Paget* [1950] 1 KB 252, 261.

protection of the interests of losers that they could avail of a right to reverse the unjust enrichment of a finder. The finder's liability would certainly not compel the kind of conduct envisaged by Donaldson LJ, and moreover it seems that the loser is more fully protected (and the finder more incentivised to seek him out) by his potential claim for conversion.

As to the liability question, there is some authority to suggest that losers can bring claims against finders based on unjust enrichment, but the position is far from unequivocal. In *Holiday v Sigil*,[96] the plaintiff lost a £500 banknote, which the defendant found and lodged at a bank. The plaintiff recovered the value of the note in an action for money had and received.[97] Before the court the plaintiff proved only facts relating to his acquisition of the note; facts relating to its loss; and facts suggesting that the defendant was present at the locus and on the occasion of the loss. Abbot CJ directed the jury to find for the plaintiff if it was 'satisfied that the plaintiff lost this note, and that the defendant found it'.[98] Burrows uses this case to support the possibility that a claim based on unjust enrichment avails in finding situations,[99] but the substance of the action is unclear.[100] After a similar fashion is the claim in *Moffatt v Kazana*,[101] where, as we have seen, the plaintiffs recovered the value of the banknotes discovered in a chimney flue. *Holiday* was not cited there, but again the majority of the evidence related to proof of the plaintiff's title to the money, and Wrangham J was satisfied that if the money 'belongs to the plaintiffs, the plaintiffs are entitled to judgment for that amount'.[102] Whilst the reporter and the judgment refer to the plaintiffs' claim as 'an action for the recovery of the money from the defendant', there are references towards the end of the judgment which suggest that the defendant refused to redeliver the notes on a demand from the plaintiffs. This would be consistent with liability for conversion or detinue. The report tells us

---

[96] (1826) 2 Car & P 177.

[97] *Ibid.*

[98] *Ibid.* See generally *Goff and Jones*, 2-026.

[99] A Burrows, *The Law of Restitution* 2nd edn (London, Butterworths, 2002) 185–6.

[100] W Swadling, 'Ignorance and Unjust Enrichment: the Problem of Title' (2008) 28 *OJLS* 627, 636; and B McFarlane, *The Structure of Property Law* (Oxford, Hart Publishing, 2008) 334–6. Swadling argues generally that *indebitatus assumpsit* for money had and received could be used against wrongdoers, identifying as a typical case 'the defendant who by sale converted a chattel to which the claimant had a better title': (2008) 28 *OJLS* 627, 633. This is not disputed in general, but it does cause Swadling to lean in favour of a wrongs-based analysis to *Holiday* (although he notes the existence of the doubt) when perhaps this is difficult to square with the judgment. The defendant certainly converted the note when he lodged it in his bank account, but understood literally, the direction from Abbot CJ lays no emphasis on the facts of that conversion. If it was correct to say that the plaintiff's claim to recover the value of the banknote would be established if 'the plaintiff lost this note, and … the defendant found it', then the plaintiff's claim seems not to depend on a conversion, at least to the extent that, as we have seen, 'finding' does not without more constitute a conversion. This seems to lend some support to the argument that the claim in *Holiday* depended on unjust enrichment.

[101] [1969] 2 QB 152.

[102] *Ibid* 154.

nothing about the relevant sequence of events: we do not know how it was that the plaintiffs learned of the defendant's find, or what steps if any were taken to recover the monies prior to litigation. So whilst at first blush the judgment in *Moffatt* is consistent with liability based on unjust enrichment, it seems equally consistent with liability in tort.

To this slender authority we can add a general doctrinal problem. On the orthodox modern view, prima facie liability in unjust enrichment arises where the defendant (a) has been enriched; (b) at the expense of the claimant; and (c) this enrichment was unjust.[103] In cases of finding, it seems possible (though by no means uncontroversial)[104] to make an argument in support of the first two criteria. Even where a finder does not also convert the goods, she is arguably enriched inasmuch as she receives control of an asset easily realisable in monetary terms through its sale.[105] And if she is enriched, it is certainly possible for the loser to show that this enrichment was at his expense, that in effect being the substance of the decisions in *Holiday* and *Moffatt*.[106] The difficulty is whether the enrichment in these circumstances can properly be regarded as unjust. In a case of accidental loss, it is plain that the loser has no intent to transfer any benefit to the finder. By definition he has no intention at all that his goods should leave his custody. In *The Law of Restitution*, Birks argued that this kind of 'ignorance' in transfer should be recognised as an 'unjust factor'.[107] It was 'the most extreme

---

[103] See generally P Birks, *Unjust Enrichment* 2nd edn (Oxford, OUP, 2005) 39; Burrows, above n 99 at 15–51; *EPL*, 18.11; *Goff and Jones*, 1-015–1-016.

[104] See R Stevens, 'Three Enrichment Issues' in A Burrows and Lord Rodger of Earlsferry (eds), *Mapping the Law: Essays in Memory of Peter Birks* (Oxford, OUP, 2006) 62–64, noting the existence of controversy as to whether properly there can be enrichment where title is not transferred to the defendant, but preferring the view that there can; and compare Swadling, above n 100, arguing that properly a defendant cannot be enriched at the expense of the claimant where the claimant retains title to the asset in question. This is discussed further below.

[105] P Birks, 'Property and Unjust Enrichment: Categorical Truths' [1997] *NZLR* 623, 654–5. It is the fact of potentially realisable value that would constitute the enrichment rather than the actual realisation of that value through sale, which would of course be a conversion.

[106] Birks, above n 103 at 73, citing *Holiday* and *Moffatt*. See also *Lipkin Gorman v Karpnale* Ltd [1991] 2 AC 548. That was a three-party case, where the House of Lords considered the liability of the defendant casino to pay to the claimant firm of solicitors a large sum of money, representing funds surreptitiously withdrawn from the claimant's client account (and gambled away) by a partner of the firm. Mitchell argues that, whilst the facts of the case in reality were much more complex, 'the model which their lordships applied was that in which X finds C's money and gives it to D': *EPL*, 18.47.

[107] P Birks, *The Law of Restitution* rev edn (Oxford, Clarendon Press, 1989) 140–6, citing *Moffatt*. Compare Krebs, arguing recently that the idea of ignorance as an unjust factor remains undeveloped in English law: T Krebs, 'The Fallacy of "Restitution for Wrongs"' in A Burrows and Lord Rodger of Earlsferry (eds), *Mapping the Law: Essays in Memory of Peter Birks* (Oxford, OUP, 2006) 392–3. In the second edition of *Unjust Enrichment*, Birks argued that English law has moved away from this general approach, dealing with the question whether a given enrichment is unjust according to a more civilian 'absence of basis' approach, rather than the elucidation of specific 'unjust factors': P Birks, above n 103 at ch 5. This argument has not found acceptance in the literature (see eg *EPL*, 18.40–18.45).

case on, or more accurately before, the spectrum of vitiated intention'. Burrows[108] and Mitchell[109] agree, though Burrows concedes that there are few decisions on the two-party scenario typified by a finding dispute.[110] Elsewhere, however, there is persuasive resistance. Swadling denies generally that ignorance can be the basis of a claim in unjust enrichment.[111] In the circumstances of ignorance the claimant's property rights are not transferred to the defendant, but persist in the claimant,[112] and the proper action for one who retains property in disputed goods, as does a loser, must be premised on the continuation of those rights. In English law this means recourse to the law of wrongs, not to unjust enrichment.[113] Notice if this is correct, inasmuch as it argues against recognition of ignorance as an unjust factor, simultaneously it bites on the prospects of arguing that the defendant is enriched at the expense of the claimant.[114] Indeed, the argument rejects ignorance as an unjust factor precisely because in the circumstances of ignorance the defendant is not enriched at the expense of the claimant.[115]

Even if we were to overcome these objections, and allow that a finder is unjustly enriched by the simple act of taking and keeping, it is not clear that the resultant obligation to reverse that enrichment would compel the kind of conduct envisaged in *Parker*. Donaldson LJ is aiming at a form of specific restitution. The finder is supposed to care for the goods and take steps to acquaint the loser with their whereabouts. The goal is that losers and lost items are reunited.[116] But the unjust enrichment of a finder in these circumstances would raise only an obligation to make restitution of the value she received. If anything, this serves as a disincentive to finders who are thinking about locating a loser. The finder who locates the loser will in any case be bound to deliver up the goods if the loser asks for them: it would be a conversion not to do so. The finder who does nothing does not convert the goods. She will be answerable for any enrichment she has received if the loser ever identifies her, but that is much less likely to happen if she says nothing.

Accordingly, it is difficult to see that a finders' liability in unjust enrichment would add very much to the legal protection of the loser. Probably a loser is

---

[108] Burrows, above n 99 at 182.

[109] *EPL*, 18.46–18.51. There, 'no intent' is considered to be 'the strongest example of deficient intent', and 'deficient intent' is an 'unjust factor'.

[110] Burrows, above n 99 at 185–6, citing *Holiday*.

[111] Swadling, above n 100.

[112] *Ibid* 642–3; W Swadling, 'A Claim in Restitution?' (1996) *LMCLQ* 63, 64–5; G Virgo, *The Principles of the Law of Restitution* 2nd edn (Oxford, OUP, 2006) 131–2.

[113] See generally W Swadling, 'Unjust Delivery', in A Burrows and Lord Rodger of Earlsferry (eds), *Mapping the Law: Essays in Memory of Peter Birks* (Oxford, OUP, 2006) 283–7. *Goff and Jones* shares this view, doubting whether, without more, ignorance is a ground of recovery: *Goff and Jones*, 4-001.

[114] Swadling, above n 100 at 642–3.

[115] *Ibid* 657–8; B McFarlane, *The Structure of Property Law* (Oxford, Hart Publishing, 2008) 334–6.

[116] [1982] QB 1004, 1017.

better advised to sue on the basis of a wrong.[117] Even if a finder's liability in unjust enrichment exists, additional proof of the simple fact of demand and refusal will ground an action for conversion, and there the claimant has some prospect that the goods themselves will be returned to him, not just their value.[118] Moreover, the law of unjust enrichment has no analogous provision to section 3(2) of the Limitation Act 1980, such that a finder's liability for unjust enrichment will necessarily lack the incentivising force of her liability for conversion.[119] The most that could be said is that the rhetoric of liability for unjust enrichment would provide a reason for a finder to act in favour of a loser ('I have received an enrichment at the expense of the loser; this is unjust; I must take steps to reverse it'), but we will see that it is a weak reason compared with that provided by a combination of conversion and theft.

# Obligations and Policy

We began this chapter with the proposition in *Parker* that a finder owes certain duties to the loser of goods. However, we have seen that there is no common law authority to suggest the specific imposition of positive obligations on finders; that it is at least doubtful that finders can be classed as bailees; and that the content of the supposed obligations is not necessarily entailed by general duties of tort or unjust enrichment. Accordingly, and overwhelmingly, we are left to conclude that Donaldson LJ's dictum is not an accurate statement of the law.

We have already seen enough to suggest that Donaldson LJ's treatment of the obligations point affords but one example of a wider problem with the judgment in *Parker*. The text contains several apparently definitive propositions which are neither germane to the facts nor demonstrable on the authorities,[120] and relies on

---

[117] On the view of Swadling and *Goff and Jones*, a claim for wrongful interference is the *only* suitable avenue in these circumstances: an action in unjust enrichment is 'never appropriate if the right to immediate possession remains in the claimant and the defendant is in a position to return the goods; the plaintiff then has his remedies for wrongful interference': *Goff and Jones*, 1-027.

[118] Torts (Interference with Goods) Act 1977, s 3; *Clerk and Lindsell on Torts*, 17-83–17-87. Actions for unjust enrichment attract no equivalent provision. Birks thought that this was quite proper. He argued that a claimant's election to bring an action based on unjust enrichment supposed a renunciation by the claimant of his title. Correlatively, in a claim for wrongful interference with goods, the claimant effectively insisted on the continuation of his title, which made appropriate the award of specific recovery: Birks, above n 103 at 66–7. This theory of elective renunciation is not uncontroversial.

[119] As we have noted already, the argument on the existence of that incentive is developed fully in Chapter 7.

[120] Thus we find opinion on the rights of trespassing and dishonest finders, the rights of those who find in the course of their employment, and the equivalence of the occupation of ships and motor cars to the occupation of a building for the purpose of resolving doubts as to possessory title: [1982] QB 1004, 1009–10, 1017, 1018. In the case of wrongdoing and employee finders, Donaldson LJ's central

over-lengthy citations offering no support for the propositions canvassed.[121] So far as the obligations proposition is concerned, it seems clear that this was motivated by public policy concerns. The law must meet the needs of society,[122] and in this respect the guiding idea was:

> the need to have common law rules which facilitate rather than hinder the ascertainment of the true owner of a lost chattel.[123]

Counsel for British Airways had argued that to effect this policy a possessor of land should always have a better right than a finder, because the loser of goods was likely to retrace his steps and make inquiries at the place of loss.[124] Donaldson LJ resisted such a wide rule in favour of possessors of land, because in effect it would leave the finder without any prospect of reward.[125] A finder needed to have some incentive to report her find. If she stood to gain nothing, she might pass by a discovered object and say nothing, or worse yet take up her find and conceal its discovery.[126] Implicit in this is that the recognition of property rights in finders fulfils an important policy objective, but such recognition must be tempered from the other end. It is not enough to recognise rights in finders, for this by itself does not promote ascertainment of the loser of a chattel. Donaldson LJ's answer was to subject the finder's conduct to specific obligations, which would usually include the duty 'to inform the occupier of the land of the fact that the article has been found and where it is to be kept'.[127] Accordingly, the obligations are posited to achieve balance. They are designed to qualify the finder's acquisition of right, and thereby produce a legal position which (i) gives the finder sufficient incentive

---

contention was that the finder's acquisition of rights in the find should be qualified. This argument is considered, and ultimately dismissed, in Chapter 6.

[121] Roberts, above n 26 at 685.

[122] [1982] QB 1004, 1017.

[123] [1982] QB 1004, 1017.

[124] [1982] QB 1004, 1006 (Stephen Desch QC). The case report in *Parker* does not record any authority or comment relied on by counsel for this proposition, but it is not unreasonable to assume it owed some debt to the US literature, where a similar policy objective has been canvassed as the basis for a similarly suggested rule: see EH Warren, *Cases on Property* 2nd edn (Cambridge, MA, Harvard Co-operative Society, 1938) 116; Anon, 'Comment on Lost, Mislaid, and Abandoned Property' (1939) 8 *Fordham Law Review* 222, 234–5.

[125] [1982] QB 1004, 1017. English law has never recognised any general entitlement to payment of a reward; indeed, finders are not normally entitled to recover expenses. Contrast the position in the United States whereby legislation several states allow recovery of expenses by finders, and some require payment of rewards: see Chapter 7.

[126] [1982] QB 1004, 1017. Of course, in other legal systems this problem was avoided by positing some form of guaranteed entitlement for the finder, even where goods were found on land belonging to another. At Roman law, under certain conditions, finders and possessors of land were entitled to an equal share in things found by chance: J Inst II.1.39; WW Buckland, *A Textbook of Roman Law* 2nd edn (Cambridge, Cambridge University Press, 1932) 218–19. In Ireland, the Brehon law responded in a similar fashion, though there the size of the finder's share would vary on a sliding scale referenced to the circumstances of the find. For example, 'the more remote the place where an article is found, the greater the proportion of its value goes to the finder': F Kelly, *A Guide to Early Irish Law* (Dublin, Dublin Institute for Advanced Studies, 1988) 123.

[127] [1982] QB 1004, 1017.

to intervene in the situation (to take up the item, rather than to pass by); but (ii) simultaneously compels her to report her discovery, preventing windfall gains and ensuring so far as possible that information about the find becomes available to the loser.

Whilst much of the judgment in *Parker* is worthy of criticism, it is almost impossible to disagree with this political sentiment.[128] To the extent that we respect the continuing property rights of losers of goods, we must have laws which strive to give real effect to those rights. The loser is entitled to have his thing, and we must get it back to him, or at least account to him for its value. This ethical imperative has been recognised in one form or another for thousands of years, often in a manner even more stringent than that suggested by Donaldson LJ. The Mosaic Codes compel intervenient action on discovery of loss. They forbid finders to ignore lost goods, demanding specific restitution to losers and care in the interim.[129] Our law would seem to fail if it did not provide a similar impetus for restoration.[130] Accordingly, it seems absurd to suggest, as here we have done, that such obligations do not exist at common law.

The objection, though, is not to the policy conclusions drawn, but rather to the manner in which their realisation has been conceived. Later it will be argued that English law actually does implement these policy aims,[131] but it does not do so in the manner suggested by Donaldson LJ. His Lordship's proposed obligations do not exist, and to suggest that they do exist is to distort the authorities and read into them propositions for which they cannot stand. This was exactly the mischief decried by Goodhart when he objected to inventive academic rationalisations of *Bridges*, *Elwes* and *Sharman*, and it seems that the lesson has not been learned. The next two chapters of this work urge doctrinal accuracy. They consider the nature of the finder's right, and the extent to which the cases allow that right to be limited by certain extraneous circumstances. But doctrinal accuracy should not imply political deficiency. Although we must conclude from the cases that a finder always acquires a property right and is not constrained by specifically imposed

---

[128] For a general assertion that such a policy should be the basis of the law relating to finders, see EP Morton, 'Public Policy and the Finders Cases' (1946–47) 1 *Wyoming Law Journal* 101.

[129] 'If you see your brother's sheep or ox straying, do not ignore it but be sure to take it back to him. If the brother does not live near you or if you do not know who he is, take it home with you and keep it until he comes looking for it. Then give it back to him. Do the same if you find your brother's donkey or his cloak or anything he loses. Do not ignore it'. (Deuteronomy 22:1-3, New International Version).

[130] Particularly bearing in mind the general context of property protection in English law. In English law, property rights are always protected through the law of obligations: we never offer direct vindication of property rights in our courts: *EPL*, 17.318–17.321; P Birks, 'Personal Property: Proprietary Rights and Remedies' (2000) 11 *KCLJ* 1. If there is no *obligation* to restore lost goods, prima facie the law's protection of the loser's *property* right is deficient. In a society where the protection of property and possessions is considered a basic human right (European Convention on Human Rights, First Protocol, Art 1) this could be a critical failing.

[131] It also achieves effective resource allocation and (therefore) dispute resolution by providing clearly for the long-term use of a find in the event that its loser cannot be found. The argument on the execution of these policies is made in Chapter 7.

obligations, her behaviour *is* curtailed by other rules of property, crime and tort, and correctly understood, English law delivers a law of finds which achieves sensible policy aims. Accordingly, the final chapter emphasises the importance of reasoning across the apparently discrete categories of property, obligations and crime when stating the policy of our law relating to finders. We will see that we need not distort our basic doctrines, nor modify existing authorities, to achieve sensible results.

# 5

## Possession and the Rights of Finders

The foregoing chapters establish that, in English law, finding cases depend on possession. Contests between possessors of land and finders are resolved according to which party can establish the earliest possession on the facts. Nothing turns on the factual classification of the goods in any sense, and the finder owes no special duty to the loser in virtue of her status as finder. A finder is only a possessor, in the sense that the only grounds for her claim to legal entitlement to the object of her find are the facts of her possession. She has no pre-existing legal relationship to the object or to its loser, and she comes to it without express authority. So, as the law stands, insofar as a finder has any property right in respect of the object of her find, that right must be premised on, and must result from, the facts of her possession. In this chapter we consider the nature and extent of this right.

Whilst modern cases involving finders are undoubtedly premised on an evaluation of the relativity of the respective rights of finders and rival claimants,[1] the cases do not contain much express analysis of the nature or quality of those rights. When Pollock came to consider the rights of possessors,[2] he started with the general availability of possessory protection (through trover in the case of goods and ejectment in the case of land),[3] before abstracting from that availability to offer a substantive account of the rights in question. The first part of this chapter traces the development of Pollock's argument, placing it in the context of contemporaneous decisions on trover and ejectment. We will see that although the argument is far from uncontroversial, Pollock considered the possessor to acquire a property right in the fullest sense, transmissible in the manner appropriate to the thing in question, and attracting the standard advantages of ownership. Inasmuch as the modern finding cases unquestionably apply Pollock's understanding of the facts of possession, they are also consistent with his view that these facts generate this kind of right. That being the case, the second part of the chapter considers the extent of the right, arguing that once created it should be regarded as continuing even beyond the cessation of the original facts of possession. On this view the

---

[1] See *Parker v British Airways Board* [1982] QB 1004, 1008; *Waverly BC v Fletcher* [1996] QB 334, 338–40, 346.

[2] P & W, ch II, Pt III, p 91 *et seq.*

[3] P & W, 91.

finder acquires a property right which binds the whole world, except one able to prove an earlier, and therefore better right to the goods in question.

# Possession as a Source of Property Rights at Common Law

In Chapter 2 we located the origin of our modern theory of possession in the writings of Holmes and Pollock late in the nineteenth century. We noted that each owed a heavy debt to Roman law, at least insofar as they conceived of possession as depending on proof of two discrete factual elements, ie some degree of factual control over the object in question, and some degree of intention to exclude others from interfering with it. It cannot be emphasised strongly enough that each of these writers regarded these twin elements as facts. Their legal significance was that when demonstrably present in a given person they pointed to the existence of a 'definite legal relation' between that person and the thing possessed.[4] In addition, Pollock's account disclosed a further distinction between possession acquired with the consent of some previous possessor and possession acquired without such consent.[5] Pollock was careful to suggest that consensual changes of possession were 'not fully determined' by the facts of control and intention, inasmuch as the consent of the transferor was 'a real element' in the transferee's 'power of enjoyment and control'.[6] The exact import of this observation is a matter of some doubt,[7] but for now it is enough to note that a finder who acquired

---

[4] P & W, 28; Holmes, *CL*, 214–15. See also JW Salmond, *The First Principles of Jurisprudence* (London, Stevens and Haynes, 1893) 190.

[5] Thus, Pollock's whole scheme purported to rest on a 'fundamental division' between 'voluntary' and 'involuntary' changes of possession, between acts of 'delivery' on the one hand, and 'occupation or taking' on the other: P & W, 43–4.

[6] P & W, 43–4; also Holmes, *CL*, 214–15.

[7] In a later chapter Pollock seems to suggest that the resultant relation is the same on whichever set of facts possession is proved (P & W, 91), which would tend to suggest that the distinction between consensually-acquired and original possession is largely redundant. On the other hand, it is theoretically possible that there is a difference between the kind of right created on a consensual delivery of possession and the kind which arises on proof of control and intention, and this proposition is still evident in some of our most recent books. See eg R Goode, *Commercial Law* 3rd edn,(London, LexisNexis UK, 2004) 31–5, 42, where 'possession' is conceived as the foundation of two interests, ie 'general' and 'limited' interests. The contrast between the two is highlighted by consideration of a recalcitrant hirer of goods: '[The bailee] has a right to continue in possession on the terms of the bailment and, since no one else has a better right, he has an indefeasible title to his limited interest as bailee. But suppose that, in defiance of his bailor's rights of ownership, the bailee asserts dominion over the goods ... [T]hough ineffective as against the bailor, [the assertion] is nevertheless good against the rest of the world, since it is supported by possession and possession is recognised by English law as a root of title. The position of the recalcitrant bailee is now reversed. From being the holder of an indefeasible title to a limited interest he has become the holder of a relative title to an absolute interest': Goode, *ibid* 33; but compare generally W Swadling, 'The Proprietary Effect of a Hire of Goods' in NE Palmer and E McKendirck, (eds), *Interests in Goods* 2nd edn (London, LLP, 1998) 514–18.

possession was certainly in the latter category. Her acquisition might be a justified trespass if she took with intention of saving the thing for its owner;[8] it would be wrongful, and subject to the law on larceny, if she took for herself;[9] but in neither case did it occur with the express consent of the loser.[10] On Pollock's thesis, then, a finder can establish a 'definite legal relation' to the object of her find insofar as (and because) she can establish the twin possessory facts of control and intention, and this of course is borne out by the cases decided in modern times, as we saw in Chapter 2.

In arguing for the existence of this 'definite legal relation', Pollock's major premise is that possession makes available legal protection. His treatment of 'title by possession' begins with this proposition:

> Existing possession, however acquired, is protected against any interference by a mere wrongdoer; and the wrongdoer cannot defend himself by showing a better title than the plaintiff's in some third person through or under whom he does not himself claim or justify.[11]

Pollock thought that this proposition was true equally of goods and land, in the actions of trover and ejectment respectively,[12] and treated trover and ejectment coterminously is his consideration of the right resulting from possession.[13] Since the accuracy of his whole argument depends on the truth of this assimilation, we consider first the extent to which it was correct to regard possession as the basis of trover and ejectment respectively, before moving to discuss Pollock's substantive account of the resultant right.

## Possession as the Basis of Trover

To the modern lawyer, there is nothing startling in the proposition that actual possession gives title to sue in conversion.[14] Accordingly, it seems a fairly orthodox rationalisation of trover to say that it lay to protect a right to possess goods, and that it was available to a possessor on proof of possession alone. However, it is likely that our understanding of the action in these terms owes a heavier

---

[8] P & W, 84.

[9] P & W, 84–5.

[10] Nowadays, within the category of non-consensual possession, nothing very much turns on the distinction between rightful and wrongful taking from the finder's point of view. Our laws of theft and conversion being premised on a wide concept of appropriation, it really makes very little difference to the finder's liability to the loser that she can formally excuse *trespassory* interference: see Chapter 7 for consideration of the applicable rules of theft and conversion, and their intended effect on the behaviour of finders.

[11] P & W, 91; and see Holmes, *CL*, 211, 241–2, 244.

[12] P & W, 91.

[13] P & W, 28, 85, 91.

[14] See generally *Clerk and Lindsell on Torts*, 17-40; Goode, above n 7 at 62; ELG Tyler, and NE Palmer (eds), *Crossley Vaines' Personal Property* 5th edn (London, Butterworths, 1973) 46.

debt to Pollock and his contemporaries than we might realise. A good deal of intellectual rationalisation of the cases occurred at the end of the nineteenth century. For the proposition that one who is able to establish possession of goods can (on that basis) sue for conversion, our modern books typically rely on *Armory v Delamirie*, yet curiously *Armory* was not cited at all by Pollock.[15] Instead, Pollock relied on *Jeffries v Great Western Railway Co*,[16] or more accurately, on the following proposition from Serjeant Williams' notes to *Wilbraham v Snow*,[17] which was approved by the judges of the Exchequer Chamber in *Jeffries*:

> Possession with an assertion of title, or even possession alone, gives the possessor such a property as will enable him to maintain this action [trover] against a wrongdoer.[18]

The latter part of this passage so closely resonates with *Armory* that it seems strange Pratt CJ's judgment was not cited directly by Pollock. Stranger still is that in *Jeffries* the question whether proof of possession was sufficient to allow trover against a wrongdoer was treated as a novelty. The plaintiff proved possession of certain trucks which had been seized by the defendants, and which the plaintiff claimed to have held under assignment from one Owen (a bankrupt). The defendants claimed under a subsequent assignment from Owen, and produced evidence tending to show that the assignment to plaintiff was fraudulent and void,[19] prompting at least one of the judges to treat the plaintiff as a wrongdoer in possession.[20] Counsel for the plaintiff argued that 'mere possession is sufficient title against a wrongdoer', but the authorities given were roundly denied;[21] and when, in reliance on Williams' notes, Wightman J put the same proposition to the defendants, counsel retorted: 'There is no decision to that effect'.[22] Yet ultimately the court accepted the proposition, and framed its decision in language which looks familiar in light of our understanding of *Armory v Delamirie*. So Lord Campbell CJ confirmed that 'against a wrongdoer possession is title';[23] Wightman J spoke of 'the prima facie right arising from possession';[24] all of their Lordships

---

[15] The judgment in *Armory* was reproduced by RS Wright in his part of the work, and cited for the general proposition suggested here, ie that a possessor might maintain trover: P & W, 149. Pollock did cite *Armory* in the first edition of *The Law of Torts* (which was published slightly earlier than the *Essay on Possession*), and connected it with *Jeffries v Great Western Railway Co* (discussed immediately below), albeit in a footnote: F Pollock, *The Law of Torts* (London, Stevens & Sons, 1887) 300 fn (q).

[16] (1856) 5 E & B 802.

[17] (1845) 2 Wms Saund 47. *Wilbraham v Snow* itself was decided in 1670: see 1 Mod 30, and the further reports cited below.

[18] (1845) 2 Wms Saund 47, approved (1856) 5 E & B 802, 805, 806, 808; cited P & W, 92.

[19] (1856) 5 E & B 802, 803.

[20] *Ibid* 807 (Crompton J).

[21] *Ibid* 803–4 (Crompton J, in argument).

[22] *Ibid* 804.

[23] *Ibid* 805.

[24] *Ibid* 806.

approved the statement from the notes to *Wilbraham v Snow*;[25] and all denied to the defendants the ability to plead a *jus tertii* defence.[26]

It seems possible that, as it was originally understood, *Armory* was not about possession, or at least that the plaintiff's right did not arise as a result of possession in the factual sense employed by Pollock. The short judgment in *Armory* makes no express mention of possession as a source of the right,[27] and neither do most reports of *Wilbraham v Snow*.[28] Instead, *Wilbraham* depended on a concept of special property, according to which a non-owner in possession of goods with the consent of their owner was allowed to bring trover for the goods because he was accountable to the owner for their value. In *Wilbraham* itself, a sheriff was allowed to recover goods taken out of his possession following their lawful seizure. The court reached its decision by analogy with the legal position of carriers, allowing trover to the sheriff because by law he was accountable for the value of goods seized.[29] In such cases the plaintiff's right appears to be premised on his legal responsibility for the goods, and that responsibility in turn premised on the lawful nature of his possession.[30] It seems possible that, to the lawyers of its day, *Armory* would have been understood in the same way. Significantly, in Williams' notes to *Wilbraham v Snow*, the chimney sweep's boy was treated as a 'lawful' possessor,[31] the only conceivable reason (recalling the law of charity discussed in Chapter 1) being a supposition that the boy had taken the goods to save them for their owner such that he would have had a defence to proceedings for trespass. In other words, perhaps the chimney sweep's boy could maintain trover because he had made himself responsible for the safety of the jewel. There are traces of this understanding in *Bridges v Hawkesworth*, where, in disputing the claim of the plaintiff finder, counsel urged the court to consider whether he did 'take to himself the charge of these notes, or make himself liable for the advertisements'.[32] In *Jeffries*, though, where the evidence tended to suggest that the plaintiff was a wrongdoer, this special property construction could not technically have been possible. In this sense, it could be that it was the fact that the plaintiff was a

---

[25] *Ibid* 805, 806, 808.

[26] *Ibid* 805, 807–808.

[27] We are told only that '[t]he finder of a jewel, though he does not by such finding acquire an absolute property or ownership, yet he has such property as will enable him to keep it against all but the rightful owner, and consequently may maintain trover': (1722) 1 Stra 505.

[28] (1670) 1 Mod 30; 1 Ventris 52; 1 Lev 282; 2 Keble 588.

[29] *Ibid.*

[30] See this helpful description of 'special property' from counsel for the plaintiff in *Webb v Fox*, where an uncertified bankrupt was allowed trover of goods lawfully in his possession: 'Special property is the mere possession of property by one, with the assent of the true owner: the possessor is liable over to the person who has the absolute property for any damage that may be done to it, and in respect of that liability he may maintain trover for it': (1797) 7 TR 391, 393. Cf Holmes, disputing the development of this doctrine, and preferring the view that the right called 'special property' arose only in consequence of the facts of possession: Holmes, *CL*, 242–3; and likewise JW Clerk, 'Title to Chattels by Possession' (1891) 7 *LQR* 224, 236.

[31] (1845) 2 Wms Saund 47.

[32] (1851) 15 Jur 1079, 1081 (Hake, appearing for the defendant).

*wrongdoer* in possession which was the novelty in *Jeffries*,[33] and which explains why *Armory v Delamirie* was not cited to the court. However, once the ability of a wrongdoer to maintain trover has been recognised, it immediately becomes meaningless to insist on consent or accountability as the basis of recovery. If the wrongdoer in possession without consent can have trover, a fortiori the literal bailee or similar possessor with a positive duty to account to some other for the value of goods. In other words, after *Jeffries*, the right of a person actually in possession to proceed in trover for some conversion of goods need only depend on proof of possession in the bare factual sense. Correlatively, there is no need to lay emphasis on the lawful nature of special property. This latter at least was the view of Holmes, who argued specifically that special property 'did not mean anything more' than possession.[34]

Consistently with these last suggestions we find that authorities in the late nineteenth and early twentieth centuries treat *Armory* and the earlier cases on trover as depending on proof of possession alone. In *South Staffs Water Co v Sharman*, the county court judge found for the plaintiffs on the basis of *Armory*,[35] and (as we have seen) that verdict was upheld by the Divisional Court. In *The Winkfield*, Collins MR referred to *Armory* and *Jeffries* in the same paragraph to support the view that 'a long series of authorities' established that in trover 'possession is good against a wrongdoer'.[36] In a like manner, Holdsworth treated *Armory* as a possession case,[37] as did Cyprian Williams in the later editions of *Williams on Personal Property*.[38] No doubt this process of rationalisation was not completely linear: there are instances much earlier than *Jeffries* where it appears that *Armory*

---

[33] Even 30 years after *Jeffries* was decided, Pollock himself expressed some equivocation on the view that a title acquired by wrongful possession availed in trover. In the first edition of *Pollock on Torts*, we read that: 'The authorities do not clearly decide, but seem to imply, that it would make no difference if the de facto possession violated by the defendant were not only without title, but obviously wrongful': F Pollock, above n 15 at 300.

[34] Holmes, *CL*, 242. See to the same effect J Williams, *Principles of the Law of Personal Property* (London, H Sweet, 1848) 23; HW Elphinstone and JW Clark (eds), *Goodeve's Modern Law of Personal Property* 2nd edn (London, Sweet and Maxwell, 1892) 19; Clerk, above n 30 at 236.

[35] [1896] 2 QB 44, 45.

[36] [1902] P 42, 54. See also *Glenwood Lumber Co Ltd v Phillips* [1904] AC 405, 410; *Eastern Construction Co Ltd v National Trust Co Ltd* [1914] AC 197, 209 (PC).

[37] '[T]he rule laid down [in *Armory*] follows from the root principle of the common law of possession, that the possessor is prima facie owner, and has all the rights of an owner except as against one who can show a better right': Holdsworth, *HEL*, 7, 426; see also 449–50.

[38] *Armory* is used to support the proposition that 'one who is merely in possession of goods, even by wrong, is said to have a title against all except the true owner': TC Williams (ed), *Williams on Personal Property* 18th edn (London, Sweet and Maxwell, 1926) 49, 52. In the 14th edition of 1894, TC Williams had offered a major revision of the original text. In the preface he recorded that the bulk of the new material concerned 'the ownership of goods, and its history, and … the possession and alienation of goods, and the title thereto': 14th edn (London, Sweet and Maxwell, 1894) v. The preface to the 14th edition records a 'sense of obligation' to Holmes and Pollock, and acknowledges a benefit from discussions with Maitland: *ibid* vi. In earlier editions, Joshua Williams discussed *Armory*, and spoke of a finder being 'entitled to possession', but his description of the right acquired by the finder lacks the fullness of description evident in TC Williams' account: Williams, above n 34 at 23–4, and see further below.

was treated as a matter of mere possession.[39] But we can be sure that legal writing in the nineteenth and twentieth centuries had a tremendously clarifying effect on this branch of law, and after Pollock no one seems to doubt that proof of possession alone is sufficient to bring proceedings in trover.[40]

## Possession as the Basis of Ejectment

It is instructive to note that in the land law of the nineteenth century we find a parallel development, as possession came to be treated as the basis of entitlement to sue for ejectment. By the middle of the seventeenth century, the action of ejectment had become in practice the principal means for protecting freehold interests in land, and this position was consolidated by the abolition of the old real actions in the nineteenth century.[41] The common law orthodoxy was that the generation of freehold estates in land (and therefore the ability to try a freehold estate in ejectment), depended on seisin.[42] It has been suggested that in its original sense seisin bore a close factual resemblance to possession,[43] but equally certain is that it came to bear a technical legal meaning.[44] Relevant proof of this, were it needed, is found in the origins of the action for ejectment itself. Very late in the fifteenth century, a species of the writ of trespass called *ejectio firmae* was allowed to a termor in order that he might achieve specific recovery of his term.[45] Previously, specific recovery had been unavailable to him because he could not have the assize of novel disseisin for the very reason that he lacked seisin.[46] According to Maitland, the word 'possession' eventually appeared in the English texts to explain the interest of the termor, and distinguish it from that of the person seised.[47] The termor had possession, and therefore ejectment

---

[39] See eg *Sutton v Buck* (1810) 2 Taunt 302 (Lord Mansfield CJ and Lawrence J); JW Smith, *A Selection of Leading Cases on Various Branches of the Law* 2nd edn (London, A Maxwell, 1841) 264 (there is no discussion of *Armory* in the 1st edition of 1837).

[40] See generally JW Salmond, *The Law of Torts* (London, Stevens and Haynes, 1907) 308–14.

[41] See generaly AWB Simpson, *A History of the Land Law* 2nd edn (Oxford, Clarendon Press, 1986) 144–52.

[42] J Williams, *The Seisin of the Freehold* (London, H Sweet, 1878) 7. Correlatively, disseisin generated rights of entry. On seisin generally, see J Williams, *The Seisin of the Freehold* (London, H Sweet, 1878); HW Challis, *The Law of Real Property* (London, Reeves & Turner, 1885) 76; FW Maitland, 'Seisin of Chattels' (1885) 1 *LQR* 324, 'The Mystery of Seisin' (1886) 2 *LQR* 481, 'The Beatitude of Seisin' (1888) 4 *LQR* 24, 286; and Holdsworth, *HEL*, 3, 88.

[43] P & M, II, 30, noting the etymological connections between possession and seisin.

[44] There were specified sets of circumstances according to which seisin could be acquired, ie 'either by devolution from the preceding tenant or by some wrongful act which amounted to disseisin, abatement, intrusion, or discontinuance': AD Hargreaves 'Terminology and Title in Ejectment' (1940) 56 *LQR* 376, 381. See generally P & M, II, 34–40.

[45] Baker, *Introduction*, 300–1, citing *Gernes v Smith* (1499) B & M 179–80 (KB).

[46] FW Maitland, 'The Seisin of Chattels' (1885) 1 *LQR* 324, 336–7; and generally exploring the reasons for denying the assize of novel disseisin to a termor: P & M, II, 109 *et seq.*

[47] Maitland, above n 46 at 337.

as originally understood; the person seised had an estate, and had entry or his action if he was disseised.[48]

By means of an elaborate fiction, the action of ejectment came to be available to freeholders.[49] It was trite that the action was relative,[50] but the plaintiff must prove his case. He recovered on the strength of his own title, and could not rely on any defect or weakness in the title of the defendant.[51] Possession became an important index of proof. The facts of possession were taken as evidence of seisin in fee,[52] and early in the nineteenth century they were accepted as conclusive in the absence of evidence to the contrary. In *Doe v Dyeball*,[53] the plaintiff proved a lease to him and a year's possession, and was allowed to maintain ejectment against the defendant who forcibly turned him out of a room. Against the objection that the plaintiff proved no title, Lord Tenterden CJ replied 'there is ample proof; the plaintiff is in possession and you come and turn him out, you must show your title'.[54] In *Doe v Cooke*,[55] the plaintiff proved 23 years' possession under a lease prior to the last 10 years, when it was not disputed that the defendant had been in possession. The court took it for granted that the plaintiff's earlier possession established a prima facie case, and held that the defendant could only succeed on proof of a title 'of a higher description' than that of the plaintiff.[56] In the absence of this evidence the court favoured the earlier possession, and found for the plaintiff.[57]

In the middle of the nineteenth century, some judges were prepared to depart from the orthodox notion that possession was merely a mechanism for proving seisin. The language of the judgments began to suggest alternatively that possession itself was a source of freehold estates in land. In *Asher v Whitlock*,[58] one

---

[48] P & M, II, 36–7.

[49] For a lively and concise explanation see Simpson, above n 41 at 147–9. The fictions of ejectment have a nominal plaintiff, Doe, ousted by a casual ejector, Roe. Doe claimed possession under a lease, from which subsequently he was ousted by Roe. The true plaintiff in ejectment was the grantor of Doe's hypothetical lease ('the lessor of the plaintiff'). The fiction achieved the effect of allowing him to try his title against the true ejector by enjoining the latter to defend the action in Roe's stead. Roe would inform the true ejector that an action had been commenced against Roe, which action Roe planned not to defend. The idea was that, fearing the entry of judgment by default, which would see the nominal plaintiff recover his term, the defendant would be moved to defend the action. He would only be allowed to do so on the condition that he did not deny the lease to Doe and the ouster by Roe. Accordingly, the only issue to be tried was whether Doe's lessor (the true plaintiff) or the defendant had the better title to the land.

[50] 3 Bl Comm, Ch 11.

[51] *Roe d Haldane and Urry v Harvey* (1769) 4 Burr 2484, 2487 (Lord Mansfield).

[52] *Peaceable d Uncle v Watson* (1811) 4 Taunt 16, 17 (Lord Mansfield); JH Williams and WB Yates, *The Law of Ejectment* (London, Sweet and Maxwell, 1894) 227.

[53] *Doe d Hughes v Dyeball* (1829) 1 M & M 346 (KB).

[54] *Ibid.*

[55] *Doe d Harding v Cooke* (1831) 7 Bing 346 (CP).

[56] *Ibid* (Alderson J).

[57] See also *Doe d Smith and Payne v Webber* (1834) 1 Ad & E 119 (KB).

[58] *Asher and Wife v Whitlock* (1865–66) LR 1 QB 1. But see also *Doe d Pritchard v Jauncey* (1839) 8 Car & P 99; *Doe d Mary Carter v Barnard* (1849) 13 QB 945, 948.

Thomas enclosed land from the waste and built a cottage. By his will he devised the land and cottage to his wife for life or until she remarried, remainder to his only daughter 'in fee'. At the date of Thomas' death, the limitation period had not expired. The plaintiff claimed as heir at law of the daughter. The defendant was the second husband of the wife, who continued to reside in the cottage after the wife's death. On the question whether Thomas could have maintained ejectment against the defendant,[59] Cockburn CJ thought it 'too clear to admit of doubt' that he could have done so,[60] but framed the proposition solely in terms of Thomas' possession:

> 'On the simple ground that possession is good title against all but the true owner, I think the plaintiffs entitled to succeed, and that the rule should be discharged'.[61]

That this was an unorthodox approach becomes clear through the contrasting opinion of Mellor J, who was more faithful to the dogma. His Lordship agreed that Thomas acquired an estate interest in the land, but this was because 'the fact of possession is *primâ facie* evidence of seisin in fee'.[62] Similarly, in the slightly earlier case of *Doe v Barnard*,[63] Patteson J held that possession raised a presumption of seisin in fee, and that this fee would descend to an heir.[64] In argument, counsel for the plaintiff attempted to rest the necessary right on possession alone, but the proposition was roundly denied:

> the ground [of saying that an actual possessor can maintain ejectment] would not be that possession alone is sufficient in ejectment (as it is in trespass) to maintain the action; but that such possession is prima facie evidence of title, and, no other interest appearing in proof, evidence of seisin in fee.[65]

As is apparent from such diverging opinions, it seems that in the nineteenth century there was real debate about whether seisin or possession was the proper basis of a freehold estate in land, and therefore of title to sue for ejectment. Evidence of equivocation on the issue is provided by the various judgments of the Court of Appeal in *Rosenberg v Cook*.[66] The defendant had purchased certain land from a railway company via a conveyance that was ultra vires the company and void. The plaintiff contracted to purchase the land from the defendant, but later he learned of the defect in the defendant's title and brought an action to recover the deposit paid under the contract. The plaintiff argued that the contract should be set aside because the defendant had contracted to sell a freehold interest in the land whereas he held only a revocable licence to go on to the land.[67] The

---

[59] See below for discussion of the second aspect of *Asher*, ie the transmissibility of Thomas' interest.
[60] (1865–66) LR 1 QB 1, 5.
[61] *Ibid* 6.
[62] *Ibid*.
[63] *Doe d Mary Carter v Barnard* (1849) 13 QB 945, 948.
[64] *Ibid* 951.
[65] *Ibid* 953.
[66] (1881) 8 QBD 162 (CA).
[67] *Ibid* 164.

Court of Appeal rejected that claim, holding that the defendant held an original freehold estate in the land, but the language of the judgments oscillates between seisin and possession as the source of the defendant's right. Jessel MR noted first that a 'disseisor' acquired 'a title good against all the world, except against those who might be proved to have a better one',[68] but framed his conclusion in terms of possession:

> The simple fact is that the [defendant] had a possession in this case, so that a fair sale of that possession is perfectly good.[69]

Brett LJ seems to have estimated the defendant's right in terms of possession, and reasoned clearly that 'possession would give a title' before rather ambiguously adding that the title in question was 'similar to that of a disseisor or a trespasser'.[70] Cotton LJ, on the other hand, firmly attributed possession as the cause of the defendant's title, and did not at all employ the language of seisin. The defendant had 'actual possession', and a 'sufficient possession to ripen into a title under the Statute of Limitations'.[71]

The commentators too were divided. Hargreaves argued that developments in the action of ejectment had 'not altered the principles derived from the real actions'.[72] He was very clear that, as a matter of fact, a plaintiff in ejectment must prove seisin in a technical sense,[73] and whilst he accepted that proof of possession was good evidence of seisin in fee in the absence of an alternative explanation for the plaintiff's possession,[74] abridgements of this proposition (such as those found in *Asher*) that connected possession with the generation of an estate were to be rejected as hinging on 'loose terminology' attributable to 'the sentimental liberalism of the [eighteen] fifties'.[75] Holdsworth took an opposing position, considering possession the foundation of a general right, and connecting this with an emergent recognition in English law of an absolute conception of ownership like the Roman *dominium*.[76] Others explored the middle ground. The first *Williams on Real Property* to cite *Asher* was the seventeenth edition,

---

[68] *Ibid* 165.
[69] *Ibid* 165.
[70] *Ibid* 166.
[71] *Ibid* 166.
[72] Hargreaves, above n 44 at 381.
[73] Or 'possession' for recovery of a chattel interest, the contradistinction serving to emphasise the point that proof of 'possession' was not enough for a freeholder: (1940) 56 *LQR* 376, 380, 381. 'A plaintiff who relies on a right of entry derived from a former seisin must show that the possession in question was in fact seisin, and many of the cases deal with the evidence which is necessary to establish this': (1940) 56 *LQR* 376, 381.
[74] 'Mere possession is never a title. At most it is evidence of seisin. It is only when this evidence is not rebutted that possession can create a title by investing the tenant with a freehold estate derived from seisin': (1940) 56 *LQR* 376, 391.
[75] (1940) 56 *LQR* 376, 387.
[76] WS Holdsworth, 'Terminology and Title in Ejectment: a Reply' (1940) 56 *LQR* 479.

prepared by TC Williams.[77] It acknowledged the orthodoxy that possession was evidence of seisin in fee, but equally spoke of 'title' being 'founded on possession', and 'wrongful' possession as generating a fee simple estate.[78] Lightwood thought it impossible to deny that possession 'is itself the source of a right of possession',[79] but his description seemed to indicate that this right was qualitatively different from that of the person seised in fee,[80] and he continued to insist on the truth of the established doctrine.[81] As we move through the twentieth century it becomes more common to treat possession alone as the basis of title: the second edition of Cheshire is to this effect;[82] and Megarry and Wade took the view from the first.[83] But the point seems never authoritatively to have been resolved,[84] and even in the 1980s an eminent commentator regarded it as unsettled.[85] Pollock for his part seemed heavily influenced by Maitland's opinion that possession and seisin were originally synonymous,[86] and so whilst in places his essay holds closely to the dogma,[87] ultimately he conflated possession and seisin, arguing that 'seisin is the legal result of de facto possession'.[88] It seems plain that at one stage the law was much more technical than this, but Pollock thought it 'unnecessary to speak of the details of the old law',[89] and in considering *Asher*

---

[77] TC Williams (ed), *Williams' Principles of the Law of Real Property* 17th edn (London, Sweet and Maxwell, 1892) 531. As was the case in revising the 14th edition of the text on personal property, the 17th edition of *Real Property* was 'to a large extent a new book': at iii. Again the preface acknowledges a debt to Maitland: at iv.

[78] *Ibid* 531. The same passage remains in the 24th edn: RA Eastwood, *Williams' Principles of the Law of Real Property* 24th edn (London, Sweet and Maxwell, 1926) 703.

[79] JM Lightwood, *Possession of Land* (London, Stevens & Sons, 1894) 125.

[80] *Ibid*.

[81] *Ibid* 123.

[82] A 'person who enters into possession … acquires an estate in fee simple which will descend to his heirs and which becomes a possible subject of disposition': CG Cheshire, *The Modern Law of Real Property* 2nd edn (London, Butterworths, 1927) 782. The 1st edition was more faithful to the language of disseisin: CG Cheshire, *The Modern Law of Real Property* (London, Butterworths, 1925) 703.

[83] 'Possession by itself gives a good title against all the world, except someone having a better legal right to possession': RE Megarry and HWR Wade, *The Law of Real Property* (London, Steven & Sons, 1957) 891.

[84] Recently in *Pye v Graham*, the House of Lords confirmed that, for the purposes of the Limitation Act 1980, time begins to run as soon as possession is taken 'in the ordinary sense of the word', but the judgment is silent as to the technical cause of the adverse possessor's rights, as opposed to the mechanism for extinguishing the owner's rights: *J A Pye (Oxford) Ltd v Graham* [2003] 1 AC 419, 435.

[85] Simpson, above n 41 at 154. Possibly the argument is not of enormous practical significance. Even Hargreaves acknowledged that cases where the relaxed terminology was employed still reached decisions in conformity with the law derived from the real actions: (1940) 56 *LQR* 376, 387–8. The object of Hargreaves' concern was principally the textbooks, and the extent to which the looser terminology would prevent the law from there being stated accurately: (1940) 56 *LQR* 376, 388, 398; and see generally AD Hargreaves, 'Modern Real Property' (1956) 19 *MLR* 14, esp 17–19.

[86] P & W, 47.

[87] For example, P & W, 49–50, 94.

[88] P & W, 53.

[89] P & W, 94. Interested readers were referred to FW Maitland, 'The Beatitude of Seisin' (1888) 4 *LQR* 24, 286.

and the related authorities he spoke only in the language of possession and dispossession.[90]

## From Remedy to Right

Having thus consigned the difficulties of seisin, Pollock could easily speak of trover and ejectment as equivalent procedures. Accordingly we read that:

> Under the old procedure an actual possessor might sue either in trespass for the wrong to his possession, or in a form of action founded on right to possess (ejectment for land, trover for goods). In the latter alternative, his right, being derived from his own actual possession, was still not allowed to be disputed by a wrongdoer, and he had the same advantages as if he had sued in trespass. In other words, possession is equivalent to title as against a mere wrongdoer, and this is a substantive rule of law not affected by forms of action'.[91]

As we have seen, already this conclusion is the result of considerable (and potentially novel) rationalisation,[92] but having in these terms identified a general 'right to possess', Pollock switched his focus from the remedial procedures of trover and ejectment to an elucidation of the legal rights of potential claimants. His starting point was the generality of the possessor's protection. Since the cases made clear that the possessor's right was exigible against any defendant, and not vulnerable to a defence of *jus tertii*,[93] it followed that:

> possession confers more than a personal right to be protected against wrongdoers; it confers a qualified right to possess, a right in the nature of property which is valid against every one who cannot show a prior and better right.[94]

Once the law had gone so far as to recognise this right accruing to the possessor, Pollock thought that necessarily it must go further, offering protection not just to the possessor, but also to her successors and assigns.[95] The possessor would deal with her goods. She would sell them, give them, or bequeath them, and her transferees should be afforded the same degree of legal protection, because 'the general reasons of policy are at least as strong in their favour ... their case at least as meritorious'.[96] Accordingly, Pollock thought that the right arising from

---

[90] At one point in the discussion of title there is a readily apparent switch in Pollock's language from 'seisin' to 'possession': P & W, 95 *et seq*.

[91] P & W, 91.

[92] J Gordley, *Foundations of Private Law: Property, Tort, Contract, Unjust Enrichment* (Oxford, OUP, 2006) 59–61.

[93] At least not where the plaintiff had been in actual possession of the goods at the time of the conversion. Where she could not demonstrate such possession, a line of authority seemed to hold that a *jus tertii* could be set up in defence to a count of trover: *Leake v Loveday* (1842) 4 M & Gr 972; P & W, 92. More recently, the soundness of this latter principle has been questioned: see G Battersby, 'The Present Status of the *ius tertii* Principle' (1992) *Conv* 100.

[94] P & W, 93.

[95] P & W, 93.

[96] P & W, 93.

possession must also be capable of transfer,[97] and his statement of the right took on a very substantive flavour:

> As against strangers, the right founded on possession has the incidents of ownership and is transmissible according to the nature of the subject matter: we may say compendiously that *Possession is a root of title.*[98]

This statement is a good deal broader than the label 'right to possess' suggests. Pollock is here arguing that possession generates an entitlement, that it creates a property right in the fullest sense, attracting the standard advantages of ownership, and differing from ownership only insofar as it will yield to one who can prove a better (because earlier) right to possess.[99] In other words, the right founded on possession differs from ownership only by *degree* and not by quality: it has the content of ownership, but it will be vulnerable to a commensurately better right. Holmes ventured a similar, though conversely framed proposition,[100] and certainly the position finds support in the ejectment cases we have been considering. In *Asher v Whitlock*, having decided that Thomas could have maintained ejectment against the defendant, the court held further that Thomas' interest was devisable and that ejectment could be maintained by his daughter and her heirs.[101] *Doe v Jauncey* and *Doe v Barnard* also endorse the general principle that the right acquired in these circumstances is devisable even before the expiry of the relevant limitation period,[102] but it is the general structure of the law that lends the greatest support to Pollock's argument. It was well settled that in its fictional form ejectment put at issue the freehold title of the true plaintiff. To the extent that possession generated a right to proceed for ejectment, it must also generate a freehold estate if a successful suit was to have any meaning. In other words, the substantive effect of possession, ie that it created a freehold estate in land, was already clear from the procedural learning on ejectment.[103] The achievement of

---

[97] Pollock speaks in these categorical terms, but of course this sentence does not express a conceptual necessity. We might just as well confine the transferee's entitlement to protection to his own ability to prove the facts of actual possession (compare the approach in Goode, above n 7 at 33). Pollock poses this objection, but resists it because 'when possession is conceived as a substantive right in the nature of property, valid against all merely extraneous intrusion, there is no reason for not holding it to be capable of the same kinds of transfer and devolution as property itself': P & W, 22–3. Really, then, the proposition doing all the work in Pollock's theory is that possession generates a property right because it generates a right to general protection in trover or ejectment.

[98] P & W, 22. See also at 93, where the argument is unfolded, and where the phrase 'possession is a root of title' also appears. The quotation reproduced above is from Pollock's summary of the 'rules' of possession, which forms an introduction to the main part of the essay.

[99] Salmond concurs in this: Salmond, above n 4 at 190.

[100] 'But what are the rights of ownership? The are substantially the same as those incident to possession': Holmes, *CL*, 245. See also Salmond, above n 4 at 189–90; TC Williams (ed), *Principles of the Law of Personal Property* 14th edn (London, Sweet and Maxwell, 1894) 44–8; J Crossley Vaines, *Personal Property* (London, Butterworths, 1954) 39–41.

[101] (1865–66) LR 1 QB 1, 6.

[102] *Doe d Pritchard v Jauncey* (1839) 8 Car & P 99, 102 (Coleridge J, directing the jury); *Doe d Mary Carter v Barnard* (1849) 13 QB 945.

[103] Subject of course to the caveat noted above on the relation between seisin and possession.

Pollock was to rationalise the matter from the other end, considering the nature of the right in isolation from the procedure of the remedy.[104] In this sense no novel proposition of law is involved, but our focus is laid squarely on the right, and the rhetoric of freehold estates confirms rather than denies that it 'has the incidents of ownership and is transmissible according to the nature of the subject matter'.[105]

We might question whether the learning on goods lent itself as readily to this conclusion. Instructively, in his eight-page treatment of 'title by possession', Pollock referred only to one other case on goods (which was *Buckley v Gross*)[106] for the proposition (discussed below) that a right generated by possession could not avail to the possessor once it had been lawfully divested.[107] It is clear that the majority of his argument hinged on the land law. It is possible that the notion of special property, drawn from the earlier trover cases, did not lend itself to correlativity with a freehold estate in land, though Holmes probably would have disputed this.[108] Nevertheless, as far as goods are concerned, the relative lack of cited decisions gives Pollock's account the appearance of novelty, and it would not be unreasonable to conclude that the ejectment cases were the greater influence on his substantive account of the right arising by possession.[109]

Seeming to operate generally against Pollock's conclusions on the rights of possessors is the tendency of the courts, both in ejectment and trover, to regard their conclusions in favour of successful plaintiffs as presumptions. In *Jeffries*, Lord Campbell CJ spoke of 'a presumption of law ... that the person who has possession has the property',[110] and similar dicta are found in the ejectment cases.[111] Understood literally, a *presumption* that a possessor had title need not involve any commitment to the nature of the rights actually held by the possessor. In theory we could affirm that 'as against' a particular defendant a particular possessor could be regarded as having property (for the sake of dispute resolution), but at the same time assert that in reality he had no rights.[112] The better view, however, is that these cases do not depend on presumptions.[113] As has been suggested recently, presumptions 'properly-so-called are methods of proof of facts, and no fact is here in issue'.[114] In the ejectment cases considered above,

---

[104] We might readily attribute such rationalisation to some sense of intellectual freedom on the part of jurists recently freed from the constraints of the forms of action. For a general view on the legal technique of reasoning from remedy to right, see P & M, II, 31, suggesting that the pattern is 'spiral' rather than circular.

[105] P & W, 22, 93. As Coke commented, 'fee ... legally signifieth inheritance ... and simple is added for that it is descendible to his heires generally': 1 Co Inst, Ch 1, 1.

[106] (1863) 3 B & S 566.

[107] P & W, 99–100.

[108] Holmes, *CL*, 242–3, noted above.

[109] And see the opinion of Parke B in *Elliott v Kemp*, tending to suggest that the position in relation to land was clarified earlier than in relation to goods: (1840) 7 M & W 306, 312.

[110] (1856) 5 E & B 802, 806.

[111] For example: *Doe d Mary Carter v Barnard* (1849) 13 QB 945, 951, 953 (Patteson J).

[112] This seems to be the approach of RS Wright in his part of the essay: P & W, 149.

[113] Pollock, above n 15 at 300.

[114] *EPL*, 4.418.

and very clearly in *Jeffries*, the plaintiff had actually proven possession before the court.[115] Accordingly, the question in the cases concerned the legal inference to be drawn from facts *already proven* by evidence. In these circumstances, it is not technically possible for a claimant to benefit from any presumption,[116] and it seems analytically more accurate to regard possession as the source of a definite legal relation.

Whilst the idea that possession generates a relatively good property right had a heavy influence on later commentators,[117] it is worth noting that the finding cases themselves contain little by way of express comment on the issue; indeed the language of the judgments is entirely equivocal. Although the most recent are framed in terms of the *rights* of the parties, they disclose no analysis of the nature of those rights. In truth, the question has been avoided in reliance on *Armory v Delamirie* or, as in Lord Russell CJ's pivotal judgment in *Sharman*, on some general rehearsal of Pollock's view. Thus in *Parker*, despite a conviction that there was no decision binding on the Court of Appeal, and the accordingly portentous rehearsal of the court's 'duty to extend and adapt the common law in the light of established principles and the current needs of the community',[118] Donaldson LJ did little more than reproduce the 250-year-old judgment in *Armory*:

> a finder of a chattel, whilst not acquiring any absolute property or ownership in the chattel, acquires a right to keep it against all but the true owner or those in a position to claim through the true owner or one who can assert a prior right to keep the chattel which was subsisting at the time when the finder took the chattel into his care and control.[119]

Of course, this dictum was a qualification of *Armory*. It made plain that there were right-holders other than the 'true owner' to whom the finder's rights would yield. But (a) this was not a new qualification;[120] and (b) the dictum wholly failed to discuss or answer the interesting question about the nature of this 'right to keep'. We are told no more about the right in *Parker*. We might have expected a Court of Appeal freed from the constraints of the forms of action, and exercising its duty to adapt common law authorities to modern life, to give more thought to the substance of the right it was recognising. As it is, insofar as they employ the language

---

[115] Indeed, on *Asher*, it was exactly that the plaintiff had proved *possession* rather than seisin which was the dominant controversy: see Lightwood, above n 79 at 111, 124.

[116] *EPL*, 4.418. Compare D Fox, 'Relativity of Title in Law and at Equity' (2006) *CLJ* 330, 331, which asserts, with reference to the nineteenth century authorities, that an adverse possessor of land benefits from an 'evidential presumption' that she holds under a fee simple estate.

[117] TC Williams (ed), *Williams' Principles of the Law of Real Property* 17th edn (London, Sweet and Maxwell, 1892) 531; Lightwood, above n 79 at 1; TC Williams (ed), *Principles of the Law of Personal Property* 14th edn (London, Sweet and Maxwell, 1894) 44–5; Cheshire, above n 82 at 782; Megarry and Wade, above n 83 at 891; AM Honoré, 'Ownership' in AG Guest (ed), *Oxford Essays in Jurisprudence* (Oxford, OUP, 1961) 140; AP Bell, *Modern Law of Personal Property in England and Ireland* (London, Butterworths, 1989) 76–82; S Gleeson, *Personal Property Law* (London, FT Law & Tax, 1997) 54; Goode, above n 7 at 31.

[118] [1982] QB 1004, 1008.

[119] *Ibid* 1017.

[120] It was identified in similar terms by the Manitoba Court of Appeal in *Bird v Fort Frances*.

of rights, the judgments in *Parker* and the other cases remain heavily dependent on the work of Pollock, though since *Sharman* they are at least consistent with Pollock's general view, ie that a finder of goods, because of her possession, acquires a general property right to the object of her find, which right attracts the standard advantages of ownership and will avail against all those incapable of proving a better, because earlier, right.

Some questions must remain as to the authoritative basis of Pollock's thesis. It is entirely clear that the core of the argument was an assimilation of trover and ejectment, a deep conviction that since each depended solely on proof of possession each raised a right to possess protected to the full extent of the law. This proposition could equally well be regarded as heresy or genius rationalisation. Certainly, insofar as it related to goods it depended to some extent on a resolution of the old cases on special property; on ejectment, it depended on an outright conflation of possession and seisin. Accordingly it would seem at least to be arguable (a) that trover and ejectment were not technically as synonymous as Pollock's major premise would suggest; and (b) that the role of possession in each was not as clear as the premise would suggest. We have tried to show that the general trend of the cases does lend some support to Pollock's view, but much further research is needed in this area. For now, and as we seek later to show that English law as currently understood produces a satisfactory law of finders, it will be enough to have established that our finding cases depend on Pollock's understanding of possession, and Pollock thought that possessors acquired relatively good property rights in the things they possessed. To this extent, that most pervasive idea in our law of finds, ie that a finder does acquire some property in the object of her find, continues to depend for its validity on the old learning of the forms of action, notwithstanding their long abolition from the common law.

# The Extent of the Finder's Right

Accepting that by possession a finder acquires a property right in her find, a second question arises as to the extent of that right. It is plain that for so long as she remains in actual possession of a chattel, a finder will be able to resist any wrongful interference with it. Much more difficult is the question whether a finder's rights outlive the facts of possession. Would these rights survive a subsequent loss of the chattel? Can a finder sue for a subsequent conversion when she is not also the possessor at the time of that conversion? Does possession 'confer a right to possession which outlives possession itself?'[121]

---

[121] NE Palmer, 'Bad Apples and Blighted Windfalls: Finding, Bailment and the Fruits of Crime' in F Meisel and P Cook (eds), *Property and Protection: Essays in Honour of Brian Harvey* (Oxford, Hart Publishing, 2000) 1, 10; and generally Palmer, *Bailment*, 1422–31.

At the extreme end of a spectrum of negative answers to this question is the opinion of Winfield, who seems to hold that a finder cannot sue for conversion unless she was actually in possession of the goods at the time of the alleged conversion.[122] The immediate difficulty for this opinion is that the decided cases are against it. Indeed, in almost all the cases where a finder successfully has asserted a right in respect of some conversion of goods, the finder has been out of the possession at the time of the conversion. In *Armory v Delamirie*, the finder had passed the ring to the goldsmith's apprentice, who passed it in turn to his master, after which the conversion occurred. In *Bridges v Hawkesworth* the notes were likewise surrendered to the shop owner, who kept them safely and advertised their loss. The finder had been out of actual possession for three years before he asserted his right against the defendant. *Parker* follows more or less the same course, and yet a clearer example is *Hannah v Peel*. There, the plaintiff handed his discovered brooch to the police. After two years the police returned it to the defendant owner of the premises. He sold it to a firm of jewellers, and they resold it at a profit. The brooch was gone, and it was clear that the plaintiff had not been in actual possession of it at the time of the defendant's conversion. Yet Birkett J allowed the plaintiff to sue on the strength of the right he acquired by finding,[123] and awarded damages to the plaintiff representing the price obtained by the defendant as a result of his unlawful sale.[124]

Prima facie, then, the cases suggest that a finder can sue for conversions committed when she is not in actual possession of the goods. A fortiori, she must have a right which outlives the facts of possession. However, at least three arguments exist to counter this first impression. They relate to (i) the estoppel which at common law prevents a bailee from denying the title of his bailor; (ii) the decision in *Buckley v Gross*; and (iii) the effect of a subsequent conversion on the rights acquired in virtue of possession. We will deal with each of these in turn, but it suffices now to say that none will be thought effective to deny that the right arising from possession can survive the loss of possession. On the contrary, each serves to confirm that the finder acquires a general property right in respect of the goods in question.

## The Estoppel Argument

Atiyah explained *Armory v Delamirie* on the basis of a bailment between plaintiff and defendant, and specifically on the common law rule that a bailee is estopped from denying the title of his bailor.[125] Palmer follows suit, using the existence of this rule to argue generally against the recognition of any right in the finder

---

[122] PH Winfield, *A Textbook on the Law of Tort* (London, Sweet and Maxwell, 1937) 397.

[123] [1945] 1 KB 509, 521.

[124] That is to say, £66. The London jewellers resold the brooch for £88 one month after buying it from the defendant: [1945] 1 KB 509, 510.

[125] PS Atiyah, 'A Re-Examination of the Jus Tertii in Conversion' (1955) 18 *MLR* 97, 106.

which outlives the facts of her possession.[126] The 'bailee's estoppel' has long been recognised at common law,[127] and is said to be based on considerations of commercial necessity.[128] Essentially, it admits a doubt about the bailor's title, but denies to the bailee the ability of impugning that title by raising a plea of *jus tertii* in defence. As such, it is accepted that the estoppel applies even where the bailment is made without any colour of title, as where the bailor is a thief.[129] However, the view taken here is that the estoppel argument is not properly applied to the resolution of finding disputes.

Despite the views of Palmer and Atiyah, there are at least three reasons why we should dispute the application of the bailee's estoppel argument to finding disputes. The first is quite simply that it is a hindrance to analysis. Inasmuch as it stops a defendant from impugning the title of his bailor, it also stops commentators from facing directly the question as to the extent of the right arising from the facts of possession. When this is combined with the language of 'presumption' discussed above, the result is that a large part of the law of possessory title collapses into empty rhetoric. When a finder is in actual possession of found goods at the time of their conversion, she recovers on the strength of her presumptive title; when she is out of possession, she can recover from any transferee on the basis of the bailee's estoppel at common law. No decision is necessary as to whether her right outlives the facts of possession. The question is squarely avoided. Rather than offering a cogent and doctrinally cohesive account of this fundamental component of our personal property law, we posit a pragmatic solution that serves only to obscure its true extent. This is not satisfactory. It is also a fatal flaw in an argument such as Palmer's which attempts to deny the general extent of possessory title by relying on the existence of the estoppel. Even if judges actually have applied the estoppel in resolution of finding disputes, that takes us nowhere. At most it is a partial denial of the assertion that a finder's rights outlive her possession. We know that the right need not have done so in a given case: the estoppel would have allowed the finder to recover from her bailee *even if* she had *no continuing title*. But we do not know the converse, ie that the finder's rights must not outlive her possession. That question is simply avoided, and nothing close to clear doctrinal analysis is achieved.

Secondly, this estoppel has not been invoked in the resolution of any case. Whilst it might offer an explanation of cases such as *Armory, Bridges* and *Parker*, where on the facts there is an immediate transfer of possession from finder to defendant (and so clearly, to that extent, a bailment), the estoppel argument is

---

[126] 'It is difficult to envisage any right, other than one arising from his possession, which a finder can ever enjoy in lost goods; or how any remedy can consequently lie once that possession has been lost': Palmer, *Bailment*, 1426.

[127] See *Biddle v Bond* (1865) 6 B & S 225, and the cases listed there.

[128] *Cheesman v Exall* (1851) 6 Ex 341, 346 (Martin B).

[129] *Biddle v Bond* (1865) 6 B & S 225; Palmer, *Bailment*, 267.

not the avowed basis of any of them. Palmer concedes this.[130] We have seen that in *Armory*, the boy's ability to sue was an incremental extension of the availability of trover, made in a legal climate dominated by rigid forms of action; and even allowing for this, Pratt CJ's conclusion was positively that the boy had 'property' in the jewel, not that the defendant was estopped from denying any right that he *might* have. In *Bridges*, Patteson J purported to confirm the existence of this general right in finders, and could not find any title in the defendant to oust it, having reasoned by analogy to the common law duties of innkeepers. In *Parker*, Donaldson LJ thought that the claimant 'prima facie ... had a full finder's rights'.[131] The defendant board could 'not assert any title to the bracelet based upon the rights of an occupier', and accordingly could not resist Parker's claim.[132] These cases are expressly about the existence of relatively better legal rights in the finder at the time of the defendant's conversion. They are not about estoppels, which would entail precisely the opposite conclusion, ie an admission of doubt about the finder's right, but a refusal to allow the defendant to impugn it with evidence of a better right elsewhere.

The proponent of the estoppel view does receive a little more help from *Bird v Fort Frances*,[133] where the police were described as bailees of a quantity of banknotes found by a young boy, and were held to owe an obligation to return them.[134] But even this case is difficult. The police were not the immediate transferees from the boy, who had deposited the monies with his mother after the finding. The police took the money without lawful authority from the custody of the mother. In the circumstances, the court thought that the best construction of that transaction was that the mother voluntarily had surrendered the monies to the police. Accordingly they were her bailees, and owed an obligation to return the goods. The boy's ability to sue on these facts was premised on an argument which, again, confirms rather than denies that he had a right to the banknotes which survived the loss of their possession to his mother. Citing a lengthy passage to the same effect from Holmes, McRuer CJHC concluded that:

> The mere fact that the plaintiff's possession may have been interrupted does not necessarily deprive him of the right to maintain an action against someone who wrongfully dispossesses his successor in possession.[135]

Clearly this contemplates that a finder's right has the potential to outlive the facts of her possession, at least to the extent that she can restrain wrongful

---

[130] '[Estoppel] analysis might ... have been *(but was not)* applied in *Parker* ..., *Bridges* ..., [and] *Armory*': NE Palmer, 'Bad Apples and Blighted Windfalls: Finding, Bailment and the Fruits of Crime' in F Meisel & P Cook (eds), *Property and Protection: Essays in Honour of Brian Harvey* (Oxford, Hart Publishing, 2000) 1, 12 (emphasis added).

[131] [1982] 1 QB 1004, 1018.

[132] *Ibid* 1018.

[133] [1949] 2 DLR 791.

[134] *Ibid* 800.

[135] *Ibid* 800.

interference with the actual possession of her own transferees.[136] On this basis, *Bird* is at best equivocal authority for the view that these cases can be resolved according to an estoppel argument. Indeed, so far as it appears, the only decision in which the bailee's estoppel has been invoked expressly is that of Blayney J at first instance in *Webb v Ireland*.[137] The Irish Supreme Court overturned the decision on that point by allowing the state a defence of title paramount. On the majority view, the state was not estopped from denying the title of the plaintiff finders to the Derrynaflan Hoard,[138] because it had taken a transfer of the hoard from the defendants,[139] and the defendants had a better title than the plaintiffs.[140] On this analysis, the decision in *Webb* entails no answer to any question on the extent of the finders' rights, and no further guidance is to be gleaned from this case on this issue. Even if the plaintiffs' rights did outlast loss of possession, they would not oust the superior claim of the state.

A third reason for discounting the estoppel argument, is that there are (admittedly only a few) cases where there is no bailment on the facts,[141] yet an out of possession finder has been able to recover the value of the found goods. One

---

[136] Note that the court in *Bird* also considered the possibility of overcoming objections based on the boy's loss of possession by joining his mother as a party to the action. This had not been argued before the court, and accordingly was 'dismissed from further consideration': [1949] 2 DLR 791, 800. If the point had been taken, and the mother joined, the judgment would have been deprived of a usefully clear statement on the extent of the boy's possessory rights.

[137] [1988] ILRM 565, 571, relying on *Roger, Sons & Co v Lambert & Co* [1891] 1 QB 318, and thus on the opinion of Blackburn J in *Biddle v Bond* (1865) 6 B & S 225, which was there cited. Note, however, in the paragraph immediately following citation of *Roger*, Blayney J opined: 'the duty to restore the hoard arose when [the plaintiffs' solicitors wrote] requesting the return of the hoard. When the request was made, the plaintiffs had the right to immediate possession of the hoard'. This analysis renders the case a straightforward action in detinue, and the plaintiffs' success does not depend on the existence of any estoppel. Hence, even here, there exists a doubt about whether the estoppel argument is soundly applied to finding cases.

[138] 'One of the most significant discoveries ever made of Christian art', the hoard consisted of a ninth century chalice, and various other silver and bronze artefacts: [1988] ILRM 565, 583; JM Kelly, 'Hidden Treasure and the Constitution' (1988) 10 *Dublin University Law Journal* 5.

[139] [1988] ILRM 565, 586–8 per Finlay CJ (Henchy and Griffith JJ concurring). The remaining judges dissented on this point, agreeing with Blayney J that the estoppel could be allowed on the facts: [1988] ILRM 565, 599 (Walsh J), 606 (McCarthy J).

[140] Because they were the owners of the land on which the hoard was found: [1988] ILRM 565, 590. Walsh and McCarthy JJ seemed to leave open the question whether the state had acquired from the landowners any title paramount to that of the plaintiff finders, each being more or less unpersuaded of the circumstances in which landowners would acquire a possessory interest in goods found on or in their land: [1988] ILRM 565, 600, 607. They were prepared to find for the state, however, on the basis of its inherent claim to 'all objects forming part of the national heritage', and to that extent agreed that the state's appeal should be allowed: [1988] ILRM 565, 604 (Walsh J); also 609 (McCarthy J).

[141] Palmer says that *Deaderick v Oulds*, the case which is the subject of this paragraph, is capable of explanation on bailment grounds 'only if one adopts a highly synthetic and possibly circular notion of bailment': 'Bad Apples and Blighted Windfalls: Finding, Bailment and the Fruits of Crime' in F Meisel and P Cook (eds), *Property and Protection: Essays in Honour of Brian Harvey* (Oxford, Hart Publishing, 2000) 1, 20.

example is *Deaderick v Oulds*.[142] There, the servants of the defendant found certain walnut logs entangled in a drift off the Nolichucky River in Washington County, Tennessee. The servants took possession of these logs for the defendant, believing them to be logs previously lost by him, though there was no conclusive evidence that this was the case.[143] They cast them again on the river, intending that they be carried by the tides to a boom made by the defendant further downstream. Eventually one of the logs was washed up on the lands of the plaintiff. Presumably after some enquiry, the plaintiff ordered the defendant not to remove the log from his land. The defendant then seized the log as his own, but the plaintiff replevied it, demanding that the defendant prove his title, and suspecting that it belonged to one Wilson, who had also lost logs on the river. The Supreme Court of Tennessee found for the defendant, denying the plaintiff's ability to replevy the log. Giving judgment, Lurton J held that the defendant's servants had taken possession of the log when they found it in the drift, and:

> This right of possession was not lost by the log subsequently drifting upon the land of the plaintiff, and the defendant had a right to take and hold this log against all but the true owner, or one having a superior right of possession.[144]

It is difficult to imagine a case where goods claimed could more clearly be out of a finder's actual possession at the time of subsequent wrongful interference. The possessed log had been cast on a river, the currents of which had washed it up on land never intended as its destination. This was physical control absolutely relinquished, with no power or possibility of that control being retaken unless the log should eventually be caught in the defendant's boom.[145] Only the most strained constructive possession could regard the defendant's control as continuing in these circumstances, and in any event the judgment is clear. Notwithstanding the absolute loss of the physical power of dealing with the log, notwithstanding that it was irretrievably out of the defendant's actual possession, the court held that the defendant's possessory rights continued, and could not be displaced unless the plaintiff could show a better right.[146]

*Clark v Maloney*[147] was decided on facts similar to *Deaderick*. The plaintiff found logs floating on water and moored them. They broke free, and were later found and taken by the defendant, who refused to redeliver them to the plaintiff. Despite the loss of his actual possession, the plaintiff first finder could maintain trover against the defendant second finder. Holmes referred to the facts of this

---

[142] (1887) 5 SW 487 (Supreme Court of Tennessee). See also *McFadyen v Wineti* (1909) 11 GLR 345 (Supreme Court of New Zealand); *Russell v Wilson* (1923) 33 CLR 538 (High Court of Australia).

[143] (1887) 5 SW 487, 488.

[144] *Ibid*.

[145] Indeed, before any of the reclaimed logs had reached the boom, it had given way, 'and the defendant was obliged to rely on catching his logs upon the banks of the stream and islands below the broken boom': *ibid* 487.

[146] *Ibid* 489.

[147] (1840) 3 Harr (Del) 68.

case in his lecture on possession, and abstracted the ruling to a general principle about the durability of possessory rights.[148] Once it had been accepted that the facts of possession were capable of generating a legal right to goods, there was no need further to suppose that those facts must continue in order for the legal right to persist. Although we accept that consideration and promise are necessary elements in the creation of a contact, we do not say that they must continue to exist until performance if a right of action on the contract is to be sustained.[149] Neither should we insist on continuing intention and control as a ground of the right arising on possession. Thus, there is no reason in principle to suggest that a possessory right should end when possession is lost.

All of this tends to suggest that the estoppel argument should not be advanced in explanation of the finding cases. At best it is an ex post facto rationalisation, not to be found within the ratio of any case. At worst, it risks obscuring the true extent of rights arising from possession, which, following the view of Holmes, have at least the potential to outlive the facts which generate them. In addition we should note a recent view that the bailee's estoppel is no longer available at common law, having been substantially abrogated by section 8 of the Torts (Interference with Goods) Act 1977.[150] If this is correct, it will force courts and commentators much more expressly to inquire after the nature of possessory rights whenever a bailment is made with doubtful title. However, the view may go too far. It is generally thought that the common law on *jus tertii* defences has survived the implementation of the 1977 provisions, at least where the common law defence is not inconsistent with the operation of the statute.[151] The section 8 defence is premised on the ability of the parties to an action to identify a named third party who can be joined as a defendant having a better right to the subject matter of the dispute.[152] Only rarely will this be a possibility in modern finding disputes, where generally the identity of the loser is unknown. At least we can say that the section 8 provisions did not help the protagonists in *Parker* or *Waverly*, nor would they have aided the defendants in *Armory*, *Bridges* or *Hannah*. Accordingly it seems to be accepted that the common law *jus tertii* provisions are still operative in finding cases, and to this extent, and subject to the views expressed above, we can expect that the bailee's estoppel would still be available to a court considering a finding dispute. But a court choosing to avail of the argument would be on shaky ground. The estoppel argument is a manifest hindrance to thorough analysis of possessory rights, and seems never to have been invoked successfully as the ratio of any decided finding dispute.

---

[148] Holmes, *CL*, 236.

[149] *Ibid*.

[150] GS McBain, 'Modernising and Codifying the Law of Bailment' (2008) *Journal of Business Law* 1, 50; G McMeel, 'The Redundancy of Bailment' [2003] *LMCLQ* 169, 180–1.

[151] Palmer, *Bailment*, 285.

[152] Section 8(1); CPR Pt 19, R 5A. See *Clerk and Lindsell on Torts*, 17–78.

## Cases of Divested Rights

Any legal recognition that the facts of possession are capable of generating a right to goods which outlives the cessation of possession entails a further, correlative proposition: when that right has been divested lawfully, the possessor's title is at an end, and he no longer has grounds to sue. Obviously, a finder who sells or gives away her interest in found goods cannot thereafter complain of wrongful interferences with them. But after this fashion too is the decision in *Buckley v Gross*,[153] which unless properly understood, has the effect of indicating that rights resultant from possession cannot outlast possession. Some tallow had melted following a severe fire at warehouses below London Bridge. Some of it was collected by a stranger, and sold to the plaintiff. Shortly thereafter the plaintiff was arrested, and charged with possession of tallow supposed to have been stolen or unlawfully obtained. The charge was dismissed, but the magistrate ordered that the tallow be detained pursuant to certain powers contained in the Metropolitan Police Act 1839. Later, it was sold to the defendants at the direction of the Police Commissioner, in exercise of similar powers. The plaintiff sued the defendants for conversion. At trial, Blackburn J found for the defendants, but with leave reserved to move to enter a verdict for the plaintiff if an appeal found that the plaintiff had sufficient property to maintain the action.[154] The court discharged the rule, being very clearly of the opinion that there was no property in the plaintiff because he had no possession.[155] But the reason for this was not the factual loss of actual possession, but rather that such rights as the plaintiff had enjoyed in the tallow had been divested by the order of sale pursuant to the powers in the Metropolitan Police Act. The plaintiff 'who had nothing but bare naked possession (which would have been sufficient against a wrongdoer) had it taken out of him by virtue of this enactment'.[156] Therefore, whilst it would not be an inaccurate summation of the ratio of *Buckley* to say that the plaintiff 'had no property at the time of the conversion' because his 'possession was gone',[157] this loss of possession is attributable to statutory divesting, rather than the cessation of possessory facts.

*Buckley* is complicated by evidence of some doubt on the nature of the title acquired by the defendants. Cockburn CJ seemed inclined to the view that theirs was an original title made 'under the authority of justice',[158] though presumably not a title which would withstand suit from the owner of the tallow. The appellate judgment of Blackburn J certainly seems to hold that the owner's right to the tallow survives, but he thought that the defendants' title was derived from the police; that the police held as bailees of the owner ('their possession was the possession of

---

[153] (1863) 3 B & S 566.
[154] *Ibid* 568.
[155] *Ibid* 572, 573, 576.
[156] *Ibid* 572 (Cockburn CJ).
[157] *Ibid* 573 (Crompton J).
[158] *Ibid* 571.

the true owner'); and that accordingly the defendants were amenable to suit from the owner, but not from the plaintiff. Whatever the true nature of the defendants' title, however, it is clear for our purposes that *Buckley* does not offer any reason to suppose that the right resultant from possession ends when the facts of possession end.

## The Effect of a Subsequent Conversion

*Buckley v Gross* is interesting because the claimant sued someone not immediate to him in the chain of possessors: the police had taken the tallow from the plaintiff, and later sold it to the defendant.[159] Of course, on the facts of the case, there is no possibility that the plaintiff could have maintained an action against the defendant (any rights of the plaintiff in respect of the tallow had been divested in the exercise of the statutory powers),[160] but an interesting question arises as to the general ability of a possessor to maintain this kind of claim. Suppose a finder (P2) takes possession of a chattel. Subsequently it is converted by P3, and later still it comes to the hands of P4. It is beyond doubt that P2 can maintain an action against P3, but can P2 sue P4 to recover the value of the goods? There is little or no direct authority on this question,[161] but recently David Fox has argued that, in general, the answer should be negative:

> once a person with a purely possessory title to a chattel has been dispossessed, he loses his title to it. He acquires in substitution a purely personal right of action in trespass or conversion against the person who wrongfully dispossessed him.[162]

If this is right, it imposes an obvious limit on the extent of a possessor's rights: they are 'vulnerable to extinction'[163] by the wrongful act of a third party. But before considering the merits of this argument, we ought to reject any connection between a possessor's loss of title and *dispossession*. Where land is concerned, it is enough to generate a right of action to recover land that possession is taken by someone else,[164] but the same is not true of goods. As we have seen, by taking possession of goods, P3 does not necessarily commit a conversion,[165] or a trespass,[166] and so there does not necessarily occur any event sufficient to generate a concomitant right of action in P2. If the general contention of Fox's argument is right, it

[159] *Ibid* 567.
[160] *Ibid* 572; and see generally above.
[161] In most cases where a finder has sued successfully for conversion, the defendant has been an immediately subsequent wrongdoer, as was the case in *Armory*, *Bridges* and *Parker*. Possibly an exception is *Hannah v Peel*, where the finder sued the owner of the premises on which he had found the brooch. The police had delivered the brooch to the defendant, and it would not be impossible to construe this delivery as a conversion.
[162] D Fox, 'Relativity of Title in Law and at Equity' (2006) *CLJ* 330, 344.
[163] *Ibid*.
[164] *J A Pye (Oxford) Ltd v Graham* [2003] 1 AC 419, 435.
[165] See Chapter 4.
[166] See Chapter 1.

would be much more correct to say that *on subsequent wrongful interference with goods*, P2 loses her title and acquires in substitution a purely personal right of action against the wrongdoer, P3. This is a small point, but it makes plain that any loss of the possessor's rights is not attributable merely to the cessation of the possessory facts which created those rights, and so we avoid the same mischief threatened by misinterpretations of the dicta in *Buckley* above.

The general contention that rights arising from possession are lost on commission of a subsequent wrong is supported by orthodox accounts of adverse possession of land prior to the reforms of the nineteenth century.[167] Originally the perception was that a proprietor of land lost his fee simple estate when he was disseised, acquiring in substitution a right of entry on the land,[168] which right of entry might in turn be 'tolled',[169] leaving the disseised with a right of action available through the cumbersome procedures of the old real actions.[170] There could only ever be one fee simple estate in respect of given land, and that estate was necessarily vested in the person seised of the land for the time being. In the nineteenth century, reforms of the law of real property made it possible for a dispossessed proprietor to alienate his right of entry inter vivos[171] or by will;[172] and it also became possible to convey an estate in land without formally allowing the transferee to enter on the land.[173] It was plausible to treat the dispossessed proprietor as if he had a continuing estate in the land: he still had a readily marketable interest. Accordingly, the orthodox construction ceased to be persuasive, and it is sensible to regard the fee simple of the proprietor as subsisting even though adverse possession has been taken by another.[174] It is just possible that this newer theory is not so readily applicable to goods,[175] but neither is the orthodox theory

---

[167] Fox, above n 162 at 349.

[168] FW Maitland, 'The Mystery of Seisin' (1886) 2 *LQR* 481, 482.

[169] For example, following a transfer made by the adverse possessor, and non-claim for a year and a day: Co Litt 245 b. See generally Simpson, above n 41 at 41–3.

[170] Most of the real actions were abolished by the Real Property Limitation Act 1833. This Act also abolished the rules on tolling rights of entry, and provided a general limitation period of 20 years for the exercise of rights of entry. See generally Simpson, above n 41 at 152–3.

[171] Real Property Act 1845, s 6.

[172] Wills Act 1837, s 3.

[173] Real Property Act 1845, s 2, allowed an estate in land to be conveyed by deed of grant as opposed to 'livery of seisin'. In 1925, livery of seisin was altogether abolished: Law of Property Act 1925, s 51.

[174] From the inception of her possession, the adverse possessor has her own fee simple estate, which exists contemporaneously with, but ranks subordinately to, the estate of the proprietor. The latest edition of Megarry and Wade notes that 'there is no absurdity in speaking of two or more adverse estates in the land, for their validity is relative': C Harpum, S Bridge and M Dixon (eds), *Megarry and Wade's The Law of Real Property* 7th edn (London, Sweet and Maxwell, 2008) 4-009. Contrast N Curwen, 'The Squatter's Interest at Common Law' (2000) *Conv* 528, esp 534–5, arguing generally that nothing in the Limitation Acts has served to alter the classical position that there can only be one fee simple estate, necessarily vested in the person seised of the land.

[175] Fox notes that whilst rights in action in respect of goods generally have been considered assignable since the Judicature Act 1875, 'the rules prohibiting the maintenance of actions may nonetheless prevent the assignment of causes of action in tort'. For his own part, Fox doubts whether any useful policy objective is served by this proposition where the tort in question relates to property rather than persons: Fox, above n 162 at 351.

analogously applied to personal property. Generally, we do not assume that when goods are converted an owner out of possession loses his ownership interest, retaining only a cause of action against the immediate wrongdoer. This much is clear from Fox's own analysis, where he contrasts the position of a claimant relying on a right resultant from possession with that of the 'owner with an indefeasible title, P1'.[176] Whereas P2 might maintain his cause of action only against P3, having no claim against the later wrongdoer P4, 'P1 could recover damages from P3 for the conversion of a chattel, even though P3 did not wrongfully dispossess P1'.[177] If the analogy with old land law is to have any force, it would need to be true that P1 lost his ownership interest on the occurrence of a subsequent wrong, acquiring in substitution a right of action against the wrongdoer. That this is not so shows that the modern law of personal property cannot be aligned to the old law of real property, and affirms that there is no necessary conceptual connection between existing possession and subsisting rights.

Although it is framed in terms of the extent of the right resulting from possession, Fox's position really articulates a perceived difference in the content of the rights of 'owners' and 'possessors'. Driving this perception of difference is the idea that possession raises only a *presumption* that the possessor is owner.[178] Fox attributes P1's ability to maintain a claim against P3 to the 'indefeasible title' of P1: P1 'has a right to possession which is enforceable against third parties generally'.[179] By contrast, P2 has no such generally enforceable right. She can maintain a claim against P3,[180] because in an action against P3 the facts of her possession justify an inference that she was owner of the goods in question at the time of the alleged interference; but on the same logic, she cannot maintain a claim against P4, because at the time of P4's conversion there are no facts to justify an inference that she is owner.[181] Thus, P1 has a general property right in respect of the goods in question; P2 has only a right to maintain proceedings against an immediate wrongdoer, which right of action is derived from a presumption operating against the defendant. However, as we noted above, the better view of the decided cases is that the possessor's claim never depends for its success on a presumption.[182] Presumptions are methods of proof of facts. In a successful case against P3, the facts of P2's possession have been proven, and the true question is as to the legal significance of these facts *given that they have been proven*.[183] The

---

[176] *Ibid* 348.

[177] *Ibid*.

[178] *Ibid* 340, 345–6.

[179] *Ibid* 348.

[180] Of course, the identity of P3 is irrelevant, and in this sense on Fox's analysis it looks like P2 has a generally exigible right. P2 can maintain her action against anyone who happens to be the immediately subsequent wrongdoer, but this is obviously not the same as holding that she can enforce her right against anyone who comes later in time to the goods in question.

[181] Fox, above n 162 at 345–6.

[182] Pollock, above n 15 at 300; see above.

[183] *EPL*, 4.418.

answer, as Holmes and Pollock gave it, is that the facts of possession generate a property right in respect of the goods possessed.[184] Once we have conceived of possession as a mechanism for generating (as opposed to presuming the existence of) a right, there is no reason to deny that P2 might assert her previously generated right against P4, *unless* (i) *generally* there is reason to hold that title to goods never withstands a subsequent conversion, property rights in every case being substituted for a personal right of action against the wrongdoer; or (ii) *specifically* there is some policy reason to deny P2 the same measure of legal protection afforded to P1. Since we continue to suppose that someone in the position of P1 might maintain a claim against every subsequent wrongdoer, we ought to reject the first of these possibilities. On the second, Fox does suggest that 'the policy of protecting possession only goes so far as to give P2 a right of action in trespass or conversion against P3',[185] but his only reason is again that the presumption of title in P2 would not avail against P4. The other weakness he supposes in P2's position result from the premise that she has no continuing title,[186] and do not suggest any wider policy decision to treat her as having some qualitatively different interest in the goods. Moreover, at least so far as finders are concerned, the policy arguments probably run in the other direction. In Chapter 7 we will see that finders have a role to play in the process of reuniting lost goods with their loser. Given this strategic position, it would make little sense to defeat the rights of the finder on the occurrence of a subsequent wrong.[187]

# Finders as (Relative) Owners

Appreciating that possession need not continue for the resultant right to subsist helps us to be very precise about the legal significance of possession in finding scenarios, and in other cases where a claimant can have no other basis for her claim than the facts of control and intention. These facts are relevant to acquisition. In modern language they are causative events.[188] Their significance is precisely that, when demonstrably present, they result in the acquisition of a property right in respect of the goods in question. But without more, that the facts of possession cause the possessor to acquire a legal right in respect of the goods tells us nothing about the content of the right acquired. That question can only be answered by evaluating the substance of the possessor's position under the law. Pollock

---

[184] Holmes, *CL*, 236; P & W, 22, 93.

[185] *Ibid* 345.

[186] So, whilst noting correctly that without physical possession P2 might make a gift of her interest in the goods only by deed (*Irons v Smallpiece* (1819) 2 B & Ald 551, 552), Fox adds that 'the most [s]he could assign would be a cause of action to recover the chattel', which assumes, rather than proves, that her title is lost on subsequent wrongful interference: Fox, above n 162 at 351.

[187] Thanks to Norma Dawson for this observation.

[188] PBH Birks, 'Introduction' in PBH Birks (ed), *English Private Law* (Oxford, OUP, 2000) xli.

observed the possessor's general ability to maintain an action against a subsequent wrongdoer, and the general transmissibility of her right, and concluded that the right amounted to ownership.[189] His conclusion is bolstered by the language of contemporaneous judgments in ejectment, which came to regard possession as a mode of acquiring a fee simple estate, the most extensive interest in land known to the common law. The terminology is not so neat in the case of goods,[190] but Pollock thought the general effect of the proposition was equally applicable to goods and land. So the finder of goods acquires by her possession a property right in the goods, which right has the content (or 'the incidents') of ownership.[191] Finders are owners of the things that they find, subject only to the weakness that their rights will not avail against one able to establish an earlier right in respect of the goods. Finders are *relative* owners of the things that they find.

For some time, the question why a possessor should be considered to have any legal rights in respect of the thing possessed has troubled legal philosophers. The question had much exercised German minds attempting to rationalise the Roman law.[192] Their accounts were connected with the wider philosophical positions of Kant and Hegel, but such connections are not to be found in the common law. Indeed, the doctrines of the common law offer no independent philosophical justification for why possession results in the acquisition of a property right, and Holmes was specifically determined to distance them from the a priori theories which had influenced the German accounts.[193] Instead, as we have seen, the common law's justification is internal: possession generates a property right because the best available rationalisation of our legal procedure shows this to be the case. As such, the law on possession serves only to emphasise the close connection between procedure and substance in common law reasoning. This connection is well known, but it is still likely to disappoint the reader searching for some over-arching explanation for why possessors are to be treated as owners. There would be merit in investigating this issue further. Perhaps it is possible to offer a modern defence of the idea that a possessor is a relative owner without referring to the learning we have inherited on trover and ejectment. Perhaps too there is warrant to depart from the old ideas, and to re-evaluate the content of rights acquired by possession. But we leave these questions for another day, because so far as finders are concerned, there is reason to suppose, perhaps conversely, that the proposition drawn from the forms of action produces sound practical results. In some respects this argument is counter-intuitive. At least, it seems excessively advantageous to the finder to treat her as an owner when somewhere there is a

---

[189] P & W, 91, 93.

[190] We return to this issue in the Epilogue.

[191] P & W, 22; Holmes, *CL*, 236.

[192] FC von Savigny, *Treatise on Possession; or the Jus Possessionis of the Civil Law* (E Perry (trans), London, Sweet, 1848) Bk One, s II; JM Lightwood, 'Possession in the Roman Law' (1887) 3 *LQR* 32.

[193] Holmes *CL*, 206. See also RWM Dias and GBJ Hughes, *Jurisprudence* (London, Butterworths, 1957) 308.

loser of goods, whose continuing property it should be the law's first concern to protect. Moreover, in the next chapter the finder's advantage will appear to increase. We are going to see that it makes no difference to the finder's acquisition of a property right that she dishonestly conceals her find, or that she commits a trespass to land in the course of the find; indeed, we will see that that no extraneous circumstance will qualify the finder's acquisition of right. In every case where a finder takes possession of goods she acquires in respect of them a property right, even if she is a thief. In Chapter 7 we will explain how this disproportionately wide property rule allows us to achieve sound policies. Read in the light of countervailing rules of crime and tort, it provides strong incentives for a finder to take reasonable steps to locate the loser, but justifies her continued retention of the goods in the event that the loser cannot be found. Where other common law jurisdictions have implemented specific legislation to regulate the position of finders, the legislation has aimed at exactly these policies. So we will argue that the English law of finders, wedded though it is to old rationalisations of old legal procedures, is coherent from the perspective of policy.

# 6

# Qualifications on the Acquisition of Right

Occasionally it has been suggested that in certain circumstances a finder's acquisition of right should be qualified, denied or necessarily defeated, notwithstanding the ability of the finder to establish her possession of the chattel. Specifically, it has been thought relevant to the question of acquisition that the finder was (a) dishonest; (b) a trespasser to land; (c) an employee; or (d) on private premises at the time of the find. This chapter considers the extent to which the cases provide support for the view that a finder's acquisition of right should be qualified in these circumstances. It argues that in no circumstance are there grounds for holding that a finder acquires anything less than those rights ordinarily consequent on possession, though sometimes she incurs additional liabilities or will necessarily be vulnerable to a better right. This establishes a very wide proposition as the basic doctrine of our property law relating to finders: in every case where a finder takes possession of goods, she acquires in respect of them an ownership interest.

## Dishonesty

The majority of our decided finding cases involve finders who were considered by the courts to have behaved commendably or honestly, usually because the finder reported the loss and/or made some effort to trace the loser.[1] What difference does it make where the contrary is true, and a finder forms the intention of concealing her find and keeping it for herself? A necessary first observation is that such a finder risks criminal liability for theft. Indeed, the belief that it was right to punish those who fraudulently converted their finds was a significant factor in the development of larceny at common law. In Chapter 1, we saw how cases like *Thurborn* incrementally stretched the fundamental concept

---

[1] See Chapter 4, commenting on *Bridges v Hawkesworth* (1851) 15 Jur 1079; *Hannah v Peel* [1945] 1 KB 509; *Parker v British Airways Board* [1982] QB 1004; and *Waverly Borough Council v Fletcher* [1996] QB 334.

of 'taking', and in the end produced a specific offence of larceny by finding. The Theft Act 1968 has preserved the substance of these rules,[2] and a prosecution lies against the finder who appropriates goods with the relevant dishonest intentions.[3] In the next chapter we argue that the existence of this offence provides an incentive for finders to behave responsibly, and in particular, when combined with other rules of property and tort, encourages the reporting of found goods to the police. Here the concern is with the proprietary effect of dishonesty. Two contentions are evident from our books: first, that the finder's right is somehow qualified when she takes with dishonest intentions; secondly, that a better proprietary right necessarily exists in the possessor of the locus of the theft when goods are taken feloniously from that place. On the authorities it is doubtful that either of these propositions can be supported. Whilst they are understandable reactions to the moral culpability of dishonest takers, they cannot be established on the doctrines of the common law, and in fact there are good reasons of public policy for *not* altering those principles to achieve more palatable results.

## Qualifying the Dishonest Finder's Rights

As the common law developed its theory of possession in the twentieth century, it was easy to find suggestions that the theory should not be applied for the benefit of dishonest possessors. Harris thought that if a finder could be punished criminally when she took with dishonest intentions, '[s]he surely ought not to acquire in civil law any possessory remedies'.[4] The difficulty was that there were not any cases to suggest this. Harris gave his opinion in reference to *Hibbert v McKiernan*,[5] but that was a case where the court decided that a possessor of land had a better right than a subsequent taker, not that the taker had no rights.[6] Nonetheless, the opinion persisted, and in *Parker* Donaldson LJ suggested that the rights of a finder should be qualified where she takes with dishonest intentions. Specifically, his lordship proposed that, in contrast to an honest finder, a dishonest finder has only a 'frail title', enough to restrain immediate physical interference, but something qualitatively less than the ordinary rights of a finder, and probably unavailable against a subsequent honest taker.[7]

Authoritatively, these contentions rest on dubious ground. Donaldson LJ conceded that there was no clear decision on the point,[8] and made the suggestion in

---

[2] D Ormerod and DH Williams (eds), *Smith's The Law of Theft* 9th edn (Oxford, OUP, 2007) 106.
[3] Theft Act 1968, s 2(1)(c).
[4] DR Harris, 'The Concept of Possession in English Law' in AG Guest (ed), *Oxford Essays in Jurisprudence* (Oxford, OUP, 1961) 96.
[5] [1948] 2 KB 142.
[6] See Chapter 2, and further below.
[7] [1982] QB 1004, 1010.
[8] *Ibid* 1010.

reliance on *Buckley v Gross*[9] and *Bird v Fort Frances*.[10] On the basis of the former, his lordship opined that dishonest possessors 'are unlikely to risk invoking the law, particularly against another subsequent dishonest taker, and a subsequent honest taker is likely to have a superior title'.[11] We saw in the last chapter that, correctly understood, *Buckley* holds that it is not possible to assert a right created by possession once that right has been lawfully divested. Without more, it has nothing to say about the rights of a wrongful possessor where no divesting authority has been exercised. Indeed, in *Buckley* itself, Cockburn CJ treated that question as open, and considered its decision unnecessary to any ruling in the instant case.[12] Consistently, in *Bird*, McRuer CJHC treated the judgments in *Buckley* as casting 'no light … on what would have been the result if it had not been for the provisions of the statute, and the plaintiff had been in the position of asserting his felonious possession against a wrongdoer'.[13] Therefore it is entirely wrong to use *Buckley* to suggest anything about the creation or general exigibility of a dishonest finder's rights. As for the contention that dishonest possessors are unlikely to have resort to the law, later cases have shown this to be false,[14] and in any event it rather begs the question. Dishonest finders ought to be able to have recourse to law if they have rights in the things they find. That in general they do not litigate claims affords a painfully trite explanation of why there was no decided case on the point at the time of *Parker*, but it offers no comment on the question whether the law does or should recognise their rights in the first place.

In *Bird v Fort Frances*, McRuer CJHC had no doubt that the plaintiff had taken the monies wrongfully, and distinguished the facts from *Bridges* and *Hannah*.[15] It was accepted on the usual authorities that a wrongful possessor could maintain conversion for goods wrongfully taken from her possession,[16] and so the question was whether the possibility that the taking was felonious made any difference. This was answered in the negative, and for this reason McRuer CJHC declined to rule whether the plaintiff was a thief on the facts:

'The conclusion I have come to is that it is not necessary for me to decide whether the taking was with felonious intent or not, as I think in this case the same result flows. In my

---

[9] (1863) 3 B & S 566.

[10] [1949] 2 DLR 791.

[11] [1982] QB 1004, 1010.

[12] (1863) 3 B & S 566, 571. See also Blackburn J at 574.

[13] [1949] 2 DLR 791, 797.

[14] *Costello v Chief Constable of Derbyshire* [2001] 1 WLR 1437 (CA); *Gough v Chief Constable of West Midlands Police* [2004] EWCA Civ 206.

[15] [1949] 2 DLR 791, 798.

[16] Given for this proposition in the judgment are *Armory v Delamirie* (1722) 1 Stra 505; *Daniels v Rogers* [1918] 2 KB 228; *Graham v Peat* (1801) 1 East 244, 246; *Jeffries v Great Western Railway Co* (1856) 25 LJQB 107; *Eastern Construction Co v National Trust Co* [1914] AC 197, 209–10; *Glenwood Lumber Co v Phillips* [1904] AC 405, 410; P & W, 91–3, 171–87; TC Williams (ed), *Williams on Personal Property* 18th edn (London, Sweet and Maxwell, 1926) 51–2.

view the authorities with which I have dealt justify the conclusion that where A enters upon the land of B and takes possession of and removes chattels to which B asserts no legal rights, and A is wrongfully dispossessed of those chattels, he may bring an action to recover the same'.[17]

On the facts of *Bird*, the possibly felonious plaintiff was allowed to recover the full value of the banknotes, plus the interest which had accrued on defendant's bank account. McRuer CJHC made an order directing that this sum be paid into court, where it would be held to the credit of the plaintiff until his twenty-first birthday. There was absolutely nothing to suggest that this plaintiff was being treated any differently from any other dispossessed possessor, in fact it was quite the contrary. Accordingly, it is impossible to use *Bird* as authority for the proposition that a dishonest finder has something other than those rights normally consequent on possession, and quite remarkable that Donaldson LJ supposed that the case could be deployed in this way.

If *Bird* supposes that a dishonest possessor acquires an ordinary possessory title, *Costello v Chief Constable of Derbyshire*[18] puts it beyond doubt that this is the position at common law. The Court of Appeal was unequivocally clear that:

> as a matter of principle and authority possession means the same thing and is entitled to the same legal protection, whether or not it has been obtained lawfully or by theft or by other unlawful means. It vests in the possessor a possessory title which is good against the world save as against anyone setting up or claiming under a better title.[19]

On the facts of *Costello*, this proposition was applied to allow the claimant to recover a car which it was believed he had stolen,[20] and also damages for its wrongful detention. The car had been taken from him and retained by the police pursuant to certain powers of seizure contained in sections 19 and 22 of the Police and Criminal Evidence Act 1984. But these provisions gave the police only a temporary right to detain the car for the limited purposes of the statute.[21] Such a right would not avail against the claimant after the expiry of the statutory purposes, because the claimant had acquired rights in the car as a consequence of his possession. That this possession had been acquired dishonestly made no difference. The claimant still acquired a right in respect of the car, and was entitled to rely on this right without reference to the circumstances in which it was obtained.[22] His

---

[17] [1949] 2 DLR 791, 796 (McRuer CJHC).

[18] [2001] 1 WLR 1437 (CA): noted J Getzler, 'Unclean Hands and the Doctrine of Jus Tertii' (2001) 117 *LQR* 565, 567; G Battersby, 'Acquiring Title by Theft' (2002) *MLR* 603.

[19] [2001] 1 WLR 1437, 1450 (Lightman J, Keene and Robert Walker LJJ concurring).

[20] The claimant was released on bail, and no criminal proceedings were brought against him in relation to the car. In the instant case, however, the trial judge was satisfied that the car had been stolen: [2001] 1 WLR 1437, 1439.

[21] *Ibid* 1441.

[22] *Ibid*. Lightman J prefixed this conclusion with a useful discussion on the effect of wrongdoing and illegality on civil relationships generally, largely based on *Tinsley v Milligan* [1994] 1 AC 340 (HL), and the more recent decision of the Court of Appeal in *Webb v Chief Constable of Merseyside* [2000] QB 427. Both *Webb* and *Costello* were followed by the Court of Appeal in *Gough v Chief Constable of*

dishonesty triggered no special rule to take the case outside of the normal rules.[23] Accordingly, on the authorities, the better view is that a dishonest finder, like any dishonest possessor, will in the ordinary way acquire a relatively good right in the object of her find. Donaldson LJ's suggestion that a dishonest finder acquires 'very limited rights' is without foundation. If Mr Parker had taken the bracelet with dishonest intentions he would still have had a better right than the British Airways Board.[24]

Probably this proposition seems counter-intuitive from a public policy perspective. At the least, it is difficult to sympathise with a rule which prima facie results in the reward of wrongdoers. Giving judgment in *Costello*, Lightman J was mindful of this 'natural moral disinclination' towards the recognition of possessory title in thieves,[25] but thought it did not offer sufficient ground to deprive the possessor of protection. On the contrary, there were public policy reasons for *not* denying protection to the thief. Lightman J relied on *Webb v Chief Constable of Merseyside*.[26] There the police had seized money from the claimants on the suspicion that it represented the proceeds of drug trafficking. Had the claimants been convicted of such an offence, the conviction would have triggered statutory powers for the confiscation of the money. In the absence of a conviction, the Court of Appeal thought it improper to manipulate the common law position of the parties in order to achieve a result more attractive from the perspective of public policy.[27] Essentially it was articulating a constitutional principle about the proper functioning of civil courts. Once possession has been recognised as the source of a proprietary entitlement, for a court to deny that right (even to one accepted on the balance of probabilities as a criminal)[28] amounts to 'expropriation by a public authority'.[29] Such expropriation can only ever be justified on the basis of unambiguous statutory authority.[30] Where there is none, it is constitutionally correct to uphold the possessor's right, and consistent with public policy to deny the incremental extension of the confiscation powers of the police.[31]

None of this is intended to cast any doubt on the situation where expropriation powers are clearly defined by legislation. Governments can and do create

---

*West Midlands Police* [2004] EWCA Civ 206, paras 15 and 29, though Potter LJ expressed dissatisfaction at the availability of civil actions for recovery goods obtained unlawfully: *ibid* para 48.

[23] Compare *Tamworth Industries v Attorney-General* [1991] 3 NZLR 616, 623, where the court was very clear that the claimant failed to establish a right in respect of monies found on land demised to him because he had not exhibited the required degree of intention to control the premises, and not because of strongly held suspicions that the monies had been raised by the claimant through the sale of cannabis.

[24] G Battersby, 'Acquiring Title by Theft' (2002) *MLR* 603, 610.

[25] [2001] 1 WLR 1437, 1450.

[26] [2000] QB 427 (CA).

[27] *Ibid* 446–7 (May LJ).

[28] The judges in both *Webb* and *Costello* found that the respective claimants had committed the respective offences according to civil standards of proof: [2001] 1 WLR 1437, 1440.

[29] [2000] QB 427, 446.

[30] *Malone v Metropolitan Chief Commissioner* [1980] QB 49, 62 (Stephenson LJ).

[31] See Battersby, above n 24 at 609.

confiscatory procedures which bite on criminal assets.[32] In the context of theft, courts today have powers to compel the restoration of stolen property,[33] or to make orders depriving a thief or suspected thief of property in her possession.[34] The existence of such powers serves to answer the paradox of a common law rule recognising the existence of property rights in thieves. The property rule must not be read in isolation, but understood in the light of countervailing rules of criminal law and tort. If a thief is a possessor she acquires those rights ordinarily consequent on possession, but those rights might be taken away from her by statutory authority, and even if she retains her right, she will still hold it subject to the general law of obligations. So, whilst on the authorities we are bound to acknowledge that the felonious possessor is the holder of a property right, this does not necessarily mean that she will make a windfall gain from her activities. On the criminal side, we have expropriation authorities, and if these do not meet the policy aim of preventing thieves from profiting from their wrongdoing we might extend them by further legislation. On the civil side, a dishonest possessor (as any possessor) is bound to answer for the value of the goods to any person better entitled. All in all, it seems most consistent with the authorities, and nowhere near the affront to moral judgement which it appears at first blush, to suggest that a dishonest possessor, and therefore a dishonest finder, acquires in the usual way those rights consequent on possession. Dishonesty is no qualification on the generation of finder's rights.

## Recognising a Better Right in a Third Party

Even if a dishonest finder has a property right in the thing she finds, some cases appear to suggest that a possessor of land will always have a better right to goods found on and stolen from his land. In this way, dishonesty might serve to qualify the finder's rights, not by preventing their creation, but by providing for the existence of a better right in a third party. This was the view recently in *R v Rostron*,[35] where the Court of Appeal upheld convictions for theft on facts superficially similar to *Hibbert v McKiernan*.[36] The defendants had recovered 'lost' golf balls

---

[32] See Getzler noting that even shortly after *Costello* was decided, 'the statutory wind ... [seemed] to be blowing the other way' as the Labour Government announced plans to create the criminal assets recovery agency: J Getzler, 'Unclean Hands and the Doctrine of Jus Tertii' (2001) 117 *LQR* 565, 567.

[33] Powers of Criminal Courts (Sentencing) Act 2000, s 148, which replaces the procedure under s Theft Act 1968, s 28. See generally Ormerod and Williams, above n 2 at 14.27–14.57. For the position under the Theft Act and a historical overview see JK Macleod, 'Restitution under the Theft Act' (1968) *Crim LR* 577.

[34] *Buckley v Gross* offers an example of the latter, and today the position is regulated by the Police Property Act 1897. Under s 1(1), where any property has come into the possession of the police in their investigation of a suspected offence, a magistrate's court may make an order for delivery of the thing in question to a person appearing to be its owner, or, in the absence of such a person, any other order which the court thinks fit. See generally Ormerod and Williams, above n 34 at 14.60–14.65; *Irving v National Provincial Bank Ltd* [1962] QB 73 (CA).

[35] [2003] EWCA Crim 2206; [2003] All ER (D) 269.

[36] [1948] 2 KB 142.

from the water hazards of a golf course in Leicestershire, intending to offer them for resale.[37] The court accepted that the golf balls had been abandoned by their owners, but thought it authoritatively clear that the owners of the golf course had a proprietary interest in the balls:

> [A]s every law student learns when studying criminal law, on the authority of a well-known case called *Hibbert and McKiernan*, for the purposes of theft the owners of golf courses are regarded as having the property and control of lost golf balls for their own purposes.[38]

In Chapter 2 we argued that the better view of *Hibbert* is that the successive courts applied orthodox principles of possession and found the club members better entitled to the golf balls insofar as they were able to prove a prior right on the facts of control and intention.[39] We could dispose of its relevance quickly were it not for the opinion of Lord Goddard CJ, which appears to suggest that the circumstances of theft are relevant to the generation of title in the possessor of land:

> Every householder or occupier of land means or intends to exclude thieves and wrong-doers from the property occupied by him, and this confers on him a special property in goods found on his land sufficient to support an indictment if the goods are taken therefrom, not under a claim of right, but with a felonious intent.[40]

Elsewhere, it has been argued that, despite some terminological differences, Lord Goddard's judgment should be read as endorsing a similar position to the other members of the court.[41] Clearly, in large measure the passage above rests the right of the club on their intention to exclude interference with things found on the land, and this is entirely consistent with the theory of possession discussed in Chapter 2. At most, we might take the reference to intention to exclude thieves and wrongdoers as establishing a general evidentiary presumption in favour of the possessor of land (discharging him from the burden of proving his manifest intention to possess goods), and so deal with stolen goods in the way we deal with buried or attached goods. The difficulty is that, in *Hibbert*, the intention to exclude the recovery of lost golf balls was actually proven as a matter of fact, and only Lord Goddard suggested the manifestation of this fact could be generally presumed. Accordingly, it seems preferable to regard *Hibbert* as a case where the

---

[37] The court noted considerable commercial activity in the recovery and resale of 'lake balls' from the hazards of golf courses. Mantell LJ did not doubt that in many cases such trade could be carried on quite legitimately: 'Indeed, we are told that there are companies with very considerable turnovers who deal in ... lake balls and one can imagine all sorts of ways in which such property could come on to the market without any prior offence having been committed': *ibid* para 6.

[38] *Ibid* para 16, Mantell LJ giving the judgment of the court. Accurately, this is the dictum of Potter LJ, delivering judgment in the second defendant's appeal against sentence. It is expressly approved and reproduced by Mantell LJ at the given paragraph.

[39] See also the discussion of the *Button B Pennies Case* in OR Marshall, 'The Problem of Finding' (1949) 2 *Current Legal Problems* 68; see Chapter 2.

[40] [1948] 2 KB 142, 149–50.

[41] R Hickey, 'Stealing Abandoned Goods: Possessory Title in Proceedings for Theft' (2006) *Legal Studies* 584, 591–3.

club's right was established in the usual way, ie by proof of the twin elements of control and intention. As for the suggestion that the generation of the club's right is conditional (the intention to exclude is sufficient *if* the golf balls are taken with felonious intent, and not under a claim of right), this should not be followed. It is difficult to see why the criminal intentions of a taker should make any difference to a possessor of land's acquisition of goods lost on his land. The better view is that the civil law of property determines title issues in theft proceedings, and there the orthodoxy is that dishonesty makes no difference to the allocation of rights in goods.[42]

Accordingly the better view of *Rostron* is that the club members only have a better right to the golf balls than the felonious finders if they have succeeded in making out their right on the ordinary rules of possession. This might have produced some difficulties on the facts of *Rostron* which were not wholly considered,[43] but in any case the general point is clear: dishonesty does not operate to qualify the rights of a finder. It does not affect the generation of those rights, nor does it contribute to the generation of better rights in a possessor of land.

# Trespass to Land

It has often been suggested that the rights of a finder should be qualified when her find is made on the land of another and she is committing a trespass to that land at the time of the find.[44] Despite the fact that trespass has been a live issue in virtually none of the decided cases,[45] the opinion has persisted, and in *Parker* Donaldson LJ formulated a specific doctrinal qualification. Where a finder was a trespasser to land, a special rule of the common law gave a better title to the person vis-à-vis whom he was a trespasser:

> The fundamental basis of this is clearly public policy. Wrongdoers should not benefit from their wrongdoing. This requirement would be met if the trespassing finder

---

[42] See Ormerod and Williams, above n 2 at 77, 83.

[43] Hickey, above n 41 at 598–600; see Ormerod and Williams, above n 2 at 83.

[44] See eg Harris, above n 4 at 96; Law Reform Committee, *Eighteenth Report (Conversion and Detinue)*, Cmnd 4774 (1971) 48.

[45] In the vast majority of cases the finder has been lawfully on the premises at the time of her find (*Bridges, Elwes, Sharman, Hannah, Bird, Parker*). In others, she has certainly been a trespasser, but that has not influenced the outcome of the case (*Hibbert, Waverly*). Harris thought that in *Hibbert* 'the Divisional Court laid some emphasis on the fact that the appellant had trespassed on the course', but this is misleading. The fact that the club had engaged the services of a police constable to ward off trespassers was relevant proof of the club's intention to possess the lost balls, and so relevant evidence of a better title in the club. Without more this says nothing about the rather different question as to Hibbert's rights, if any, in the golf balls. For the passage cited from Harris see above n 4 at 96. In *Waverly*, Auld LJ overruled the first instance decision of His Honour Judge Fawcus and held that Mr Fletcher necessarily committed an act of trespass in digging to excavate his find. But the judgment in favour of the council was based squarely on its ability to set up a prior right on the facts of possession: [1996] QB 334, 350.

acquired no rights. That would, however, produce [a] free-for-all situation ... in that anyone could take the article from the trespassing finder. Accordingly, the common law has been obliged to give rights to someone else, the owner ex hypothesi being unknown. The obvious candidate is the occupier of the property upon which the finder was trespassing.[46]

Immediately it is tempting to resist this argument by pointing out that it was obiter. The Court of Appeal was considering the claim of a finder lawfully present in the airport lounge, and no discussion of the position of trespassers was necessary to the resolution of the case. A more telling argument against Donaldson LJ's proposition is that in many cases involving a trespasser it would add nothing. Consider first the situation where a buried object is removed from the land of another. There is no prospect of a right superior to that of the possessor of land arising in any person who comes later in time to the object than its burial. That is the effect of the evidentiary concession to proof of possessory intention in cases where objects are found buried in land.[47] Irrespective of whether or not the taker has permission to be on the land, the possessor of land will have a better right.[48] Any talk of trespass here is a red herring.

The same reasoning will apply to objects taken from the surface of land, where the possessor of land successfully manifests an intention to control objects found on that land. Certainly this is true of the decision in *Hibbert v McKiernan*, where the defendant was a trespasser. Early in his judgment, Donaldson LJ records of that case:

> The indictment named the members of the club ... as having property in the balls, and it is clear that at the time when the balls were taken the members were very clearly asserting such a right, even to the extent of mounting a police patrol to warn off trespassers seeking to harvest lost balls.[49]

The presence in the club members of a property interest in the golf balls subsisting at the time they were taken would make it impossible for Donaldson LJ to rely on the defendant's act of trespass as a cause of the club's rights. Quite clearly, the acquisition of the right is temporally prior to the trespass. The events causing the right here are the club's factual control of the land coupled with an intention to control golf balls found on that land, this latter manifested by the presence of the police constable with the special duty. The defendant's act of trespass is not a material fact. It is again a red herring.

It is not so easy to dismiss the relevance of trespass where a possessor of land fails to manifest an intention to control lost objects lying unattached on his land.

---

[46] [1982] QB 1004, 1009.
[47] See Chapter 2.
[48] Unless, of course, the taker can set up a title through the true owner or someone who has an interest prior to the interest of the landowner which arises at the point of burial. But in that case, the taker sets up a derivative title, and does not in any real sense rely on his taking: see generally *Moffatt v Kazana* [1969] 2 KB 152.
[49] [1982] QB 1004, 1009.

Suppose in *Parker* the claimant had been present in the executive lounge without the permission of the British Airways Board. Applying unqualified rules of possession would entail holding that the trespasser could recover the value of the bracelet from the Board, and thus could profit from his wrong. It was the desire to discourage this kind of wrongful profit that prompted Donaldson LJ to propose that the rights of the trespassing finder should be given to the possessor of land, and certainly it is not difficult to sympathise with his view. The problem is that, inasmuch as the common law knows of a principle which denies the ability of wrongdoers to make profit from their wrongs,[50] this principle has never seemed particularly prominent when it comes to the proprietary consequences of trespass to land. The cardinal example is provided by the law of adverse possession of unregistered land, where, as we have seen, the possessor takes a fee simple estate in the disputed land.[51] Not only is the commission of a trespass instrumental in the generation of this property right, it also triggers the start of the limitation period, which on its expiry might see the right confirmed as the best available in the land at issue.[52] Far from being a hindrance to the squatter, his trespass has the potential to cause and confirm property rights.[53]

Even if we get past these concerns, there are further difficulties with Donaldson LJ's formulation. In the main, it is not clear what would cause the generation of the right in the possessor of the trespassed land. It could be the act of trespass itself, but necessarily this would involve some adherence to a general proposition that property rights can arise in a third person on the commission of a wrong, which proposition seems at least doubtful.[54] Alternatively (and this seems Donaldson LJ's contention) full rights could arise initially in the trespassing finder and then immediately be transferred to the occupier. But even if we tolerate a fictitious transfer, insofar as the right of the occupier is derived from the finder it would seem difficult for the finder also to retain the 'frail title' proposed by Donaldson LJ. To this extent, the comments in *Parker* on the relevance of trespass to the acquisition of rights by a finder seem unpersuasive. The better view is that in our law of property, trespass to land makes no difference to the nature or substance of a finder's rights. It is only possible to defeat the claims of trespassing finders in the

---

[50] See the now well-known case of *Riggs v Palmer* (1889) 115 NY 506, where the court mindful of this maxim ruled that the law did not allow a grandson to take his grandfather's inheritance, the former having murdered the latter; and the comments of Ronald Dworkin in *Law's Empire* (Oxford, Hart Publishing, 1998) 15–20.

[51] *JA Pye (Oxford) v Graham* [2003] 1 AC 419; *Asher v Whitlock* (1865) LR 1 QB 1. On the doctrines of adverse possession, see generally C Harpum, S Bridge and M Dixon (eds), *Megarry and Wade's The Law of Real Property* 7th edn (London, Sweet and Maxwell, 2008) ch 35.

[52] Limitation Act 1980, sch 1, para 1.

[53] Notice that there is no reason to suppose that the proposition about a trespasser to land's acquisition of right applies any less strongly where title to the land is registered. Even though the terms of sch 6 to the Land Registration Act 2002 contemplate an adverse possessor making an application to be registered as proprietor, at common law he still acquires a fee simple estate from the inception, and by reason, of his possession: see K Gray and SF Gray, *Elements of Land Law* 4th edn (Oxford, OUP, 2005) 3.37.

[54] Certainly its correctness is disputed: *EPL*, 4.406–4.412.

usual way, ie by proof of a better possessory title. And here, of course, is the answer for the possessor of land worried about trespassing finders wrongfully profiting from articles found on his land. The possessor of land will necessarily defeat the claim of any finder if he manifests an intention to control objects found on the land.[55] He is free to take steps to do so. If he does not, his claim to found goods has no proprietary base, and effectively he forfeits his right to assert an interest against a finder, even where the finder is a trespasser.

# Employment Relationships

In a like manner to the trespassing finder, from time to time it has been urged that a finder should not acquire any rights in an object which she finds in the course of her employment: instead, they vest in her employer. There seems a remarkably high degree of consensus about this rule. Holmes acknowledged it, and conceded it as an anomalous exception to his general theory of possession,[56] and this proposition remains today. The most recent edition of *Crossley Vaines* says that 'chattels found by a servant in the course of his employment belong to his master'.[57] Bridge seems to agree,[58] as did Donaldson LJ in *Parker*. There we read that:

> Unless otherwise agreed, any servant or agent who finds a chattel in the course of his employment or agency and not wholly incidentally or collaterally thereto and who takes it into his care and control does so on behalf of his employer or principal who acquires a finder's rights to the exclusion of those of the actual finder.[59]

In *Parker*, of course, the point was obiter.[60] Moreover, only *Appleyard*[61] was considered in support of the proposition, and there it was obiter too. Whilst McNair J would have been prepared to hold that finders were obliged to hand over their

---

[55] Where the article in question is found buried in land, the possessor of land is relieved from this burden of proof, and will necessarily have a claim in priority to that of the finder.

[56] Holmes, *CL*, 227.

[57] ELG Tyler and NE Palmer (eds), *Crossley Vaines' Personal Property* 5th edn (London, Butterworths, 1973) 420.

[58] M Bridge, *Personal Property Law* 3rd edn (Oxford, Clarendon Press, 2003) 25. Here, Bridge says only that the employee must account to the employer for the find, and does not say expressly that rights are acquired by the employer. However, since he sees the application of employment principles in this instance as a corollary to 'the rule that the employee does not possess, but merely has custody of, the master's chattels' (as to which see below), it seems safe to say he is supposing that the employee finder does not acquire any rights. In any event, he takes the point as 'emerging from *Parker*', which also suggests agreement with this proposition.

[59] [1982] 1 QB 1004, 1017 (Donaldson LJ). See also *Clerk and Lindsell on Torts*, 17–51.

[60] Donaldson LJ recognised that there was 'no evidence that [Mr Parker] was in the executive lounge in the course of any employment or agency and, if he was, the finding of the bracelet was quite clearly collateral thereto'. [1982] 1 QB 1004, 1018.

[61] *City of London Corporation v Appleyard* [1963] 1 WLR 982.

find to a direct employer,[62] on the facts there was a superior possessory title to the banknotes in the possessor of land,[63] and this rendered it 'strictly unnecessary ... to decide' the employment point.[64] It was the same with *South Staffs Water Co v Sharman*,[65] where Lord Russell CJ based his verdict for the plaintiffs on their possession of the premises, having applied Pollock's theory of possession. Although the defendant finder was the servant of the plaintiff engaged to clean Minster Pool, this relationship formed no part of the Divisional Court's decision. Indeed, Lord Russell CJ did not mention the point at all. In *Hannah v Peel*, however, counsel for the plaintiff finder sought to distinguish *Sharman* by arguing that it was a 'sufficient explanation' of that case that the finder 'as the servant or agent of the water company, though he was the first to obtain the custody of the rings, obtained possession of them for his employers ... and could claim no title to them for himself'.[66] The point was accepted by Birkett J, though clearly it had formed no part of the decision in *Sharman*. Ironically, Birkett J had criticised Lord Russell CJ's summation of *Bridges*, finding it 'a little remarkable' that his Lordship emphasised the public nature of the shop when Patteson J had expressly disclaimed the relevance of such publicity. Here, it seems, Birkett J is guilty of similar offence. We might pause to notice in general that such red-herring statements are at least part of the reason why rationalisation of the finding cases is so difficult. For now, though, it is enough to observe that these leading cases (*Parker*, *Appleyard*, *Hannah*, *Sharman*) have nothing definitive to say on the employment question. We could leave them to one side, save insofar as they can be taken as evidence of a general trend which favours the idea that employers acquire rights in objects found by their employees.

There are a few cases which do appear to hold expressly that when an employee finder takes possession of a discovered chattel, she takes possession on behalf of her employer. In *M'Dowell v Ulster Bank*,[67] a porter in a Belfast bank found a parcel containing £25 in single bills. He was sweeping the floor at the time, performing a regular after-hours cleaning duty. He behaved honestly, handing over the notes to the branch manager, 'telling him how he had found them, and asking him to try and find the owner'.[68] He claimed the notes a year and a day after the date of

---

[62] [1963] 1 WLR 982, 988. McNair J approved the proposition as a general principle of law, and cited general authority including *M'Dowell v Ulster Bank* (1899) 33 *Irish Law Times* 225, discussed below.

[63] [1963] 1 WLR 982, 987–8.

[64] [1963] 1 WLR 982, 988. Having determined the existence of a relatively better title in the possessor of the premises, the real issue in *Appleyard* concerned which of the plaintiffs was that possessor, and the effect, if any, of an agreement by which the first plaintiff corporation attempted to reserve to itself any articles of value found on the demised premises: [1963] 1 WLR 982, 989–90.

[65] [1896] 2 QB 44.

[66] [1945] KB 509, 512.

[67] (1899) 33 *Irish Law Times* 225.

[68] *Ibid.*

the find,[69] the loser not having appeared. The bank refused to redeliver them, and the porter brought an action claiming their value which was ultimately dismissed by Palles CB. The learned Chief Baron was careful to distinguish the prior possession rationale which had decided *Sharman*, denying the action squarely on the basis of the employment relationship that existed between the parties:

> I do not decide this case on the ground laid down by Lord Russell in *Sharman's* case. I decide [this case] on the ground of the relation of master and servant, and that it was by reason of the existence of that relationship, and in the performance of the duties of that service that the plaintiff acquired possession of this property. I conceive that it is the duty of the porter of the Bank, who acts as caretaker, to pick up matters of this description, and to hand them over to the Bank. I hold that the possession of the servant of the Bank was the possession of the Bank itself, and that, therefore, the element is wanting which would give the title to the servant as against the master.[70]

*Crinion v Minister of Justice*[71] was after the same fashion. There an on-duty police officer was denied rights in money[72] found on a public footpath. Judge Conroy of the Irish Circuit Court held that, because the plaintiff was 'in the service of the State' when he found the money, he 'never took full possession of the money so as to establish his claim to it'.[73] Notice that if these rulings are correct, they probably entail a further rule which distinguishes between finds made in the course of employment and finds made wholly collaterally thereto;[74] or to put the matter another way, the finder's employment must be the *cause*, as opposed to merely the *occasion* of the find if the employer is to take her rights.[75] Possibly this accounts for the distinction between *Crinion* and the oft-cited Australian decision in *Byrne v Hoare*,[76] where a police officer was allowed to keep a gold ingot he found while on special duty at a drive-in movie theatre.[77] A majority of the Full Court held that the officer's discovery of the gold was 'merely incidental' to his duties at the theatre,[78] and distinguished the case where a police officer is 'told by lawful

---

[69] It seems strange that that plaintiff should have waited for a year and a day to make his claim. There was no rule to this effect in Northern Ireland, but it recalls the old learning on estrays, according to which the lord of a manor would become entitled to animals taken as lost if they were not claimed within a year and a day: 2 SS 31; 72 SS 100; Ames, HT, 379 (see generally Chapter 1). Possibly the presence of this fact in *M'Dowell* indicates the existence of an urban myth that a loser's ability to reclaim his goods was limited by the same period, leaving open the claim of the finder.

[70] *Ibid* 226.

[71] (1959) 25 *Irish Jurist Reports* 15.

[72] £184 in single banknotes: *ibid*.

[73] *Ibid* 17.

[74] [1982] 1 QB 1004, 1017.

[75] S Cretney, 'Treasure from Heaven' (1969) 119(1) *New Law Journal* 356, 357.

[76] [1965] Qd R 135.

[77] The ingot was found lying on privately owned land, which formed part of the public exit from the theatre.

[78] [1965] Qd R 135, 142 (Stable J). Gibbs J expressed the find as being 'merely coincidental', adding that the performance of the special duty was 'not the real or effective cause of the finding': *ibid* 149, 151. The dissenting judgment of Hart J argues that the find was made in the plaintiff's 'capacity as a policeman', and concludes that for that reason he is answerable for its value to the Crown: *ibid* 152, 176.

authority to go and look for something and finds it', in which case he might take no personal benefit.[79]

Notwithstanding the clarity of these decisions, analytically they leave much to be desired. In the first place, we might resist the idea (which forms the basis of the *M'Dowell* decision) that the possession of a servant is the possession of the master. This proposition derives from the old law of larceny, and is not necessarily applicable to the resolution of disputes about the acquisition of property rights. It will be recalled from the first chapter that in its earliest forms, larceny was designed to remedy an involuntary loss of possession, and was for that reason premised on some direct trespassory interference with the goods of the victim. In theory, this requirement persisted in the law of larceny until the enactment of the new offence of theft (framed in language of 'appropriation') dispensed with the need for a concept of 'taking'. In practice, it had been steadily eroded, from at least the fifteenth century onwards, in order to overcome difficult practical problems. One such problem was theft by a servant of the goods of his master. As long as trespassory interference was necessary, a servant could not be convicted of larceny for converting *animo furandi* goods with which he had been entrusted, because they were in his possession at the time of the conversion. This was an analogue of the problem with carriers.[80] When in the late fifteenth century it was determined that larceny would lie against a servant in these circumstances,[81] this was equivalent to holding that a servant did not take possession of goods entrusted to him by his master.[82] Although this translates with ease to a general principle that a servant does not have possession of the goods of his master, or as it is said, that a servant has only *custody* of goods while his master has *possession*,[83] the point of the rule was to secure criminal convictions for dishonest conduct. A rather different idea is at work in *M'Dowell*, where the actual possession of the servant is deemed to be the actual possession of the master for the purpose of generating ordinary possessory rights in the latter.

Equally unsatisfactory is the suggestion that the possessory facts are somehow qualified in the case of an employee finder (that her possession is not possession

---

[79] [1965] Qd R 135, 141. Note that an equally possible explanation of the finder's successful claim in *Byrne* is that the relation between Crown and police officer is not the usual relation of master to servant: [1965] Qd R 135, 140. But cf *Crinion* above.

[80] *The Carrier's Case* (1473) YB 13 Ed IV, Pasch, l 5 F.

[81] The earliest case given by Holmes is *The Carrier's Case* of 1473. The rules must be older, for as Turner observes *The Carrier's Case* contains dicta denying possession to several varieties of 'ministers', including household servants: *Russell on Crime*, vol II, 914. Doubt about the extent of the rule is evidenced by the statute of Henry VIII specifically providing for 'the punishment of such servants as shall withdraw themselves and go away with their master's or mistresse's caskets, and other jewels and goods' (21 Hen VIII, c 7). It is also suggested that the rules developed in a two-stage process, with a prosecution lying initially for felonious conversion of goods within the master's houses, and latterly for conversions off the premises. As to this generally, see *Russell on Crime*, vol II, 914–15.

[82] Holmes, *CL*, 226.

[83] *Russell on Crime*, vol II, 915. The Larceny Act 1916 preserved the substance of the rule by distinguishing servants from bailees: s 17.

in the 'full' sense[84]) such that some element of her acquisition is wanting.[85] There is nothing on the facts of *M'Dowell* or *Crinion* to suggest that the factual possession of the employee finder is qualitatively different to that of the finder in *Bridges*, *Hannah* or *Parker*. In both of these cases there was an assumption of factual control of a discovered object, and an evident intention to possess it (ultimately confirmed by an unheeded request to have the thing redelivered). To the extent that an employee finder is being denied those rights ordinarily consequent on possession, this denial must be attributable to some special rule of law which takes the matter outside the usual rule, and not to some defect in her possession. Holmes recognised this squarely, observing that:

> A servant is denied possession, not from any peculiarity of intent with regard to the things in his custody ... but simply as one of the incidents of his status.[86]

Holmes was able to locate the historical antecedents of these status rules in the law of slavery.[87] We might attempt a similar exercise, locating our modern rule about finder employees in a general duty to account to an employer for unauthorised profits.[88] However, we could apply this proposition without disrupting the application of our general rule on possession. Ordinarily, that an employee has received legal title to some asset in unauthorised fashion does not exclude his employer's right to have account of the profits.[89] It would seem preferable to hold that an employee finder acquires in her find those rights ordinarily consequent on possession, but at the same time must account personally to her employer for the value of the find. In other words, employment relationships do not qualify the finder's acquisition of right, but they do impose additional liabilities.[90]

# Public and Private Locations

Finally we ask what difference, if any, it makes to a finder's rights that the goods in question were found on private premises as opposed to a place to which the

---

[84] *Crinion v Minister for Justice* (1959) 25 *Irish Jurist Reports* 15, 17.

[85] *M'Dowell v Ulster Bank* (1899) 33 *Irish Law Times* 225, 226.

[86] Holmes, *CL*, 227–8.

[87] Holmes, *CL*, 228.

[88] See generally *Morrison v Thompson* (1874) LR 9 QB 480; *Parker v McKenna* (1874) 10 Ch App 96; *AG v Goddard* (1929) 45 TLR 609, 98 LJKB 743; *Reading v AG* [1951] AC 507.

[89] See eg *Attorney-General for Hong Kong v Reid* [1994] 1 AC 324 (PC).

[90] We should also note in this context that the allocation of rights in finds might be regulated by agreement of the parties: see generally *City of London Corporation v Appleyard* [1963] 1 WLR 982, but compare *Williams v Phillips* (1957) 41 Cr App Rep 5, where refuse collectors had agreed with their employer that any profits received from the sale of valuable items taken as refuse would be divided in equal shares between employer and employee. The Court of Appeal took this agreement as evidence that the defendant collectors had behaved dishonestly, but did not think it varied rights to the refuse between the parties. In this respect, the court adopted the traditional view that the refuse was in the constructive possession of the employer from the moment it was taken as refuse by the collectors: (1957) 41 Cr App Rep 5, 7, 9.

public has access. We will see that the idea that it might make *some* difference can be traced to the earliest arguments on the respective rights of finders and possessors of land, but by far the most unequivocal exposition is found in the Law Reform Committee Report of 1971.[91] The Committee was attempting to clarify the position between possessors of land and finders at a time when the law was widely considered to be unsatisfactory.[92] Adopting the in/on land orthodoxy, the Committee took it as established that where goods were found buried in land the occupier of land had a better right than a finder,[93] but thought the on land position unsettled. In cases where the finder was not also a trespasser or the servant of the occupier at the time of the find,[94] the Committee proposed the law be settled as follows for on land finds:

> a broad distinction should be drawn between premises of a private, and those of a public character, and the rule should be that where the place of finding falls within the first of these categories the occupier, and where it falls in the second the finder, should have title.[95]

This proposed rule had the benefit of apparent clarity, but also suffered from formidable defects, one of which was acknowledged in the report. The Committee recognised that the implementation of the rule involved the 'serious difficulty' of drawing a distinction between public and private places. The majority of the text in Annex 1 to the Report wrestled with this difficulty, without achieving satisfactory resolution. The Committee was concerned to foster a policy of loss reporting, and in essence differentiated private premises from public according to the availability on the premises of some person to whom the discovery of lost goods could be reported. The final paragraph of Annex 1 gives this proposed definition of 'private' premises:

> 'private' premises should include not only premises to which the public do not habitually have access but also 'managed' (or 'attended') premises to which they do habitually have access, 'managed' premises for this purpose being defined as those on which the occupier, or a servant or agent of his willing to accept custody of articles found, is normally available in reasonable proximity to the place of finding.[96]

Even if we could accept this definition as overcoming the factual difficulty of determining whether given premises were private or public in character,[97] there remain

---

[91] Law Reform Committee, *Eighteenth Report (Conversion and Detinue)*, Cmnd 4774 (1971).

[92] *Ibid* 14. It was not at all obvious that a review of the rights of finders was within the terms of reference of the committee. The inclusion of the review was justified because finding questions were 'commonly discussed in text-books on tort', and also because the question of damages recoverable by a finder in conversion was squarely within the committee's remit: at 14.

[93] *Ibid* 48. *Elwes v Brigg Gas Co* was given as authority for the view that this in land rule was 'clearly established'.

[94] As noted above, in each of these cases the Committee favoured the view that the occupier of land should always have a better right than the finder, though it admitted doubts as to whether this was so on the existing law: *ibid*.

[95] *Ibid* 49.

[96] *Ibid* 50.

[97] Even the Committee suspected that the implementation of this definition would 'prove too difficult' in practice, and proposed alternatively the creation of a closed list of 'managed' premises

problems with the idea that an occupier of land should acquire a property right in respect of goods because he is a person to whom losses can be reported. In the first place, it ignores the general function of the police to that effect.[98] More generally, at a conceptual level, it sites the cause of a property right in the factual classification of premises, and even if this could be tolerated, it is manifestly out of step with a correct reading of the cases, which have preferred to treat possession as the source of a landowner's right, and have considered the nature of the premises relevant only to the extent that it affords evidence of that possession, as we shall see.

The idea that the character of the premises can make a difference to allocation of property rights between rival claimants can be traced back to the argument on appeal in *South Staffs Water Co v Sharman*. At first instance the judge had found for the defendant finder on the strength of *Bridges v Hawkesworth*, holding that he had a right in respect of the rings good against all the world save the true owner. Before the Divisional Court, counsel for the plaintiffs had to find some method of distinguishing *Bridges*, and chose to rely on the fact that the public was freely admitted to that part of the shop where the monies had been found.[99] It is clear from the recorded argument that this distinction aimed to prove that the shop-keeper in *Bridges* did not have *possession* of the packet of banknotes because the goods were found in a public part of the shop. Conversely, counsel argued that where, as on the facts of *Sharman*, 'an article is found on private property it is in the possession of the owner of that property, although he may be unaware of its existence'.[100] It will be recalled that Lord Russell CJ relied on Pollock to decide the case in favour of the plaintiffs on the basis of their prior possession. The judg-ment recognised that *Bridges* was decided on different grounds. This, of course, was entirely accurate, but unfortunately Lord Russell CJ's explanation of *Bridges* tended to emphasise the public nature of the shop premises, rather the absence of intentional deposit. Accordingly we read that:

> The case of *Bridges v Hawkesworth* stands by itself, and on special grounds; and on those grounds it seems to me that the decision in that case was right. Some one had acciden-tally dropped a bundle of bank-notes *in a public shop*. The shopkeeper did not know they had been dropped, and did not in any sense exercise control over them. *The shop was open to the public*, and they were invited to come there ... [T]he finder then sought to recover them from the shopkeeper. It was held that he was entitled to do so, the ground of the decision being, as was pointed out by Patteson J, that the notes, *being dropped in the public part of the shop*, were never in the custody of the shopkeeper, or 'within the protection of his house'.[101]

---

(at 50), including 'shop[s] ... theatres, cinemas, football and cricket grounds, race-courses and railway stations' (at 49).

[98] Even though the Committee noted that a finder might usefully report her find to the police: at 49. See further Chapter 7.

[99] [1896] 2 QB 44, 45.

[100] *Ibid* 45.

[101] *Ibid* 47.

The phrase 'being dropped in the public part of the shop' is technically redundant. It has been correctly observed that Patteson J made no reference to the public nature of the shop premises.[102] Indeed, in the *Jurist* report of *Bridges*, the head-note specifically records that 'the place in which a lost article is found does not constitute any exception to the general rule of law, that the finder is entitled to it as against all persons except the owner'.[103] Accordingly it would have been quite wrong to suggest that the public nature of the premises per se played any deter-minative role in the resolution of that dispute. Of course, this had not been the contention of counsel, and it is by no means clear that Lord Russell meant to over-emphasise it. The passage above also notes that the shopkeeper did not exercise control over the banknotes, and this criterion is wholly consistent with the theory of possession advanced by his Lordship. Insofar as the judgment suggests that the public nature of premises affects the allocation of rights, Lord Russell relied on an argument of counsel suggesting that possession resolves disputes of this kind, but failed to connect the publicity of premises with the absence of possession in the manner intended by counsel.

The Law Reform Committee also failed to make any connection between the nature of premises and the possibility of possession, but the connection is abun-dantly clear in *Parker*. Donaldson LJ referred briefly to the 1971 report, but did not adopt its structure for resolving disputes,[104] preferring to rest a possessor of land's claim to goods found on his land on his ability to prove a manifest intention to control articles which might be on the land. However, all of the judgments in the Court of Appeal approved the view that in practice there would be circum-stances in which the existence of this intention would be so obvious as to speak for itself, and it seems this might be true where goods are found on private premises. So Eveleigh LJ inclined to the view that:

> the occupier of a house will almost invariably possess any lost article on the premises. He may not have taken any positive steps to demonstrate his *animus possidendi*, but so firm is his control that the *animus* can be seen to attach to it.[105]

Here, we see clearly the relationship between the location of the find and proof of possession. Privacy of premises is not relevant per se to the generation of rights, but only to the extent that it affords evidence of the possessory facts of control and/or intention. That is a marked difference from the 1971 report, and is sup-ported by the more recent decision of the Federal Court of Australia in *Chairman of the National Crime Authority v Flack*.[106] This case concerned a claim by a

---

[102] AL Goodhart, 'Three Cases on Possession' (1927–29) 3 *Camb LJ* 195. Patteson J did decide that the banknotes were not within the protection of the defendant's house, but this proposition was intended to recall the common law liabilities of innkeepers, and was not satisfied on the facts owing to the lack of an intentional deposit. The publicity of the locus in quo was nothing to do with it.

[103] (1851) 15 Jur 1079. See also [1982] QB 1004, 1014.

[104] [1982] QB 1004, 1008.

[105] [1982] QB 1004, 1019.

[106] (1998) 156 ALR 501.

tenant of residential premises to a briefcase containing cash lawfully taken from those premises by the police.[107] The successive judgments suggest that it can be presumed from the fact of possession of private premises that the possessor has manifested an intention to control goods found thereon. The only question is about the extent of that presumption.

The highest it could be put would be that possession of private premises always removed the need for the possessor to prove a manifest intention to control lost goods found on the premises. Some support for that proposition can be derived from *Flack*, at least where the premises in question are a private dwelling. At the trial, Hill J thought that the necessary manifestation of intention would always be presumed where the premises 'are residential premises of which the owner/occupier has exclusive possession'.[108] Heerey J agreed with this on appeal,[109] and held the fact of Mrs Flack's possession of residential premises 'sufficient to establish the requisite manifestation of intention to possess all chattels on the premises'.[110] If this view is right, it means in effect that 'goods found on private premises' operates as a categorical corollary to 'goods found in land'. They are both cases where the possessor of land is totally relieved from the burden of proving a manifest intention to control things which might be found there. However, there is reason to believe that the proposition is not so extensive in the case of private dwellings. Eveleigh LJ says that the occupier of a house will 'almost invariably possess' lost articles, but 'almost' leaves room for doubt, and it is at least consistent with his lordship's dictum that there are some circumstances in which the possessor of private premises will not possess lost goods which happen to be lying there. Foster and Tamberlin JJ took this view on appeal in *Flack*, each opining that possession of a private dwelling raised only a presumption of manifest intention, which could be rebutted on the facts.[111]

Whatever the extent of this evidentiary concession to possessors of private premises, it ought to be clear that without more it does not impact upon the *finder's* acquisition of right. A finder who takes possession of goods on private premises still acquires a property right in virtue of that possession. It is just that this acquired right will be subject (and perhaps, if the concession is strongest,

---

[107] The Australian Federal Police lawfully seized a locked briefcase containing AU$433,000 in cash. The briefcase had been hidden on residential premises, of which Mrs Flack was the tenant in possession. She denied ownership and even knowledge of the monies, but successfully claimed their recovery from the police on the strength of a prior possessory title: *ibid* 512.

[108] (1997) 150 ALR 153, 162.

[109] (1998) 156 ALR 511.

[110] *Ibid* 510.

[111] *Ibid* 506 (Foster J); 514 (Tamberlin J). Notice that if the presumption is not irrefutable in the case of private dwellings, a fortiori it would seem rebuttable in the case of private premises other than dwellings. There is a sense from Pollock onwards that a private home is the most private of locations. In *Flack*, Foster J thought that, for the purposes of the general law on possession, the occupier of a home was 'in a special position': (1998) 156 ALR 501, 506, and see too the comments of Tamberlin J at 514–15.

*necessarily* subject) to the better right of the possessor of land, who is relieved (to some extent) of the burden of proving a manifest intention to control lost goods found on his premises. Otherwise there is nothing to suggest that the finder's acquisition is qualified. She still has a right good against the world save those establishing a prior right, and will be able to resist interference from anyone coming later in time to the find.

For completeness we should add that it seems to make no difference to the resolution of disputes that the land on which a find was made was a publicly owned space. This is the effect of the decision in *Waverly Borough Council v Fletcher*.[112] The council was freehold owner of the land in question, but by certain covenants it was bound to use the land for the recreation of the public, as a 'park' within the meaning of the Open Spaces Act 1906.[113] At trial, the judge had relied on this fact to hold that the council was obliged to permit Mr Fletcher to engage in metal detecting and incidental digging,[114] and at least in part this influenced the ruling in favour of Mr Fletcher.[115] The Court of Appeal rejected any contention that the council was bound to permit metal detecting,[116] but it also went further, holding generally that the facts and obligations of public use did not oust the ordinarily applicable rules of possession. Having accepted that the council was the occupier of the park,[117] Auld LJ could 'see no basis for not applying the general rule that an owner or lawful possessor of land has a better title … or for modifying it in some way to produce a different result in the circumstances of this case'.[118] The council was able to establish a better right than Mr Fletcher to the brooch because it was found buried in the park-land.[119] Accordingly we can see that the ordinary rules of possession apply, and the finder gains no advantage from having made her find in a public space.

---

[112] [1996] QB 334. Cf an interesting discussion of the first instance decision in *Waverly*, suggesting that the question 'who owns objects found on public land' was 'a new and difficult issue': C MacMillan, 'Finders Keepers, Losers Weepers: But Who Are the Losers?' (1995) 58 *MLR* 101, 102. The Court of Appeal judgment makes the answer to this question depend on the ordinary rules of possession, and in part this seemed MacMillan's own conclusion. Her argument includes the view that the council could set up a better possessory right than Mr Fletcher (at 103, 108); but also approves the Treasure Act 1996 as a method of protecting the interest of the public in articles of historical significance (at 108).

[113] [1996] QB 334, 347.

[114] [1996] QB 334, 348.

[115] The first instance judgment also rejected the existence of any 'in/on land' distinction, and cast doubt on the council's occupation of the park by appearing to hold that the only way it could exercise effective acts of control was by prosecution for infringement of byelaws, or general resort to the criminal law: *ibid* 336, 349.

[116] *Ibid* 348–9. Metal detecting was not 'of a like nature' to other sports or pastimes, such as golf or cricket, which might involve some incidental 'disturbance of the soil': at 348.

[117] Accurately, the judgment is equivocal on whether the council was owner, occupier or possessor of the park, but in any case the court was roundly against any suggestion that the council could not exercise effective acts of control: *ibid* 350.

[118] *Ibid* 350.

[119] [1996] QB 334, 350; and see generally Chapter 2.

# A Pervasive Right

We have argued that the better view of our authorities is that a finder's right is never altered by the presence of the circumstances discussed (though in the case of employment she might find herself obligated to account to her employer for the value of the find, and in the case of private premises she might find her right subject to the necessarily better right of the possessor of land). It follows that a finder who takes possession of some thing always acquires in it a property right. Moreover, insofar as possession is the source of that right, it is a property right in the fullest sense, transmissible in the manner appropriate to the thing in question, and attracting the standard incidents of ownership. This was Pollock's view, and since 1896 we have been applying it in the resolution of finding disputes. In proprietary terms, the finder's vulnerability is only to one who can prove a better (because earlier) right, whether on the facts of possession or by some other title. In this sense, it matters not whether the finder is dishonest, a trespasser, in a private place, or an employee.

Considered in these terms, English law appears very favourable to the finder. Finders are always relative owners, and after almost 300 years, the bare statement of principle in *Armory v Delamirie* looks not too far away from the truth. Yet it would be entirely wrong to conclude from this proposition that finders can always be keepers under English law. Despite being the holder of a property right, the finder is not free to profit from the find, at least not immediately. She may not use her find with impunity, neither may she deal with it, sell it on, give it away, or in any way increase her wealth without also being answerable for its value. We have already hinted at the reason in Chapter 4. The property rule must not be read in isolation. The finder is a property holder, but her actions in respect of the chattel are constrained by the criminal law and the general law of obligations. To this issue we now turn, in order to argue that, as it stands, the English law relating to finders pursues sensible policy objectives.

# 7

## Defending the Doctrines

We have already accepted that the law of finds must meet the needs of society. The cases establish that finders acquire property rights and never incur specific obligations, but these propositions will only be worth preserving if they fulfil some desirable social purpose. In other jurisdictions, reform of the common law rules has not been uncommon,[1] and in England too there was once a call for legislative change.[2] In this final chapter, however, we defend the continued authority of our common law doctrines, arguing that they aim at useful policies and are not in need of reform.

The argument is made in two stages. First we consider modern legislative initiatives which exist to augment the common law positions in Scotland and several US state jurisdictions. Whilst provisions vary across these jurisdictions, we suggest in general that they aim at a two-tiered policy, facilitating the restoration of lost goods to their loser in the first instance, but providing alternative arrangements in favour of the finder in the event that the loser cannot be traced. Next we argue that, correctly understood, the current law in England reflects this same two-tiered structure. Central here is the contention that the laws we have already established must be read in the light of countervailing rules of crime and tort. We consider the impact on finders of certain rules of theft and conversion, and argue that, taken together with the right acquired by possession, they provide strong incentives for the finder to locate the loser, but justify her continued retention of the goods if the loser cannot be found.

## Lost Property Regulation in Other Jurisdictions

At first blush, the Scots law relating to finders seems diametrically opposed to English law. In England, in every situation a finder acquires a relatively good property right in the object of her find, and she is not under any direct obligation to seek out the loser. In Scotland, a finder acquires no property right in her find, and comes under immediate positive obligations to take reasonable care of it and to

---

[1] As to which, see further below.
[2] Law Reform Committee, *Eighteenth Report (Conversion and Detinue)*, Cmnd 4774 (1971) 48.

report the circumstances of the find to the owner of the goods or the police. The first of these propositions is true at Scots common law, according to which lost and abandoned things belong to the Crown.[3] Generally, there is provision for such things to be donated to the finder,[4] but in this case the finder's title is derivative, and it is not possible for her to acquire any common law title separately from the transfer. Specifically, it is not possible for a finder to acquire an ownership interest on the basis of possession.[5]

In recent years these common law rules have been augmented by legislation. Part VI of the Civic Government (Scotland) Act 1982 provides authoritative arrangements for the reporting and distribution of found goods. Section 73 adopts the common law's denial of right to the finder in these terms:

No person who—

(a)   finds any property appearing to have been lost or abandoned;
(b)   is the employer of a finder of such property; or
(c)   owns or occupies the land or premises on which such property is found,

shall by reason only of the finding of that property have any right to claim ownership of it.[6]

However, whilst she acquires no property right, the finder who takes possession[7] of lost or abandoned goods is immediately subjected to certain obligations. She is bound to take reasonable care of the thing, and without unreasonable delay must deliver it or report the circumstances of the find to a police constable, or to certain specified others, including the owner of the thing or the owner of the premises on which it was found.[8] Whichever of these receives the report in the first instance, the goal in every case is to reunite lost things with their losers, or in the alternative

---

[3] W Guthrie (ed), *Bell's Principles of the Law of Scotland* 10th edn (Edinburgh, Law Society of Scotland, 1989) para 1291, explaining that 'The principle on which this rests is public expediency, to avoid fraud, contests, and litigation, together with some slight purpose of adding to the public revenue'.

[4] Ibid para 1287.

[5] Scotland's possessory regime differs markedly from that operating in England: DL Carey-Miller, *Corporeal Moveables in Scots Law* (Edinburgh, W Green, 1991) 1.13. Various forms of possession are protected, but where possession creates legal rights, these are always regarded as distinct from, and inferior to, rights of property: Stair Inst.II.i.8. It is possible to acquire an original ownership interest by possession where the thing in question has never been the subject of private property rights (Stair Inst.II.i.33; Bell Prin § 1287) but this *occupatio* principle does not apply to previously owned things, which belong as we have said to the Crown: Carey-Miller, *ibid* 2.02, citing Bell Prin, § 1287.

[6] Crown rights to lost and abandoned goods are also preserved by s 78, though as we will see the statute provides further vesting arrangements which have the effect of extinguishing the Crown's title: s 78(2), (3).

[7] Technically, in Scots law 'finder who takes possession' is a tautology: used as a term of art the former implies the latter. Section 67(1) defines 'a finder' as 'any person taking possession of any property without the authority of the owner in circumstances which make it reasonable to infer that the property has been lost or abandoned'.

[8] Section 67(1).

to report the matter to the police.[9] By section 67(6), the finder who does not comply with this procedure is guilty of a criminal offence.

In the event that the find is reported or delivered to the police, further provisions specify the procedure to be followed by the chief constable. He must make arrangements for the goods to be stored safely,[10] and take reasonable steps to ascertain the identity of the owner and notify him of the location of the find.[11] If the owner claims the find within two months, the chief constable can return it to him,[12] though he has power to direct that the owner pay a reward.[13] On the expiry of two months, the chief constable can offer the thing to the finder.[14] If the finder accepts, she acquires an original ownership interest in the find in virtue of the statute,[15] subject only to a right of compensation in favour of the owner. Section 71(2) allows 'the previous owner' a year and a day to recover possession of the thing following its gratuitous transfer to the finder. The nature of the finder's right does not change on expiry of that limitation period, but she is then immune from suit, and in that sense becomes absolutely entitled to the find. Accordingly, we see a twofold emphasis in the Scots law of lost property. In the first instance, the law requires finds to be reported and strives to reunite lost things with their owners; but if this cannot quickly be achieved the law provides for the continued use of the thing by the finder, subject only to the time-limited claim of the owner.

---

[9] The other alternative candidates for delivery are some person having a right to possession of the find, or some person apparently having the authority to act on behalf of any of those named in the provision: s 67(3). Where the finder chooses to report the find to the owner of the premises, that owner comes under a similar obligation to report to the police, a right-holder or the agent of a right-holder: s 67(4)(a). If the finder reports to the agent of a right-holder, the agent is bound to report to the right-holder or the police: s 67(4)(b). Thus, there is a chain of required reporting, and it is a safe summary to say that the legislation seeks to ensure that finds are reported to one who holds a right in the find or to the police. Carey-Miller calls this 'the basic obligation' of finders: Carey-Miller, above n 5 at 2.08. See also KGC Reid, *The Law of Property in Scotland* (Edinburgh, Butterworths, 1996) para 548.

[10] Section 68(2).

[11] Section 68(3).

[12] See s 69(2). Of course, the chief constable must be satisfied that the claimant is the owner of the thing, or has a right to possession of it: s 69(2). The remainder of this subsection makes provision for delivery of the thing to the owner, including the ability of the chief constable to claim reasonable expenses incurred in the course of managing the find.

[13] Section 70(1)(a) provides that, in the event of any claim for return being made by the owner under s 69, 'the chief constable may ... order the claimant to pay to the chief constable such sum as he may determine as a reward to the finder'.

[14] Section 70(1)(b), which also contains a provision for payment of monetary reward in lieu of transfer. Note that according to s 68(4), the thing need not be offered to the finder if the chief constable considers such disposition inappropriate. No guidance is given in the statute as to the meaning of inappropriate, but Reid gives the example of a packet of drugs, and we might suppose the section would cover any contraband or harmful goods: see KGC Reid, *The Law of Property in Scotland* (Edinburgh, Butterworths, 1996) para 549. Where the chief constable does consider it inappropriate to transfer the thing to the finder, s 68(4) allows it to be sold. If it is impractical to sell, the chief constable is empowered to make such further disposal as he sees fit.

[15] Section 71(1) provides that such transfer 'shall ... vest the ownership of the property' in the finder. The same is true of any third party transferee who takes by way of disposition from the chief constable authorised under s 68.

This same emphasis is apparent across the jurisdictions of the United States, many of which have enacted legislation to supplement their common law rules on finders.[16] There is tremendous variety in the technical details of these provisions (indeed, across the various jurisdictions we will find no two lost property statutes which are exactly alike), but we will see that their intended outcome is always the same. As with Scots law, the finder who takes possession of lost goods is immediately subjected to certain obligations. Some states designate the finder a depositary for the owner, owing duties to the owner in virtue of that status;[17] others impose positive obligations of reasonable care;[18] and most allow the finder to recover expenses incurred in the discharge of her duties.[19] Usually finders are required to identify the owner if possible, making reasonable efforts to locate him,[20] though some states give finders the option simply of reporting the matter to the police[21] or advertising the find in the locale.[22] In any case, the goal is always to reunite losers with the things they have lost. Typical in this respect is section 2080 of the California Civil Code. It directs finders to inform the owner of the find within a reasonable time, and to 'make restitution without compensation'.[23]

In the event that the owner cannot be found, states posit alternative procedures for reporting and storing finds. The police are typical candidates for receiving reports,[24] as are cognate authorities,[25] and sometimes the finder is required to file an affidavit in the circuit court of the county.[26] At this point some states draw categorical distinctions in goods, such that the requisite obligations depend on the nature or (more usually) the value of the goods in question.[27] In California, where the owner is unknown, finders are bound to turn over to the police objects worth more than US$100.[28] Illinois also uses US$100 as a dividing point, but does not require the finder to deposit such items with the police. Instead, finders can retain and store found goods whatever their value, but where they are worth US$100 or more the finder must file an affidavit in the circuit court of the county,[29] with the county clerk then bearing the responsibility of causing the find to be advertised. Finders

---

[16] For a discussion of the common law rules operating in US states, see Chapter 3.

[17] Code of Alabama § 35-12-1; California Civil Code§ 2080; *United States v Crawford*, 239 F3d 1086 (2001) (Court of Appeals for the Ninth Circuit); Montana Code Annotated § 70-5-102; North Dakota Century Code § 60-01-34.

[18] Iowa Code § 556F.16.

[19] California Civil Code § 2080; 765 Illinois Compiled Statutes 1020/30; Iowa Code § 556F.14; New York Personal Property Law § 254.1.

[20] New Jersey Statutes § 46:30C-3; New York Personal Property Law § 252.

[21] Rhode Island General Laws § 33-21.2-1.

[22] Vermont 27 VSA § 1101.

[23] California Civil Code § 2080. Also 765 Illinois Compiled Statutes 1020/27; Iowa Code § 556F.6.

[24] California Civil Code § 2080.1; New Jersey Statutes § 46:30C-3.

[25] Such as the sheriff for finds outside city limits in California: California Civil Code § 2080.1.

[26] 765 Illinois Compiled Statutes 1020/27.

[27] In Michigan there is a very detailed system turning on factual classification of goods rather than a nominated value: Michigan Compiled Laws § 434.22.

[28] California Civil Code § 2080.1. And 765 Illinois Compiled Statutes 1020/27.

[29] 765 Illinois Compiled Statutes 1020/27.

must advertise lower valued items themselves.[30] In this case a typical requirement is advertisement on the door of the courthouse.[31] In Oregon, as in Illinois, goods valued at US$100 or more must be advertised 'in a newspaper of general circulation in the county', though in Oregon it is the finder who must cause the advertisement.[32] Notwithstanding these interstate differences in the details, the goal is clearly that losers are apprised of their loss. In states where lost goods can be deposited with the police, they too must make a 'reasonable attempt to ascertain the rightful owner'.[33]

Should the process of advertising fail to attract the loser, states make provision for title to lost goods to vest in the finder. Of course, one obvious difference between the Scottish and US jurisdictions is that at US state common law, finders are able to acquire property rights to lost goods.[34] In that respect, we might not feel vesting provisions to be strictly necessary in the United States, at least not in the Scottish sense of recognising an original right where none existed before. Nonetheless, this is the mechanism typically adopted by state legislation.[35] The time periods differ from state to state, and again can depend on the value or categorisation of the goods in question,[36] but overall the intended outcome is clear. In the first instance, efforts must be made to reunite lost goods with their owners; if these are not successful then the finder is entitled to the thing in the alternative. On occasion, this policy has been confirmed expressly. Prior to the introduction of the lost property rules in New York, the New York State Law Revision Commission commented that the provisions were designed to 'promote the return of the property to the owner and at the same time protect the expectations of the finder'.[37] Later, the Court of Appeals of New York referred to that comment and suggested that the laws encouraged 'responsible action' by finders.[38] The clearest statement is found in *Paset v Old Orchard Bank*, where the Appellate Court of Illinois explained that:

> [the] statute's principal purposes are to encourage and facilitate the return of property to the true owner, and then to reward a finder for his honesty if the property remains

---

[30] 765 Illinois Compiled Statutes 1020/28.

[31] 765 Illinois Compiled Statutes 1020/27; Iowa Code § 556F.8.

[32] Oregon Revised Statutes § 98.005(1).

[33] Florida Statute § 705.103.

[34] But not to *mislaid* goods: see Chapter 3 for consideration of US state common law.

[35] 765 Illinois Compiled Statutes 1020/28; Iowa Code § 556F.11; New York Personal Property Law § 257.1; North Dakota Century Code § 60-01-34; Oregon Revised Statutes § 98.005(2); Rhode Island General Laws § 33-21.2-2; Wisconsin Statute § 170.10.

[36] In Illinois and Iowa, goods valued at less than US$100 vest in the finder after six months, 12 months for goods worth more than US$100: 765 Illinois Compiled Statutes 1020/28; Iowa Code § 556F.3. In California and Rhode Island, lost goods enure to the finder 90 days after they are turned over to the police: 120 days in New Jersey: California Civil Code § 2080.2; Rhode Island General Laws § 33-21.2-3; New Jersey Statute § 46:30C-4. New York has a fourfold categorisation scheme, ranging from three months for articles valued at less than US$100 to three years for those valued at greater than US$5,000: New York Personal Property Law § 253.7.

[37] NY Legis Doc 1957, No. 65 [L], 11.

[38] *Kubli v Rosetti*, 34 NY2d 68, 72 (1974) (Rabin, J, Chief Judge Breitel and Judges Jasen, Gabrielli, Jones and Wachtler concurring).

unclaimed. The statute provides an incentive for finders to report their discoveries by making it possible for them, after the passage of the requisite time, to acquire legal title to the property they have found.[39]

Notwithstanding clear differences from the provisions operating in Scotland, these US sources point to an identical policy, and really involve very similar structures. The machinery is always two-tiered. First, a set of rules facilitates the restoration of lost items to losers, by providing for finders or others to take certain steps in pursuance of that goal, and often by directly obligating them to do so. Secondly, in the event that lost goods remain unclaimed by the loser, provision is made for the transfer of rights to some other, usually the finder. This preliminary conclusion will do well as a guide for assessing the English rules.

# Understanding English Law: Property, Tort and Crime and the Pursuit of Sensible Policy Aims

In England, the finder's legal rights begin with her possession. In every case where a finder has taken possession of some thing, she acquires in virtue of that possession an ownership interest in the find, which interest is ranked relatively to any others according to which of them was the earliest in time. But inasmuch as it is clear that in every case the finder is relatively *an owner* of the find, it does not follow that she is immediately at liberty to use it. Prior property rights in the thing withstand its casual loss. Indeed, in the absence of any clear authority to suggest that divesting abandonment is possible at common law,[40] it is likely that they also withstand its deliberate relinquishment. Accordingly, at the moment of acquisition, the finder's right is always subordinate to the right of at least one other person (ie her immediate predecessor in possession).[41] The finder is bound to respect this right. We saw in Chapter 4 that a tortious conversion occurs whenever a defendant manifests 'an assertion of rights or dominion over the goods which is inconsistent with the rights of the plaintiff'.[42] It makes no difference that this assertion is transient or even trivial.[43] Therefore, it will always be conversion for a finder to make any use of her find, never mind entirely consume or destroy it. If the maxim 'finders keepers' is supposed to imply that that a finder is at liberty to do what she likes with her find (to treat it instantly and unreservedly *as her own*) then finders can never be keepers at English law.

---

[39]  62 Ill App 3d 534, 537 (1978) (Simon J, McNamara and McGillicuddy JJ concurring).
[40]  Chapter 3.
[41]  The only exceptions to this are genuine cases of first acquisition, which today are probably limited to the capture of wild animals.
[42]  *Kuwait Airways* [2002] 2 AC 883, 1104 (Lord Steyn).
[43]  *Petre v Heneage* (1701) 12 Mod 519.

It might rightly be objected that, without more, the tort of conversion provides incomplete protection for losers of goods, for two reasons. First, as we saw earlier, whilst it is certainly wrongful for a finder to use found goods, she does no conversion merely by refusing to seek out the loser. A finder might do nothing with the object of her find. She might find it, store it, make no efforts to trace the loser, and commit no conversion. Secondly, despite the wrongness of the action, English law provides an incentive for finders to commit conversions of the things that they find. The incentive depends on certain provisions of the Limitation Act 1980. That statute gives the general time limit for actions founded on tort as six years.[44] Section 3(2) goes on to provide that, for actions in respect of conversion, the claimant's title will also be extinguished on expiry of the limitation period. Thus, if a finder commits a conversion, she will be absolutely entitled to the object of her find on the expiry of six years, providied the loser (or other prior possessor) does not assert his right within this time. On the expiry of the limitation period, the finder will be at liberty to treat the thing as her own, and the old 'finders keepers' adage begins to look true. Thus, conversion appears not only to provide incomplete protection for the rights of the loser, but also serves to incentivise conduct by the finder which ultimately could lead to the extinction of those rights. At the very least this is a paradox, but it has not been left unresolved. We will see that each difficulty is overcome by rules relating to theft.

## Theft and Entailed Behaviour

Earlier we saw that, despite technically shifting the emphasis from *actus reus* to *mens rea*, section 2(1)(c) of the Theft Act 1968 preserves the substance of the old common rules on larceny by finding and provides a defence to finders charged with theft.[45] A person is not to be regarded as dishonest if she appropriates property in the belief that the true owner cannot be found by taking reasonable steps. It is clear that the defence relates to the actual state of mind of the accused,[46] and modern texts emphasise this by observing that prima facie it matters not that the belief of the accused was unreasonable. If a defendant finder 'wrongly and unreasonably' supposes the only way to locate the loser is by drastically expensive action, on a literal reading of the Act it seems that she must be acquitted.[47] A fortiori, if the defendant wrongly but unreasonably believes that the find in question

---

[44] Limitation Act 1980, s 2.

[45] See Chapters 1 and 3.

[46] D Ormerod and DH Williams (eds), *Smith's The Law of Theft* 9th edn (Oxford, OUP, 2007) 2.271, 2.284.

[47] *Ibid* 2.284. The example given in this leading text has the defendant wrongly and unreasonably supposing that the only way to locate the loser is to buy a full-page advertisement in *The Times*. In the 5th edition of the work, JC Smith noted that even where the defendant finder knows the identity of the loser, he may not be dishonest if he believes the goods can only be restored by taking wholly unreasonable steps: JC Smith, *The Law of Theft* 5th edn (London, Butterworths, 1984) para 118.

has been abandoned, or otherwise is ownerless, such that there is no one to trace by reasonable steps, it would seem also that she must be acquitted.[48]

All of this is doubtlessly correct, and might give the impression that it is difficult to secure convictions for theft against finders. However, if a finder is to avail of the section 2 defence, she will need to lead evidence that she believed the loser could not be discovered by taking reasonable steps.[49] Whist it seems trite that the reasonableness of the finder's belief will not be evaluated by the court once that belief has been appropriately evidenced, the history of larceny and theft makes it clear that *the evidence* will be tested against inferences drawn from the facts as they appear to the court in order to determine what the finder *actually believed*. This process of interpretation will sometimes prevent the finder from establishing the existence of the relevant belief on the facts. For example, if the owner's name is on the thing, or if there is some mark on it by which he could be discovered, a finder will not succeed in making out the defence,[50] and the same is true where other circumstances of the find make it impossible for her to suggest that she believed the loser could not be traced with reasonable steps. In *Coffin*,[51] an actor lost £50 in banknotes somewhere in a theatre. A stage assistant, found the banknotes in the auditorium, and converted them to his own use. The notes were unmarked, and the actor gave evidence to suggest that the stage assistant had no way of knowing that he would have been carrying such a sum on his person. Nonetheless, the conversion was felonious. The Common Serjeant (whose opinion was later verified by Platt B) ruled that, unless a defendant made 'some endeavour, by advertisement or otherwise' to trace the loser, then he was guilty of larceny even though 'utterly ignorant' of the loser's identity at the time of the find.[52] The same result was reached in *Moore*, where the defendant converted a £10 note he found on the floor of a barber's shop.[53] Indeed, it seems that even where unmarked goods were found on a highway, that most public of public places, there might still be room for a jury to infer that the loser could have been found by taking reasonable steps, and that the defendant believed as much.[54]

---

[48] See JC Smith, 'Title to Discovered Antiquities: Theft and Possessory Title' in *Title to Finds and Discovered Antiquities*, Seminar Proceedings of the Institute of Art and Law, 3 October 1995, reading 4, 2; and Chapter 3.

[49] The burden of proof is always on the prosecution, but any defendant to a charge of theft will bear the evidential burden of ensuring that the dishonesty question is a live issue: see E Griew, *The Theft Acts* 7th edn (London, Sweet and Maxwell, 1995) 2-120.

[50] JWC Turner (ed), *Russell on Crime* 14th edn (London, Stevens, 1964) vol II, 1016, citing an anonymous and unreported decision of Lawrence J in 1804.

[51] (1846) 2 Cox CC 44 (Central Criminal Court).

[52] *Ibid*. Following the verdict, the serjeant sought the opinion of the judges at the request of counsel. The reporter notes that Platt B considered the ruling to be correct.

[53] [1861] Le & Ca 1, especially the comments of Cockburn CJ in argument, at 6–8.

[54] *R v Glyde* (1868) LR 1 CCR 139, 144 (Cockburn CJ), though on the facts of that case there was not enough evidence to convict the defendant of larceny of a sovereign coin.

This practice of interpreting the beliefs of finders in the light of an objective view of the circumstances of a case is entirely consistent with the development of larceny by finding,[55] and has crucial implications for the ways in which finders behave. In essence, the difficulty of leading evidence on a section 2 defence means that a finder is most likely to escape the inference that she was dishonest if she actually takes reasonable steps to trace the loser. In *Bird v Fort Frances*, a civil case where there was at least a suspicion that the finder was guilty of theft, McRuer CJHC opined that criminal intent could be disproved by reporting a find to the police, and we have already seen the suggestion in *Coffin* that this would be true where the finder made some other endeavour to trace the loser. Accordingly, Turner observed that:

> In cases of taking on finding, some of the strongest circumstances to rebut the impli-
> cation that such taking was felonious, will be those which show that the taker made it
> known that he had found the property.[56]

In effect, then, whilst in most cases the finder is not under a direct obligation to report her find, making it known that she has found something (whether to the police or to another appropriate person or authority) is a significant step in resisting any subsequent charge of theft. The desire to avoid criminal responsibil-ity might in itself be enough to motivate finders to report discoveries, but there is also an acquisitive incentive indirectly provided by limitation rules applicable to theftuous conversions. Since 1980, no time limit runs against a thief in respect of her conversion of stolen goods.[57] The normal time limit does run from the date of the first good faith purchase after the theft,[58] and thereafter the owner's title

---

[55] It will be recalled from Chapter 3 that the courts also used factual classifications to achieve convictions, frequently denying a defence to finders because the goods in question were not 'really lost' at the time of the taking. So in *R v Pierce* (1852) 6 Cox CC 117, it was larceny for the employee of a railway company to convert a suitcase left behind in a carriage; and in *R v West* (1854) 6 Cox CC 415, it was larceny for a market stall holder to convert a purse left behind by a customer. Earlier, we said that these were cases where the finder was not justified in believing that the loser could not be found, because the circumstances showed he was likely to return to claim the goods: see Chapter 3. It does little violence to shift the emphasis and take these as further evidence that judges and juries used the circumstances of a case to draw inferences about whether the defendant really did believe that the loser could be discovered by taking reasonable steps: *Russell on Crime*, vol II, 1015, discussing *R v Moore* [1861] Le & Ca 1.

[56] *Russell on Crime*, vol II, 1014, citing *Matthews* (1873) 12 Cox CC 489. See also McCutcheon, noting that the existence of lost-and-found facilities is relevant to the determination of the finder's actual beliefs: JP McCutcheon, *The Larceny Act 1916* (Dublin, Round Hall Press, 1989) 39; and OR Marshall, 'The Problem of Finding' (1949) 2 *Current Legal Problems* 68, 73.

[57] Limitation Act 1980, s 4(1). See generally *EPL*, 17.333–17.335; *Clerk and Lindsell on Torts*, 33-29–33-33.

[58] Limitation Act 1980, s 4(2). The drafting is extremely cumbersome. On a first reading, the provi-sions are almost impenetrable, but there seems little doubt as to their intended effect. Sections 4(1) and (2) of the Act give the general rule that the right of any person from whom a chattel is stolen to bring an action in respect of 'any conversion related to the theft' of that chattel shall not be subject to the ordinary time limits for conversion. Subsection 2 provides further that 'every conversion following the theft of a chattel' is to be treated as a conversion 'related to the theft'. But the final sentence of s 4(2) also notes exceptionally that 'if anyone purchases the stolen chattel in good faith neither the

will be extinguished on the expiry of six years,[59] but even then, the effect of the statutory provisions is such that it remains possible for the owner to sue the thief, and any other converter intermediating the theft and the good faith purchase.[60] This affords a large measure of protection to owners of stolen goods. From the point of view of a finder, it offers a radical incentive to dissociate herself from the circumstances of theft. The finder who is thief will never be able to avail of the limitation provisions to have her title confirmed as against the loser. Even if she succeeds in starting the time period by selling the thing to a good faith purchaser (indeed, even if that limit expires), she remains liable in conversion to the loser for the value of the goods. Nothing can be gained in the long run by the dishonest finder, either by keeping the goods, or by selling them. The loser will always remain a threat, and the finder will always remain liable to answer him for the value of the goods.

Accordingly, the finder has a double incentive to take reasonable steps to locate the loser of goods. Her interests will best be served by reporting her find and engaging some reasonable effort to trace the loser.[61] General practice appears to be that the police will deal with lost goods found in a street, whilst all other finds should be reported to the occupier of the premises on which they are found.[62] Note that in neither case need the finder deposit the goods with the third party, though if she does, as in *Bridges*, *Hannah* and *Parker*, the finder should bail the goods on terms which (a) require them to be kept safely for their loser; and (b) provide for their return to the finder in the event that they are not claimed by the loser. Of course, in making any effort to trace the loser the finder exposes herself to the chance that the goods will actually be claimed by him, and the consequential risk that she will profit nothing from the find, but this risk exists in

---

purchase nor any conversion following it shall be regarded as related to theft'. So, by exempting good faith purchases from any relation to a preceding theft, the statute exempts them from the general rule disapplying the time limit, and accordingly treats them as conversions in respect of which the ordinary time limit can run. See *EPL*, 17.335.

[59] Limitation Act 1980, s 3(2).

[60] The final clauses of s 4(2) in effect provide that, where an owner's title to goods has been extinguished, he may still bring an action in respect of any conversion related to a theft if that theft 'preceded the conversion from which time began to run'. So, where goods are stolen and sold to a good faith purchaser: (i) no time limit runs from the date of the theft (s 4(1)); (ii) a time limit does run from the date of the good faith purchase (s 4(1) and (2)); but (iii) even if the owner's title is extinguished six years after (ii), his action still lies against the thief, insofar as the theft preceded the conversion that commenced the limitation period. Again, see *EPL*, 17.335; *Clerk and Lindsell on Torts*, 33-33.

[61] Strictly, the finder is not required to report the find in order to avoid the implication of theft: she might do so just as well by advertising the find in an appropriate manner. But the involvement of a third party benefits the finder inasmuch as it provides external evidence of her attempts to trace the loser.

[62] See eg the guidelines of the Metropolitan Police Service at http://cms.met.police.uk/met/boroughs/islington/06advice_and_support/lost_property; and those of the West Midlands Police Service at www.west-midlands.police.uk/publications/freedom-of-information/policy.asp?id=121. The police will also deal with things lost in taxis. Public Transport providers usually make provision for lost property found on their services. Lost animals appear to be the responsibility of local councils.

every alternative scenario.[63] If the goods are not claimed by the loser, the finder is entitled to take them back. She has a continuing property right in the goods such that it would be conversion to refuse her demand for their return.[64] Moreover, when she takes redelivery of the goods, the finder can use them with impunity: it will not then be theft to convert goods because the finder can defend herself by leading evidence that she had taken reasonable steps to trace their loser. Such a non-theftuous conversion will trigger the six-year limitation period, the expiry of which will extinguish the prior rights of the loser. Accordingly, by reporting her find, the finder opens up the possibility that one day she will be absolutely entitled to the goods in question. In this sense finders can eventually be keepers, but only if (a) they have made known their finds in the first instance; and (b) the loser has not claimed the goods within the limitation period.

## Evaluating English Law

Understood in this way, English law evidences the same two-tiered structure found in the legislation of Scotland and the United States, and also in the policy observations of Donaldson LJ *Parker*.[65] Our rules about theft and theftuous conversions provide incentives for finds to be made known, and thereby encourage in the first instance that lost goods are reunited with their loser. The continuing property right of the loser explains his entitlement to have the thing (or its value) restored to him, but the relatively good property right of the finder also explains her entitlement to have the thing if the loser cannot be found. As in the legislated jurisdictions, for a certain time the loser retains the right to reclaim the goods after any redelivery to the finder, though in England this time period is provided by the general limits on his action for conversion, and the finder's right is confirmed negatively by the extinction of competing rights, rather than affirmatively, by prescription, vesting order or transfer. Be that as it may, overall the policy has

---

[63] If the finder converts the goods without report she risks application of the no time limit rule for theftuous conversion and the prospect that she will have to answer to the loser for the value of the goods at any time in the future, notwithstanding their consumption or transfer. If the finder does nothing, keeping but neither converting nor reporting the find, she does not convert the goods and triggers no time limit. She will be bound to answer an unequivocal demand for return of the goods at any point in the future.

[64] This is very clearly so in the case of the police: *Costello v Chief Constable of Derbyshire* [2001] 1 WLR 1437 (CA). In the case of possessors of land, it is complicated only insofar as the possessor of land might have a better right to the goods than the finder. Where there is a doubt, or where the possessor of land wishes to assert a prior claim to that of the finder, he might interplead to resolve the question of title. Notice, too, that where at the time of finding the finder suspects that the possessor of land has a better title, she has still the same incentive to report the find to the possessor of land even if thereby she effectively forfeits her own claim to the goods. It is very clear that theft proceedings might lie at the behest of a non-owning possessor of land (see *Hibbert* and *Rostron*), and accordingly the finder risks the adverse consequences of an implication of theft in the usual way.

[65] [1982] QB 1004, 1017. See Chapter 4.

the same direction. Losers must be sought first, but finders have an entitlement in the alternative if that process fails.

To the extent that it pursues and accomplishes the policies achieved by legislation in Scotland and the United States, the argument for comparative reform of English law is weakened. Indeed, when in 1971 the Law Reform Committee recommended legislative action, their report was premised jointly on the views that (a) the law relating to a finder's rights was in need of clarification; and (b) the law should be structured so as best to facilitate the restoration of lost goods to their loser. In Chapter 2, we argued that the first of these complaints disappears when the law is understood to revolve around the concept of possession deployed since *South Staffs Water Co v Sharman*. We might now answer to the second that the law actually does conform to the suggested structure when the concept of possession is understood in the light of countervailing rules of crime and tort.

It might still seem more satisfactory to impose on finders direct obligations to facilitate the restoration of lost goods to losers. The great advantage of so doing is that it ensures in every case that there is adequate ground for holding that *by law* a finder *must* take the required steps. If we are right about English law, the finder has an incentive to report her find only on facts which are capable of generating (at least the risk of) a conviction for theft. There might sometimes be circumstances where a finder actually does believe that a loser cannot be traced by taking reasonable steps, and can prove as much, and here the policy will break down even though as a matter of property the loser's rights are the same. However, this objection is countered by the generality of the difficulty of leading evidence on a section 2 defence. Such are the interpretative practices of the criminal courts that it would now seem almost impossible for a finder to succeed on this front where goods are found on premises to which the public have access (airport lounges, theatres, hotel lobbies, supermarkets, parks, and so on), and a fortiori to private premises, unless the finder actually has reported the find to the occupier of the premises or to the police.[66] Accordingly, the defence exists as a theoretical possibility only where goods are found on a street or highway, and perhaps too on open or remote places where it is not easy to identify a person responsible for the land. But since local police forces are prepared to accept reports of such finds, and sometimes provide telephone reporting mechanisms,[67] it must be becoming more difficult even in these circumstances to argue a belief that the loser could not be traced by taking reasonable steps. Therefore, since it is the *risk* of conviction

---

[66] *R v Coffin* (1846) 2 Cox CC 44. Public places typically have some lost-and-found facility, or at least some lost property policy, and even if in fact they do not, reporting the find to the occupier of the premises (or his employee) still provides a reasonable means of tracing the loser. McCutcheon notes that the existence of lost-and-found facilities is relevant to the determination of the finder's actual beliefs: JP McCutcheon, *The Larceny Act 1916* (Dublin, Round Hall Press, 1989) 39.

[67] Police forces happy to receive reports of lost property fond in the street by telephone include the Metropolitan Police, http://cms.met.police.uk/met; Sussex Police, www.sussex.police.uk/infocentre/content.asp?uid=230; the Devon and Cornwall Police, www.devon-cornwall.police.uk/v3/infopnt/faqs/property.htm.

for theft which provides an incentive for the finder to act, English law seems at least to be moving in the right direction inasmuch as there is a reasonable risk of conviction across the full range of circumstances, though we might concede that risk is lower by some degree where goods are found in the street.

Even if we accept that English law replicates the function of direct finder-obligations sufficiently to weaken the case for reform, we might further object that our law lacks some of the detailed arrangements found in the comparative legislation. Very obvious in this respect is the absence in English law of any provision for recovery of reasonable expenses incurred by a finder. At common law it has never been clear that there is any entitlement to expenses for safely keeping found goods. Certainly there is no general law of salvage on land such as would entitle a rescuer of goods to a lien to secure repayment of his expenditure,[68] and it has been made clear that this denial of a lien extends to finders.[69] Accordingly, a finder commits conversion if she refuses a loser's demand for delivery unless she is paid compensation.[70] There has occasionally been support for the more general view that the finder has some claim to recompense from the loser, but even this is equivocal. In *Nicholson v Chapman*, rejecting the lien argument, Erle CJ nonetheless observed that taking care of a lost thing for its loser:

> is a good office, and meritorious, at least in the moral sense of the word, and certainly intitles the party to some reasonable recompense from the bounty, if not from the justice of the owner; and of which, if it were refused, a court of justice would go as far as it could go, towards enforcing the payment.[71]

The difficulty is that there is no authority to support the opinion that such a claim is legally enforceable.[72] Indeed, in *Nicholson* itself, Erle CJ seemed equally inclined to the view that 'voluntary acts of benevolence' should incur debts sounding only in the 'moral duty of gratitude'.[73] This would leave the business of

---

[68] *Falcke v Scottish Imperial Insurance Co* (1886) 34 Ch D 234, 248.

[69] *Nicholson v Chapman* (1793) 2 H Bl 254, esp 257–8 (Erle CJ).

[70] In *Binstead v Buck* (1776) 2 Black W 1117, the plaintiff's dog strayed onto the premises of the defendant. The plaintiff located the dog some 12 months later, but the defendant refused to redeliver it until he was paid for 20 weeks' keep. This refusal was a conversion, and the plaintiff had trover for the dog. In *Nicholson v Chapman* (1793) 2 H Bl 254, a large quantity of timber belonging to the plaintiff was found washed-up on a tow-path in Putney. The defendant, under instruction from the bailiff of the manor, removed the timber to a safe place, and when later it was claimed by the plaintiff, refused to redeliver it unless paid a sum to compensate him for his efforts. In the Court of Common Pleas the jury would have allowed 2 guineas as this sum, and entered judgment in trover for the plaintiff subject to the opinion of Exchequer Chamber on whether such compensation should have been tendered before the action had been commenced. The higher court had some sympathy for the defendant's claim, but did not think the plaintiff should bear the onus of estimating and meeting those costs at the risk of being non-suited in trover. Accordingly, it was concluded that the defendant had converted the timber by refusing to redeliver it until payment of reward: (1793) 2 H Bl 254, 259.

[71] (1793) 2 H Bl 254, 258.

[72] None was given by the court in *Nicholson*. The annotator to the report suggested that such compensation might be recoverable on a plea of assumpsit for work and labour, but see Palmer discounting that possibility: Palmer, *Bailment*, 1475.

[73] (1793) 2 H Bl 254, 259.

fixing compensatory payments solely within the discretion of the loser. Given the structure of English law, this latter probably goes far enough. Generally, the common law does not compel intervention from volunteers (finders need not save or recover lost goods),[74] and correlatively does not obligate the beneficiaries of voluntarily-undertaken intervenient action to compensate those who have provided it.[75] In the case of finders, it is consistent with the general absence of common law finder-obligations that the loser owes no duty in return to compensate expenses, and yet the finder always has an incentive to intervene inasmuch as she will acquire a property right in the object of her find. Given this prospect of gain, there seems nothing unreasonable in requiring the finder to shoulder the burden of her reasonable expenses in keeping or advertising the thing.

Similar comments can explain the absence of direct provision for the payment of rewards to finders. If a finder restores lost goods in response to an advertised reward then the person offering the reward is contractually bound to honour it,[76] but otherwise there is no sign of a general common law duty to pay rewards in recognition of service.[77] Theoretically there is nothing surprising about this. Unless the relevant time limit has expired, a finder who refuses to answer the loser's demand for delivery of the thing can successfully be sued for conversion. It is not at all obvious that a finder should be entitled to expect a reward for performing an action which it would be tortious for her not to perform. As a matter of policy, it is of course desirable that finders have incentives to behave in a manner beneficial to society, but we have already seen that such an incentive exists quite independently of the question of reward.

Finally, we might observe that as it stands our law gives losers of goods much more time to recover them from finders than is normal in the comparative jurisdictions. The most generous timescale we will find in the United States is New York's three years to recover from the date when the police redeliver a lost item to its finder,[78] but that only applies to things worth US$5,000 or more. In general, short time periods of six months to a year seem to be the norm,[79] though some

---

[74] *Isaack v Clark* (1614) 2 Bulst 306, 312; *Mulgrave v Ogden* (1590) Cro Eliz 219.

[75] *Falcke v Scottish Imperial Insurance Co* (1886) 34 Ch D 234, 248. There are, of course, cases allowing recovery of benefits conferred by reason of necessity: *Re Rhodes* (1890) 44 Ch D 94; *Schneider v Eisovitch* [1960] 2 KB 430. Also compare Palmer, relying on *China Pacific SA v Food Corp'n of India; The Winson* [1982] AC 939 (HL) to support the general principle that non-contractual bailees are entitled to recover all reasonably incurred expenses, but doubting the application of this principle to finders: Palmer, *Bailment*, 1475–6.

[76] Palmer, *Bailment*, 1477. The same is true in the United States, as to which see SE Allen, 'Rewards for the Return of Lost Property: Are They Void in New York' (1950) 24 *St John's Law Review* 287.

[77] Occasionally, there has been statutory provision for the payment of rewards in defined circumstances. A very good example is the Treasure Act 1996, s 10.

[78] New York Personal Property Law § 253.7.

[79] As in Scotland: Civic Government (Scotland) Act 1982, s 71(2); Illinois: 765 Illinois Compiled Statutes 1020/28; and Iowa: Iowa Code § 556F.3.

are as low as 90 days.[80] In England, a six-year time period remains in force,[81] and perhaps there would be reason to reduce it. However, we must remember that the six-year period operates here because it is the general time applicable to conversions. To the extent we argue for the amendment of that time period, we necessarily argue for a reduction in the proprietary protection available to the loser of goods. Having accepted that the property rights of losers withstand casual loss of the relevant goods, there is no compelling ground for amending time limits in favour of finders unless we also amend the time limits for conversion generally. The finder is bound to respect prior interests, and for that reason it seems not unfair that the general time limits for conversion should govern the relative status of her rights.

Taking account of the above, it must at least be the case that the English law of finds does not present itself as a candidate for urgent reform. Our policy is geared in the right direction, reflecting the same two-tiered structure evident in jurisdictions which have adopted legislative solutions, and our law does not seem to suffer for the want of express arrangements on details such as expenses and rewards. Possibly the requirements of the law would be clearer if it was contained in a dedicated code. Certainly it would be easier to explain its operation. But having correctly understood the law of finds there seems little doubt that it aims at the accomplishment of sensible and commonly accepted policies, and it is by no means clear that its substance would be improved very much by specific legislation. If this is the case, then neither is there any need to adjust or invent common law doctrines in the name of public policy. Donaldson LJ seemed to adopt that strategy in *Parker*, but the rationale for varying the rights of finders or imposing direct obligations is considerably weakened when the behaviour of finders is understood to be constrained by existing rules of crime and tort. Indeed, in the case of the property rule, it is totally undermined. The finder's common law property right provides the incentive for her to intervene in the first place, and secures the long-term redistribution of goods in the event the loser cannot be found. Far from being a hindrance to public policy, this right is integral to its accomplishment.

Accordingly, the English law of finds appears to be coherent. This conclusion is likely to contrast starkly with the prevailing view. One eminent commentator recently described the law as a 'juridical minefield';[82] others have insisted it to be riddled with 'contradictions and flaws'[83] and have rued that the 'cases shall go on

---

[80] As in California: California Civil Code § 2080.2; and Rhode Island: Rhode Island General Laws § 33-21.2-3.

[81] Limitation Act 1980, s 2. The Law Commission has proposed wide-ranging reform of the law of limitation, which would see conversion conform to a 'core regime' comprising a primary time limit of three years and a long-stop limit of 10 years: see generally *Limitation of Actions*, Law Com No 270 (2001) 4.47–4.67.

[82] A Tettenborn, 'Gold Discovered at Heathrow Airport' (1982) *Camb LJ* 242.

[83] NE Palmer, 'Bad Apples and Blighted Windfalls: Finding, Bailment and the Fruits of Crime' in F Meisel and P Cook (eds), *Property and Protection: Essays in Honour of Brian Harvey* (Oxford, Hart Publishing, 2000) 1.

forever'.[84] It cannot be denied that our courts have made the law more difficult than it need have been. The fashion has been to bend and augment basic concepts, to propose qualifications to established rights in pursuit of the elusive policy, but this is not necessary when the full range of laws is appreciated. The great mistake of our jurisprudence on finders has been to understand the rule of property without setting it in the context of countervailing rules of crime and tort. We have not been sensitive enough to the impact of theft and conversion. When these latter are considered, there is no need to modify the property rule for the sake of policy considerations because the law can already be seen to perform the sorts of policy function that modern jurisdictions require for dealings with lost goods.

---

[84] ER Cohen, 'The Finders Cases Revisited' (1970) 48 *Texas Law Review* 1001, 1027 fn 67.

# Epilogue: The Terminology of Possession and Property

We have seen that the modern law of finders is premised on a concept of possession developed in the common law in the nineteenth century. According to this concept, where they are demonstrably present, the facts of possession (control and intention) serve to generate for the possessor a right in respect of the thing in question. This right is a property right in a very full sense. Pollock says it attracts 'the incidents of ownership'.[1] It offers access to the ordinary legal procedures for the protection of property rights in things; it might be transmitted to a third party, whether by sale, gift or succession; it affords the right to make management or use-decisions about the thing in question (for example, in a finding scenario, about how or by whom goods are to be stored while some effort is made to locate the loser). Indeed, as the finding cases show, the only defect in the property right of the possessor is that it will not afford any defence to the suit of one able to establish an earlier (and therefore better) property right in respect of the goods in question.

Probably the clarity of this conceptual position contrasts with the prevailing view of possession in the common law. Generally, possession is thought to be a hopelessly vague concept, continually changing its content and import with the exigencies of legal practice.[2] Textbook writers have considered it unsusceptible to satisfactory definition,[3] and even the most positive statements of possession in the common law retain some sense of apology for its ambiguity.[4] Yet it is abundantly clear from the writings of Holmes and Pollock that each considered 'possession' to be a causative event. There might be doubt in any given case about whether the parameters of control and intention are satisfied on the facts, but the significance of these facts *if* they are demonstrably present is that they result in the *acquisition* by the possessor of an original property right in respect of the asset in question, and this right carries with it the standard advantages of ownership. In this sense,

---

[1] P & W, 22, 93; Holmes, *CL*, 245. See also JW Salmond, *The First Principles of Jurisprudence* (London, Stevens and Haynes, 1893) 189–90; TC Williams (ed), *Principles of the Law of Personal Property* 14th edn (London, Sweet and Maxwell, 1894) 44–8; J Crossley Vaines, *Personal Property* (London, Butterworths, 1954) 39–41.

[2] Nowhere put more emphatically than by Erle CJ in his famous dictum in *R v Smith* (1855) 6 Cox CC 554, 556: 'Possession is one of the most vague of all vague terms, and shifts its meaning according to the subject matter to which it is applied'.

[3] M Bridge, *Personal Property Law* 3rd edn (Oxford, Clarendon Press, 2003) 16.

[4] PH Winfield, *Law of Tort* 4th edn (London, Sweet and Maxwell, 1948) 306: 'Our law has a fairly good working scheme of possession although it has not indulged in much scientific dissection of the idea. Its weakest spot is its slovenly terminology'.

the position of Pollock and Holmes is that possession generates an ownership interest in goods.

If the conceptual effects of this proposition are clear, the terminology is likely to jar. Personal property lawyers are suspicious of the term 'ownership'. 'English law has never had any theory of ownership' declare the editors of *Crossley Vaines*.[5] 'It is possible, and, perhaps, even desirable to write a treatise on English law without defining ownership or mentioning it as a juridical conception'.[6] We have already seen the reasons. In the first place, the common law knows of no action which directly vindicates ownership of goods, no 'pure proprietary remedy' where the claimant's ownership is at the very core of the dispute.[7] The Romans had their *vindicatio*, where a claimant would plead to be 'owner to the full extent of the law', and the liability of a defendant in possession of the thing in dispute depended solely on the success of the claimant's allegation of ownership.[8] If the judge found that the claimant was owner, he would condemn the defendant to pay the value of the thing, or to restore it, at the defendant's election.[9] In English law, the tort of conversion stands in the front line of property protection. The claimant must allege and prove wrongful interference, it is not sufficient for him to establish his right. Moreover, in conversion, possession and not ownership is at the root of the claimant's entitlement to sue; or at least, the ability of the claimant to rely on the facts of possession to prove his claim has decreased the extent to which a claimant need ever allege that he is 'owner' of the thing in question. Even someone with an unimpeachable right to goods might just as well rely on the facts of his earlier possession to justify recovery from a defendant.[10] In this sense, it is easy to see how 'ownership' has been confined to the margins of personal property law.

Still, we ought to be careful not to overstate the conceptual prevalence of possession over ownership. As much as conversion is premised on possession, in its modern form it is clearly a tort which exists to protect *rights* in things. As Lord Steyn said in *Kuwait Airways*, whenever a defendant manifests 'an assertion of rights or dominion over the goods which is *inconsistent with the rights of the plaintiff*', he converts the goods to his own use.[11] Moreover, applying Pollock's understanding of trover (and therefore conversion), the claimant who proves possession necessarily proves that he holds an ownership interest in the thing converted. So conversion puts at issue an ownership interest in goods, just as ejectment puts at issue a fee simple estate in land. Inasmuch as it protects these ownership interests, conversion can and does replicate the effects of the *vindicatio*. The mechanism is

---

[5] ELG Tyler and NE Palmer (eds), *Crossley Vaines' Personal Property* 5th edn (London, Butterworths, 1973) 39.

[6] *Ibid.*

[7] P Birks, 'Personal Property: Proprietary Rights and Remedies' (2000) 11 *KCLJ* 1, 4.

[8] WW Buckland, *A Textbook of Roman Law* 2nd edn (Cambridge, Cambridge University Press, 1932) 675.

[9] *Ibid* 658.

[10] G Battersby, 'The Present Status of the *ius tertii* Principle' (1992) *Conv* 100, 104, referring to the claimant's success in *Moffatt v Kazana* [1969] 2 QB 152.

[11] [2002] 2 AC 883, 1104 (my emphasis).

indirect: conversion requires and relies upon the commission of a wrong in its protection of property rights; but the claimant will always have an ownership interest, and the tort functions to protect this right.

There is a good deal to be said for reclaiming the use of the term 'ownership' in personal property discourse. Since the content of the right acquired by possession does not differ from ownership, we ought to give it the same name. McFarlane has made this point recently;[12] Honoré ventured a similar idea in his great essay.[13] So we would say, for example, of loser and finder, that each was *an owner* of the thing in question;[14] that each held a legal right in the thing, which right was called 'ownership'. To this extent we would abandon our use of the definite article in relation to ownership, but then in practice we are never troubled by who is *the* owner of the thing in question: we recognise instead the possibility that more than one right of the same kind might exist in respect of the same asset, and where a dispute arises between persons each having the ability to exercise the same right, we resolve the dispute according to which came earliest in time to the asset. This is exactly what we have been doing in the finding cases decided since *South Staffordshire Water Co v Sharman*.[15] When a possessor of land brings a claim against a finder, the contest turns on the relativity of their respective rights. In the case of each party, these rights depend on and result from the possessory facts of control and intention. Calling the resultant right 'ownership' really involves no new proposition of law. Simply, it reflects the very clear contention of Holmes and Pollock that the right resultant from possession has the content of ownership. We could make our writing on personal property law much clearer by accepting the force of this proposition (which is already in operation in practice), and reclaiming 'ownership' for our vocabulary.

Perhaps it too late. Perhaps we are too used to the idea that English law knows no concept of absolute ownership; perhaps it even reflects something of the uniqueness of the common law, distinguishing its tradition from the civilian systems and the influence of Roman *dominium*. Even so, if we are not happy referring to finders and other possessors as 'owners', we will need another name for the right resultant from possession which successfully explains its content. Plainly, 'possession' will not do as a substitute for 'ownership' in this context. We should not say that the loser is 'owner', but the finder has 'possession'. In the first place, using 'possession' to connote both (i) a set of facts *capable of generating* an interest in goods, and (ii) *an interest* in goods, elides necessarily separate questions about the acquisition and content of rights. This brings a ready source of confusion to our analysis. It also obscures the fact that there might be others, apart

---

[12] B McFarlane, *The Structure of Property Law* (Oxford, Hart Publishing, 2008) 144–6.

[13] 'The [possessor] has every incident of ownership except security against divesting, while the owner has every incident except present enjoyment. There is much to be said, therefore, for treating them as independent owners rather than as persons sharing a single, split ownership': AM Honoré, 'Ownership', ch 5 in AG Guest (ed), *Oxford Essays in Jurisprudence* (Oxford, OUP, 1961) 140.

[14] B McFarlane, *The Structure of Property Law* (Oxford, Hart Publishing, 2008) 145.

[15] [1896] 2 QB 44; see generally Chapter 2.

from loser and finder, holding legal property rights of the same quality in the find. These lessons are important, because sometimes personal property lawyers refer to 'possession' as if it was a nominative legal interest in goods with content to be distinguished from 'ownership',[16] but this was clearly not the case as far as Holmes and Pollock were concerned.

'Title' seems at first blush to be a more viable alternative.[17] Often it is used as shorthand for 'right to possess';[18] and it is always associated with relativity.[19] So where goods are found buried in land, the possessor of land has a 'better title' than the finder,[20] but the loser has a better title than both possessor of land and finder. However, 'title' is an ambiguous term. From its use in the books, we might fairly say that it shares the protean qualities of 'possession'. It has at least three general meanings.[21] The first is the sense we have already identified: it is used as a by-word for 'right to possess', and to this extent we might choose to use it to refer to the right resultant from possession, although even then there is a risk it would obscure the content of that right, inasmuch as it makes reference to only one of the several incidents of ownership. Secondly, 'title' refers to the facts which justify a claim to a legal right: 'in this sense, delivery, registration, seizure and succession on death may be titles'.[22] This aligns the meaning of title with causative events, so that possession *is* a title, as opposed to it *giving* or *being the root of* a title. A third sense considers 'title' to be purely a juridical notion, occupying a conceptual space between causative event and resultant right. It identifies title as a 'claim to' a right; or more specifically as 'a legal claim to the bundle of rights that is associated with the ownership of a thing'.[23] This separation of a legal-claim-to-a right and the

---

[16] R Goode, *Commercial Law* 3rd edn (London, LexixNexis UK, 2004) 25, 31–2; M Bridge, *Personal Property Law* (3rd, Oxford (Clarendon Press, 2003) 15, 30.

[17] *EPL*, 4.131; W Swadling, 'Ignorance and Unjust Enrichment: The Problem of Title' (2008) 28 *OJLS* 627, 640.

[18] PBH Birks (ed), *English Private Law* (Oxford, OUP, 2000) 4.40. The 2nd edition explains 'title' more fully in the case of goods: title is 'derived from "entitlement", that entitlement being a right to exclusive possession of the thing over which it subsists forever': *EPL*, 4.131.

[19] Note that it is not quite accurate to suggest that, in itself, 'title' is a measure of strength (contra Goode, above n 16 at 31; D Fox, 'Relativity of Title in Law and at Equity' (2006) *CLJ* 330, 333), and the same is true of 'relativity'. However, we choose to define 'title', when we say that 'titles' are 'relative' or 'relatively good', linguistically we are indicating only that titles are commensurable, that each might be judged by its weight in the balance against a competitor. The measure of weight (or strength) is priority in time. Of *any two* commensurate titles to a given asset, the earlier is always deemed better. Of *any* existing titles to a given asset, the earliest might fairly be called the best, though this question will rarely arise before a court of law.

[20] *Waverly Borough Council v Fletcher* [1996] QB 334, 345.

[21] Sometimes it also has context-specific meanings. For example, in sale of goods discourse, 'title' is sometimes used to connote the interest acquired by a buyer who benefits from one of the legislated exceptions to the rule *nemo dato quod non habet*: Sale of Goods Act 1979, ss 23–5.

[22] AM Honoré, 'Ownership', ch 5 in AG Guest (ed), *Oxford Essays in Jurisprudence* (Oxford, OUP, 1961) 134. Honoré thought this an 'earlier use' of 'title' than the modern meaning of 'right to possess'.

[23] HL Ho, 'Some Reflections on "Property" and "Title" in the Sale of Goods Act' (1997) 56 *CLJ* 571, 573; D Fox, 'Relativity of Title in Law and at Equity' (2006) *CLJ* 330, 333–4, 364. Note the doubtlessly correct observation of Fox that the connection between title and ownership is contingent: in its juridical sense, 'title' might just as well refer to a claim to any kind of legal (or equitable) right: (2006) *CLJ* 330, 333.

right itself is an analytical abstraction, but it is well known to property lawyers. It is perhaps especially applicable to the orthodox interpretation of adverse possession of land in the nineteenth century, according to which there could only ever be one fee simple estate in given land, and rival claimants were exactly that: rivals claiming to be entitled to the one fee simple estate.[24] The substantive reforms and commentary of the late nineteenth century overlooked this construction, supposing the generation of rival estates, which themselves become the subject of commensurability and competition, and for this reason it is possible that today the juridical meaning of title is an unnecessary abstraction. When I make a legal claim to a right (or to a set of rights), I mean only that certain facts exist in virtue of which law accords to me certain rights;[25] or to put it another way, that the law recognises the facts of my situation as demanding recognition or protection through legally enforceable rights. Once we conceive that relatively good versions of a given right might be acquired independently, and that these rights themselves might be ranked commensurately, the juridical notion of 'title' seems to add very little to our analysis. In any case, for present purposes, the ambiguity of the term, transgressing necessarily different questions as to the causes and content of rights, is probably enough to weaken its utility as a name for the right resultant from possession.

We might more usefully adopt an alternative drawn from the language of the Sale of Goods Act 1979. That legislation uses the term 'property' to refer to the proprietary right which must be transferred if the transaction is to be regarded as a sale.[26] As Battersby and Preston noted, the legislation purposes to define sale as involving 'the transfer of the absolute legal interest in the goods (analogous to the legal fee simple estate in land), as opposed to any lesser interest'.[27] The contrast between 'absolute' and 'lesser' interests is aimed at the content of the rights in question, not at doctrines of relativity. An 'absolute' interest, or 'general property', is an ownership interest; a 'lesser' interest, or 'special property', is a limited interest, for example the rights of a pledgee, or perhaps those of bailees generally. It does not matter that the transferor holds an absolute interest in goods which is relatively inferior to an absolute interest held by another in respect of the same goods: indeed, in a later article Battersby specifically conceives that a finder might transfer her interest in goods by sale.[28] So we might say that, in virtue of the facts of her possession, a finder acquires a general property in the object of her find.

---

[24] See Chapter 5.

[25] Holmes, *CL*, 214–15.

[26] Sale of Goods Act 1979, s 2(1).

[27] G Battersby and AD Preston, 'The Concepts of "Property", "Title", and "Owner" Used in the Sale of Goods Act 1893' (1972) 35 *MLR* 268, 271.

[28] G Battersby, 'A Re-consideration of "Property" and "Title" in the Sale of Goods Act' (2001) *JBL* 1, 2–3. See also Ho, above n 23 at 578. Of course, the finder can only transfer her own rights to the goods in question; that is, she can only pass a buyer, and a buyer can only acquire, a right which is subject to the better claim of the loser: see generally Battersby, above.

There seem to be two advantages in expressing our basic proposition like this. First, as the quotation from Battersby and Preston indicates, the term 'general property' could operate as a personal property equivalent to 'fee simple': at least, rhetorically, it could be taken to connote the greatest possible interest in goods recognised by our legal system. Analogously with the law of adverse possession, we could say that the loser of goods retains his general property in them, but by possession the finder acquires her own general property in the goods, which exists concurrently with, but is ranked subordinately to, the continuing general property of the loser. This seems adequately to reflect the substance of the law without relying expressly on the terminology of 'ownership'. At the same time, secondly, recognising that finders hold *general* property might allow us squarely to face difficult questions about the nature and extent of *limited* interests in goods. Pollock's account of possession allowed for the possibility that there was a qualitative difference between the right acquired when possession was taken independently and the right acquired when possession was taken with the consent of some grantor. He thought the grantor's consent was a real element in the grantee's acquisition.[29] It follows theoretically that there could be a qualitative difference between, say, the rights of finder and the rights of a bailee. In Pollock's own work, and in the modern law, the significance of any such difference is greatly reduced by the undoubted ability of a bailee to maintain conversion by alleging in evidence only the facts of her own possession,[30] but analytically the question remains, and it is worth exploring. It might be the case that, say, a contract of hire should be regarded as conferring a property right on the hirer distinct from the right acquired solely in virtue of the facts of possession. Although an orthodox view of current law suggests that this is not the case, even the best defence of this position recognises that there could be reason to treat the hirer's interest as a distinct property right if the appropriate policy justification was found.[31] *Perhaps* adopting the term 'general property' would simultaneously focus energy on the meaning of 'special' or 'limited' property, bringing clearer conceptual structure to our basic laws of personal property.

Whichever (and indeed, if any) of these suggestions is to be preferred, the underlying point is that the difficult terminology of our personal property law ought not to obscure the clarity of the basic conceptual relation between ownership and possession. In many ways this is the chief lesson of the law of finders. For all the difficulties in expressing ideas of ownership and possession, for all the confusion that seems to have surrounded their interrelation, common lawyers have succeeded in producing a body of law which is remarkably coherent and achieves practically sensible results. Whilst we have never settled on words to describe the right acquired by a finder in the object of her find, we have rules and

---

[29] P & W, 43–4; also Holmes, *CL*, 214–15.

[30] *The Winkfield* [1902] P 42, 54–5.

[31] W Swadling, 'The Proprietary Effect of a Hire of Goods' in NE Palmer and E McKendirck (eds), *Interests in Goods* 2nd edn (London, LLP, 1998) 526.

concepts which explain the actions she should take in respect of it, and which provide a justification for her retention of it if the loser cannot be found. Given the many centuries over which our law of finders has developed incrementally, this is no mean achievement, and perhaps it might serve as an encouragement to common lawyers struggling to bring analytical clarity to the basic concepts of personal property.

# BIBLIOGRAPHY

Aigler, RW, 'Rights of Finders' (1922–23) 21 MichiganLaw Review 664

Ames, JB, 'The Disseisin of Chattels' (1888–89) 3 Harv LR 23, 313, 337

—— 'The History of Trover' (1897–98) 11 Harv LR 277, 374

—— Lectures on Legal History (Cambridge MA, Harvard University Press, 1913)

Anon, 'Comment on Lost, Mislaid, and Abandoned Property' (1939) 8 Fordham Law Review 222

Aronovitz, AM, 'Individual Patrimonial Rights under the European Human Rights System: Some Reflections on Concepts of Possession and Dispossession of Property' (1997) 25 Int'l J Legal Info 87

Atiyah, PS, 'A Re-Examination of the Jus Tertii in Conversion' (1955) 18 MLR 97

Baker, JH (ed), The Reports of Sir John Spelman (1977) 94 SS 23

—— The Notebook of Sir John Port (1986) 102 SS 80

—— and Milsom, SFC, Sources of English Legal History: Private Law to 1750 (London, Butterworths, 1986)

—— An Introduction to English Legal History 4th edn (London, Butterworths LexisNexis, 2002)

—— The Oxford History of the Laws of England, vol VI, 1483–1558 (Oxford, OUP, 2003)

Bamforth, N, 'Finding and Possession in English Property Law' in Title to Finds and Discovered Antiquities, Seminar Proceedings of the Institute of Art and Law, 3 October 1995, reading 2

Barnes, ER, Jnr, 'Rights of Finders in Pennsylvania' (1944) Dickinson Law Review 124

Battersby, G, 'The Present Status of the ius tertii Principle' (1992) Conv 100

—— 'A Re-consideration of "Property" and "Title" in the Sale of Goods Act' (2001) JBL 1

—— 'Acquiring Title by Theft' (2002) MLR 603

Battersby, G and Preston, AD, 'The Concepts of "Property", "Title", and "Owner" Used in the Sale of Goods Act 1893' (1972) 35 MLR 268

Beale, JH, Jnr, 'The Borderland of Larceny' (1892–93) 6 Harv LR 244

Benson, P, 'Philosophy of Property Law' in JL Coleman and S Shapiro (eds), Oxford Handbook of Jurisprudence and Legal Philosophy (Oxford, OUP, 2002)

Bell, AP, Modern Law of Personal Property in England and Ireland (London, Butterworths, 1989)

—— 'Bona Vacantia' in NE Palmer and E McKendrick (eds), Interests in Goods 2nd edn (London, LLP, 1998)

Bingham, JW, 'The Nature and Importance of Legal Possession' (1915) 13 MichiganLaw Review 535

Birks, PBH, The Law of Restitution (Oxford, Clarendon Press, rev edn 1989)

—— 'Personal Property: Proprietary Rights and Remedies' (2000) 11 KCLJ 1

—— Unjust Enrichment 2nd edn (Oxford, OUP, 2005)

Birks, PBH (ed), English Private Law (Oxford, OUP, 2000)

Bond, H, 'Possession in the Roman Law' (1890) 6 LQR 259

# Bibliography

Bordwell, P, 'Property in Chattels' (1915–16) 29 *Harvard Law Review* 374, 501, 731

Bridge, M, *Personal Property Law* 3rd edn (Oxford, Clarendon Press, 2003)

Brown, CA, 'Acquiring Title to Personal Property by Adverse Possession in West Virginia' (1972–73) 75 *West Virginia Law Review* 248

Broyde, MJ and Hecht, M, 'The Return of Lost Property According to Jewish and Common Law: A Comparison' (1995–96) 12 *Journal of Law and Religion* 225

Buckland, WW, *A Textbook of Roman Law* 2nd edn (Cambridge, Cambridge University Press, 1932)

Burke, B *et al* (eds), *Fundamentals of Property* 2nd edn (Newark NJ, LexisNexis, 2004)

Burke, B, *Property* 2nd edn (New York, NY, Aspen Publishers, 2004)

Burrows, A, *The Law of Restitution* 2nd edn (London, Butterworths, 2002)

—— and Lord Rodger of Earlsferry (eds), *Mapping the Law: Essays in Memory of Peter Birks* (Oxford, OUP, 2006)

Burrows, A (ed), *English Private Law* 2nd edn (Oxford, OUP, 2007)

Calabresi, G, and Melamed, AD, 'Property Rules, Liability Rules, and Inalienability: One View of the Cathedral' (1972) 85 *Harvard Law Review* 1089

Carey-Miller, DL, *Corporeal Moveables in Scots Law* (Edinburgh, W Green, 1991)

Carman, J, *Valuing Ancient Things* (Leicester, University Press, 1996)

Carter, PB, 'Taking and the Acquisition of Possession in Larceny' (1951) 14 *MLR* 27

Challis, HW, *The Law of Real Property* (London, Reeves & Turner, 1885)

Cheshire, CG, *The Modern Law of Real Property* 2nd edn (London, Butterworths, 1927)

Chitty, J, *Prerogatives of the Crown* (London, Butterworths, 1820)

Christian, E (ed), *Commentaries on the Laws of England by Sir William Blackstone* 15th edn (London, Cadell & Davies, 1809)

Clerk, JF, 'Title to Chattels by Possession' (1891) 7 *LQR* 224

Cohen, ER, 'The Finders Cases Revisited' (1970) 48 *Texas Law Review* 1001

Coke, E, *Institutes of the Laws of England* (London, Lee and Pakeman, 1660)

Cretney, S, 'Treasure from Heaven' (1969) 119(1) *New Law Journal* 35

Crossley Vaines, J, *Personal Property* (London, Butterworths, 1954)

Curwen, N, 'The Squatter's Interest at Common Law' (2000) *Conv* 528

—— 'Title to Sue in Conversion' (2004) 68 *Conv* 308

—— 'The Remedy in Conversion: Confusing Property and Obligation' (2006) 26 *Legal Studies* 570

Curwood, J (ed), *A Treatise of the Pleas of the Crown by William Hawkins* (London, Sweet, 1824)

De Wolfe Howe, M (ed), *The Pollock-Holmes Letters* (Cambridge, CUP, 1942)

Douglas, S, 'The Abolition of Detinue' (2008) *Conv* 30

Dromgoole, S and Gaskell, N, 'Interests in Wreck' in NE Palmer and E McKendrick (eds), *Interests in Goods* 2nd edn (London, LLP, 1998)

Dugdale, AM *et al* (eds), *Clerk and Lindsell on Torts* 19th edn (London, Sweet and Maxwell, 2006)

Dworkin, R, *Law's Empire* (Oxford, Hart Publishing, 1998)

East, EH, *A Treatise on the Pleas of the Crown* (London, J Butterworth, 1803)

Eastwood, RA, *Williams' Principles of the Law of Real Property* 24th edn (London, Sweet and Maxwell, 1926)

Edwards, J, 'Possession and Larceny' (1950) 3 *Current Legal Problems* 127

Elphinstone, HW and Clark, JW (eds), *Goodeve's Modern Law of Personal Property* 2nd edn (London, Sweet and Maxwell, 1892)

# Bibliography

Epstein, RA, 'Possession as the Root of Title' (1978) 13 *Georgia Law Review* 1223

Fifoot, CHS, *History and Sources of the Common Law* (London, Stevens & Sons Ltd, 1949)

Finnis, JM, *Natural Law and Natural Rights* (Oxford, Clarendon Press, 1980)

Fisher, HAL, *The Collected Papers of Frederic William Maitland* (Cambridge, CUP, 1911) vol I

Fletcher, GP, 'The Metamorphosis of Larceny' (1976) 89 *Harv LR* 469

Ford, P and Ford, G (eds), *British Parliamentary Papers* (Irish University Press, Shannon, 1971)

Fox, D, 'Relativity of Title in Law and at Equity' (2006) *CLJ* 330

Francis, JF, 'Three Cases on Possession: Some Further Observations' (1928–29) 13 *St Louis Law Review* 11

Gerstenblith, P, 'The Adverse Possession of Personal Property' (1998–99) 37 *Buffalo Law Review* 119

Getzler, J, 'Unclean Hands and the Doctrine of Jus Tertii' (2001) 117 *LQR* 565

Gleeson, S, *Personal Property Law* (London, FT Law & Tax, 1997)

Goode, R, *Commercial Law* 3rd edn (London, LexixNexis UK, 2004)

Goodhart, AL, 'Three Cases on Possession' (1927–29) 3 *Camb LJ* 195

Goodhart, AL (ed), *Jurisprudence and Legal Essays by Sir Frederick Pollock* (London, MacMillan & Co, 1961)

Gordley, J, *Foundations of Private Law: Property, Tort, Contract, Unjust Enrichment* (Oxford, OUP, 2006)

Gordley, J and Mattei, U, 'Protecting Possession' (1996) 44 *Am Jur Comp Law* 293

Goudy, H, 'Legal Possession: Two Maxims' (1918–19) 13 *Illinois Law Review* 293

Gray, K and Gray, SF, *Elements of Land Law* 4th edn (Oxford, OUP, 2005)

Greaves, CS (ed), *Russell on Crimes and Misdemeanours* 4th edn (London, Stevens & Sons, 1866)

Griew, E, *The Theft Acts* 7th edn (London, Sweet & Maxwell, 1995)

Guthrie, W (ed), *Bell's Principles of the Law of Scotland* 10th edn (Edinburgh, Law Society of Scotland, 1989)

Hadden, T, 'Larceny by Finding: How Not to Reform the Law' (1965) *CLJ* 173

—— 'Contract, Tort and Crime: the Forms of Legal Thought' (1971) 87 *LQR* 240

Hailsham of St Marylebone (ed), *Halsbury's Laws of England* 4th edn (London, Butterworths, 1976)

Hargreaves, AD, 'Terminology and Title in Ejectment' (1940) 56 *LQR* 376

—— 'Modern Real Property' (1956) 19 *MLR* 14

Harpum, C, Bridge, S and Dixon, M (eds), *Megarry and Wade's The Law of Real Property* 7th edn (London, Sweet and Maxwell, 2008)

Harris, DR, 'Possession' in AG Guest (ed), *Oxford Essays in Jurisprudence* (Oxford, OUP, 1961)

Harris, JW, *Property and Justice* (Oxford, OUP, 1996)

Harris, MJ, 'Who Owns the Pot of Gold at the End of the Rainbow? A Review of the Impact of Cultural Property on Finders and Salvage Laws' (1997) 13 *Ariz J Int'l and Comp Law* 223

Helmholz, RH, 'Equitable Division and the Law of Finders' (1983–84) 52 *Fordham Law Review* 313

—— 'Wrongful Possession of Chattels: Hornbook Law and Case Law' (1985) 80 *Northwestern University Law Review* 1221

—— *The Oxford History of the Laws of England* (Oxford, OUP, 2004) vol I

Hickey, R, 'Dazed and Confused: Accidental Mixtures of Goods and the Theory of Acquisition of Title' (2003) 66 *MLR* 368

—— 'Stealing Abandoned Goods: Possessory Title in Proceedings for Theft' (2006) *Legal Studies* 584

—— 'Curbing the Enthusiasm of Finders' in E Cooke (ed), *Modern Studies in Property Law* (Oxford, Hart Publishing, 2007) vol IV

Ho, HL, 'Some Reflections on "Property" and "Title" in the Sale of Goods Act' (1997) 56 *CLJ* 571

Holdsworth, WS, *A History of English Law* 3rd edn (London, Methuen & Co, 1923)

—— *An Historical Introduction to the Land Law* (Oxford, Clarendon Press, 1927)

—— 'Terminology and Title in Ejectment: A Reply' (1940) 56 *LQR* 479

Holmes, OW, Jnr, *The Common Law* (New York, Dover Publications, 1991, an unabridged reproduction of the original text: Boston, MA, Little Brown, 1881)

Honoré, AM, 'Ownership' in AG Guest (ed), *Oxford Essays in Jurisprudence* (Oxford, OUP, 1961)

Hudson, A, 'Is Divesting Abandonment Possible at Common Law?' (1984) 100 *LQR* 110

—— 'Abandonment' in NE Palmer and E McKendrick (eds), *Interests in Goods* 2nd edn (London, LLP, 1998) 618

Ibbetson, DJ, *A Historical Introduction to the Law of Obligations* (Oxford, OUP, 1999)

Ing, ND, *Bona Vacantia* (London, Butterworths, 1971)

Izuel, L, 'Property Owners' Constructive Possession of Treasure Trove: Rethinking the Finders' Keepers Rule' (1990–91) 38 *UCLA Law Review* 1659

Jaffey, P, *The Nature and Scope of Restitution* (Oxford, Hart Publishing, 2000)

Johnson, JW, 'Finders' Rights in Mislaid Property' (1962) 19 *Washington and Lee Law Review* 247

Jolowicz, HF and Nicholas, B, *Historical Introduction to the Study of Roman Law* 3rd edn (Cambridge, CUP, 1972)

Jones, G (ed), *Goff and Jones: The Law of Restitution* 7th edn (London, Sweet & Maxwell, 2007)

Kaye, JM, '*Res Addiratae* and the Recovery of Stolen Goods' (1970) 86 *LQR* 379

Kelly, F, *A Guide to Early Irish Law* (Dublin, Dublin Institute for Advanced Studies, 1988)

Kelly, JM, 'Hidden Treasure and the Constitution' (1988) 10 *Dublin University Law Journal* 5

Kiralfy, AK, *The Action on the Case* (London, Sweet & Maxwell, 1951)

Kocourek, A, 'Two Problems in Possession' (1928–29) 17 *Cal Law Review* 382

Krebs, T, 'The Fallacy of "Restitution for Wrongs"' in A Burrows and Lord Rodger of Earlsferry (eds), *Mapping the Law: Essays in Memory of Peter Birks* (Oxford, OUP, 2006)

Kurjatko, A, 'Are Finders Keepers? The Need for a Uniform Law Governing the Rights of Original Owners and Good Faith Purchasers of Stolen Art' (1999) 5 *UC Davis J Int'l Law and Policy* 59

Lee, RW, *Elements of Roman Law* 4th edn (London, Sweet & Maxwell, 1956)

Lightwood, JM, 'Possession in the Roman Law' (1887) 3 *LQR* 32

—— *Possession of Land* (London, Stevens & Sons, 1894)

Macleod, JK, 'Restitution under the Theft Act' (1968) *Crim LR* 577

MacMillan, C, 'Finders Keepers, Losers Weepers—But Who Are the Losers?' (1995) 58 *MLR* 101

—— 'Burying Treasure Trove' (1996) *New Law Journal* 1346

Maitland, FW, 'Seisin of Chattels' (1885) 1 *LQR* 324

—— 'The Mystery of Seisin' (1886) 2 *LQR* 481

# Bibliography

—— *Bracton's Note Book* (London, CJ Clay & Sons, 1887)
—— 'The Beatitude of Seisin' (1888) 4 *LQR* 24, 286
Marshall, OR, 'The Problem of Finding' (1949) 2 *Current Legal Problems* 68
Martin, W, 'Treasure Trove and the British Museum' (1904) 20 *LQR* 27
McBain, GS, 'Modernising and Codifying the Law of Bailment' (2008) *Journal of Business Law* 1
McCutcheon, JP, *The Larceny Act 1916* (Dublin, Round Hall Press, 1989)
McFarlane, B, *The Structure of Property Law* (Oxford, Hart Publishing, 2008)
McMeel, G, 'Finders Weepers: *Waverly BC v Fletcher* (1995) 4 *Nottingham Law Journal* 228
—— 'The Redundancy of Bailment' (2003) *LMCLQ* 169
Megarry, RE and Wade, HWR, *The Law of Real Property* (London, Steven & Sons, 1957)
Milsom, SFC, 'Not Doing is No Trespass: A View of the Boundaries of Case' (1954) *Camb LJ* 105
—— *Historical Foundations of the Common Law* 2nd edn (London, Butterworths, 1981)
—— *Studies in the History of the Common Law* (London, Hambledon Press, 1985)
Milsom, SFC (ed), *Nova Narrationes* (1963) 80 SS
Mitchell, C, and Mitchell, P, *Landmark Cases in the Law of Restitution* (Oxford, Hart Publishing, 2006)
Mommsen, T, Krueger, P and Watson, A, *The Digest of Justinian* (University of Pennsylvania Press, 1985)
Moorman, JS, 'Finders Weepers, Losers Weepers? *Benjamin v Lindner Aviation Inc*' (1996–97) *Iowa Law Review* 717
Moreland, R, 'The Rights of Finders of Lost Property' (1927) 16 *Kentucky Law Journal* 3
Morton, EP, 'Public Policy and the Finders Cases' (1946) 1 *Wyoming Law Journal* 101
Moyle, JB (ed), *The Institutes of Justinian* (JB Moyle (trans), Oxford, Clarendon Press, 1945)
Nichols, FM (ed), *Britton* (Oxford, Clarendon Press, 1865)
Ormerod, D (ed), *Smith and Hogan Criminal Law* 11th edn (Oxford, OUP, 2005)
Ormerod, D and Williams, DW (eds), *Smith's Law of Theft* 9th edn (Oxford, OUP, 2007)
Palmer, NE, 'Treasure Trove and the Protection of Antiquities' (1981) 44 *Modern Law Review* 178
—— *Bailment* 2nd edn (London, Sweet and Maxwell, 1991)
—— 'Title to Discovered Antiquities after the *Waverly* Decision' in *Title to Finds and Discovered Antiquities*, Seminar Proceedings of the Institute of Art and Law, 3 October 1995, reading 1
—— 'Quality and Duration of the Finder's Title: Free-Standing or Free-For-All?' (1995) 3 *Art, Antiquity and Law* 223
—— 'Bad Apples and Blighted Windfalls: Finding, Bailment and the Fruits of Crime' in F Meisel and P Cook (eds), *Property and Protection: Essays in Honour of Brian Harvey* (Oxford, Hart Publishing, 2000) 1
Palmer, RC, *English Law in the Age of the Black Death* (Chapel Hill, NC, University of North Carolina Press, 1993)
Plunkett, T, *A Concise History of the Common Law* 5th edn (London, Butterworths, 1956)
Pollock, F, *The Law of Torts* (London, Stevens & Sons, 1887)
Pollock, F and Maitland, FW, *History of English Law* (Cambridge, CUP, 1898)
Pollock, F and Wright, RS, *An Essay on Possession in the Common Law* (Oxford, Clarendon Press, 1888)
Posner, RA, 'Savigny, Holmes, and the Law and Economics of Possession' (2000) 86 *Virginia Law Review* 535

# Bibliography

Radley-Gardner, O, 'Civilised Squatting' (2005) 25 *OJLS* 727

Raushenbush, WB, *Brown on Personal Property* 3rd edn (Chicago, IL, Callaghan & Co, 1975)

Reid, KGC, *The Law of Property in Scotland* (Edinburgh, Butterworths, 1996)

Riesman, D, 'Possession and the Law of Finders' (1939) 52 *Harv LR* 1105

Roberts, S, 'More Lost Than Found' (1982) 45 *MLR* 683

Russell, OW, *A Treatise on Crimes and Misdemeanours* (London, Butterworths, 1819)

Salmond, JW, *The First Principles of Jurisprudence* (London, Stevens & Haynes, 1893)

—— 'Observations on Trover and Conversion' (1905) 21 *LQR* 43

—— *The Law of Torts* (London, Stevens and Haynes, 1907)

—— *Jurisprudence* 7th edn (London, Sweet and Maxwell, 1924)

Savigny, FC von, *Treatise on Possession; or the Jus Possessionis of the Civil Law* (E Perry (trans), London, Sweet, 1848)

Schulz, F, *Classical Roman Law* (Oxford, Clarendon Press, 1951)

Shanks, E and Milsom, SFC (eds), *Novae Narrationes* (1963) 80 SS

Shartel, B, 'Meanings of Possession' (1932) 16 *Minnesota Law Review* 611

Siepp, DJ, 'The Concept of Property in the Early Common Law' (1994) 12 *Law and History Review* 29

Simester, AP and Sullivan, GR, *Criminal Law Theory and Doctrine* 3rd edn (Oxford, Hart Publishing, 2007)

Simpson, AWB, 'The Introduction of the Action on the Case for Conversion' (1959) 75 *LQR* 364

—— *A History of the Land Law* 2nd edn (Oxford, Clarendon Press, 1986)

Smith, ATH, *Property Offences* (London, Sweet and Maxwell, 1994)

Smith, JC, 'Title to Discovered Antiquities: Theft and Possessory Title' in *Title to Finds and Discovered Antiquities*, Seminar Proceedings of the Institute of Art and Law, 3 October 1995, reading 4

—— *The Law of Theft* 8th edn (London, Butterworths, 1997)

Stevens, R, 'Three Enrichment Issues' in A Burrows and Lord Rodger of Earlsferry (eds), *Mapping the Law: Essays in Memory of Peter Birks* (Oxford, OUP, 2006)

—— *Torts and Rights* (Oxford, OUP, 2007)

Street, H, *The Law of Torts* (London, Butterworths, 1955)

Swadling, W, 'A Claim in Restitution?' (1996) *LMCLQ* 63

—— 'The Proprietary Effect of a Hire of Goods' in NE Palmer and E McKendrick (eds), *Interests in Goods* 2nd edn (London, LLP, 1998)

—— 'Unjust Delivery' in Burrows, A and Lord Rodger of Earlsferry (eds), *Mapping the Law: Essays in Memory of Peter Birks* (Oxford, OUP, 2006)

—— 'Property: General Principles' in A Burrows (ed), *English Private Law* 2nd edn (Oxford, Oxford University Press, 2007)

—— 'Ignorance and Unjust Enrichment: the Problem of Title' (2008) 28 *OJLS* 627

Sweet, C, 'Possession in English Law' (1891) 3 *Juridical Review* 130

Tay, AES, 'Possession and the Modern Law of Finding' (1962–64) 4 *Sydney Law Review* 383

—— 'The Concept of Possession: Foundations for a New Approach' (1963–64) 4 *Melbourne University Law Review* 476

—— '*Bridges v Hawkesworth* and the Early History of Finding' (1964) 8 *American Journal of Legal History* 223

—— 'The Essence of a Bailment: Contract, Agreement, or Possession' (1965–67) 5 *Sydney Law Review* 239

Terry, HT, 'Possession' (1918–19) 13 *Illinois Law Review* 312

# Bibliography

Tettenborn, A, 'Gold Discovered at Heathrow Airport' (1982) *Camb LJ* 242

Thayer, AS, 'Possession' (1904–05) 18 *Harvard Law Review* 196

—— 'Possession and Ownership' (1907) 23 *LQR* 175, 314

Thomas, JAC, *The Institutes of Justinian* (Cape Town, Juta & Co, 1975)

—— *Textbook of Roman Law* (Amsterdam, North-Holland Publishing Co, 1976)

Turner, JWC (ed), *Russell on Crime* 12th edn (London, Stevens & Sons, 1964)

Tyler, ELG and Palmer, NE (eds), *Crossley Vaines' Personal Property* 5th edn (London, Butterworths, 1973)

Virgo, G, *The Principles of the Law of Restitution* 2nd edn (Oxford, OUP, 2006)

Vranesh, G and Musick, JD, Jnr, 'Finders Keepers? Or the New Statutory Laws of Treasure and Related Subjects' (1972) 5 *Natural Resources Law* 1

Warnkonig, AL, 'On the Law of Possession' (1838) 19 *Am Jurist and L Mag* 13

Warren, EH, *Cases on Property* 2nd edn (Cambridge MA, Harvard Co-operative Society, 1938)

Williams, J, *Principles of the Law of Real Property* (London, H Sweet, 1848)

—— *Principles of the Law of Personal Property* (London, H Sweet, 1848)

—— *The Seisin of the Freehold* (London, H Sweet, 1878)

Williams, JH and Crowdy, WM (eds), *Goodeve's Modern Law of Personal Property* 3rd edn (London, Sweet and Maxwell, 1899)

Williams, JH and Yates, WB, *The Law of Ejectment* (London, Sweet and Maxwell, 1894)

Williams, TC (ed), *Principles of the Law of Real Property* 14th edn (London, H Sweet, 1882)

—— *Williams on Personal Property* 14th edn (London, Sweet and Maxwell, 1894)

—— *Williams on Personal Property* 18th edn (London, Sweet and Maxwell, 1926)

Wilson, G (ed), *The History of the Pleas of the Crown by Sir Matthew Hale* (London, J Butterworth, 1800)

Winfield, PH, *The Province of the Law of Tort* (Cambridge, CUP, 1931)

—— *A Textbook on the Law of Tort* (London, Sweet & Maxwell, 1937)

Wiren, SA, 'The Plea of the *jus tertii* in Ejectment' (1925) 41 *LQR* 139

Wonnacott, M, *Possession of Land* (Cambridge, CUP, 2006)

Woodbine, GE (ed), *Henri De Bracton on the Laws and Customs of England* (SE Thorne (trans), Cambridge MA, Harvard University Press, 1968)

Worthington, S, *Proprietary Interests in Commercial Transactions* (Oxford, Clarendon Press, 1996)

—— *Personal Property Law* (Oxford, Hart Publishing, 2000)

—— 'Rehabilitating Personal Property Law as a Serious Topic for Research and Teaching' (2002) 36 *Canadian Business Law Journal* 238

—— *Equity* 2nd edn (Oxford, OUP, 2006)

# INDEX

# Index

# Index